RIVALROUS CONSONANCE:
A THEORY OF
GENERAL OLIGOPOLISTIC EQUILIBRIUM

CONTRIBUTIONS TO ECONOMIC ANALYSIS

157

Honorary Editor:
J. TINBERGEN

Editors:
D. W. JORGENSON
J. WAELBROECK

NORTH-HOLLAND
AMSTERDAM · NEW YORK · OXFORD

RIVALROUS CONSONANCE: A THEORY OF GENERAL OLIGOPOLISTIC EQUILIBRIUM

ROBERT E. KUENNE
Department of Economics
Princeton University
Princeton, NJ 08544, U.S.A.

1986

NORTH-HOLLAND
AMSTERDAM · NEW YORK · OXFORD

ISBN: 0 444 87937 4

Publishers:
ELSEVIER SCIENCE PUBLISHERS B.V.
P.O. Box 1991
1000 BZ Amsterdam
The Netherlands

Sole distributors for the U.S.A. and Canada:
ELSEVIER SCIENCE PUBLISHING COMPANY, INC.
52 Vanderbilt Avenue
New York, N.Y. 10017
U.S.A.

Library of Congress Cataloging-in-Publication Data

Kuenne, Robert E.
Rivalrous consonance.

(Contributions to economic analysis ; v. 157)
Bibliography: p.
Includes index.
1. Oligopolies. 2. Equilibrium (Economics)
I. Title. II. Series.
HD2757.3.K84 1986 338.8'2'01 85-29207
ISBN 0-444-87937-4

Printed in The Netherlands

FOR MY DAUGHTER
Carolyn Leigh Kuenne
With a Father's Love
An Academic Pride
And An Admirer's Awe

INTRODUCTION TO THE SERIES

This series consists of a number of hitherto unpublished studies, which are introduced by the editors in the belief that they represent fresh contributions to economic science.

The term 'economic analysis' as used in the title of the series has been adopted because it covers both the activities of the theoretical economist and the research worker.

Although the analytical methods used by the various contributors are not the same, they are nevertheless conditioned by the common origin of their studies, namely theoretical problems encountered in practical research. Since for this reason, business cycle research and national accounting, research work on behalf of economic policy, and problems of planning are the main sources of the subjects dealt with, they necessarily determine the manner of approach adopted by the authors. Their methods tend to be 'practical' in the sense of not being too far remote from application to actual economic conditions. In addition they are quantitative.

It is the hope of the editors that the publication of these studies will help to stimulate the exchange of scientific information and to reinforce international cooperation in the field of economics.

The Editors

PREFACE

Modern general equilibrium theory suffers from two punishing shortcomings that have kept it from the mainstream of theoretical development and diverted it to a murky backwater inhabited by an isolated covey of specialists.

First, it has failed to move away from the stultifying assumption of pure competition to realistic forms of monopolistic competition; indeed, the application of point set topology and real analysis during the last 30 years has reinforced its attachment to atomistic market structure as well as to other equally arcane regularities and simplifications.

Second, even within this artificial environment, little progress has been made in escaping the limitations of the pure deductive method that inhere in large-scale (i.e., general) systems. A priori restrictions and hypotheses have not been sufficiently exclusive of alternative states of the economic system to permit the derivation of useful qualitative theorems with empirical content. Where unambiguous theorems have been derived, more frequently than not highly unrealistic and restrictive assumptions have been adopted to that end.

Meanwhile, oligopoly theory has developed independently along equally unrealistic and sterile paths. The methodological allure of game theory, with its stress upon conflict and rivalry, continues to fascinate theorists after 40 years of disappointing application. The search for universal theories of oligopoly yielding general insights into rivalrous pricing leads researchers to blind themselves to a defining characteristic of the market structure: the sui generis quality of industries so organized.

One of the distressing characteristics of modern microeconomic theory has been its willingness to ignore its core problems of real significance in order to embrace "high-brow" methodologies of established sterility. The accumulating evidence of empirical industrial organization researchers and experimental market analysts is ignored as concerns of "lesser breeds without the Law". The theorist's important role as the explicator and codifier of the empirically observed has been largely subordinated to that of an autonomous search for determinate answers to questions generated internally by irrelevant theorizing. Who has not wondered at the utility of proving that this or that excess demand correspondence is upper semicontinuous as a step toward the proof that this or that wholly unrealistic economic system has a determinate equilibrium? Indeed, who has not encountered economic models whose sole raison d'etre, one suspects, is that of proving they have fixed points?

This book is not an appeal that theory be abandoned. Rather, it is an urging that general theoretical frameworks be infused with empiricism, operationalism, and more modest but achievable ambitions. It seeks to develop a family of frameworks with which to deal fruitfully with oligopoly within a context of industrial interdependence. It is "low-brow" in eschewing techniques that cannot be made operational, and its architecture is shaped by the desire to incorporate the empiricist's findings. It recognizes the limited generalizability of propositions relating to oligopoly, accepts the absolute necessity of specifying the model with numerical parameters, and embraces the practical need to obtain many of those parameters by heuristic means.

The work is meant to be a beginning, and the hope is that other workers will be convinced by it that the path surveyed is worth traveling.

R.E.K.
Genequil
Thompson's Point
Charlotte, Vermont

July 22, 1985

ACKNOWLEDGEMENTS

The theory and techniques in this book have been the product of a decade of thought and research. Some of it has appeared in earlier forms in articles and books listed in the bibliography.

The genesis of Chapters 1, 2, and 3 may be found in *De Economist* and *Kyklos*. Chapter 4 had its origin in work published in the *Oxford Economic Papers*. Chapter 5 owes much of its framework to articles in *Kyklos* and Energy Economics. Chapter 6 also had origins in the article in *Oxford Economic Papers*. Chapter 7's heuristic framework exploits ideas developed earlier in the Chamberlin Festschrift -- *Monopolistic Competition Theory: Studies in Impact*, published by John Wiley -- and in an article in *Applied Economics*. The techniques employed were developed and tested in the modelling of the OPEC cartel by rivalrous consonance techniques, the results of which were published in *Kyklos*, the *Journal of Business Administration*, *The Logistics and Transportation Review*, and *Energy Economics*.

I am indebted to the publishers of these journals and books for permission to draw upon this material.

At a crucial time in the development of the theory of rivalrous consonance the work was sustained in part by grants from the Rockefeller Foundation for the analysis of the OPEC cartel. I am grateful to the Foundation for such support, and especially to Drs. Laurence D. Stifel and R. Kirby Davidson for their encouragement. Of course, neither they nor the Foundation can be held responsible for errors and shortcomings.

Finally, I am indebted to Mrs. Burnette Aylor, who designed and processed the book with imagination and dedication.

SYMBOLS AND NOTATION

$\mathbf{A}$	:	Leontief technology matrix for economy
B_i	:	capacity restraint for product i
$\mathbf{B}$	:	inverse of $\mathbf{A}$
c	:	index for industrial customer
C_i	:	marginal cost of product i
C_i^k	:	firm i's kth constraint function
$\mathbf{C_k}$	:	marginal cost vector for firms k
E_i	:	firm i's extended profits
EMP_i	:	firm i's extended marginal profit
$EMCP_i$	:	firm i's extended marginal customer profit
$EMRP_i$	:	firm i's extended marginal rival profit
ETD_i	:	firm i's extended target deviation
f_i	:	product i's unit factor cost
∇f	:	gradient vector of f
$\nabla^2 f$	:	Hessian matrix of f
$\mathbf{I}$	:	intermediate demand vector
k_{ij}	:	power structure factor of firm i toward firm j
$\mathbf{K_i}$	:	row vector of $\mathbf{K}$
$\mathbf{K}$	:	power structure matrix
L_i^+	:	upper bound restraint on firm i's profits
L_i^-	:	lower bound restraint on θ_i
m_i	:	firm i's profit margin
M_i	:	lower bound restraint on firm i's sales (or) market shall of firm i, depending on context
MC_i	:	firm i's marginal cost function
MR_i	:	firm i's marginal revenue with respect to price change
MOP_i	:	firm i's marginal own profit
n	:	number of firms in an industry
N_i	:	lower bound restraint on p_i, usually taken to be zero

p_i	:	price of product i (produced by firm i)
$\bar{p}_i$	:	benchmark price of product i
$\mathbf{p_i}$	:	price vector relevant to firm's solution
$\mathbf{p}^C$	:	Cournot price solution vector
$\mathbf{p}^J$	:	Chamberlin price solution vector
$\mathbf{p_c}$	:	price vector for customers
$\mathbf{p_r}$	:	price vector for rivals
$\mathbf{Q}$	:	vector of non-price variables in firms' consumer demand functions
r	:	index for rival firm
r_i	:	firm i's actual rate of return
$\bar{r}_i$	:	firm i's target rate of return
R_i	:	firm i's reaction function
RR_i	:	firm i's rate of return function
s_i	:	target deviation for firm i
s	:	index for supplier firm
t	:	number of firms in multi-industry economies
T_i^+	:	upper bound restraint on p_i's change
T_i^-	:	lower bound restraint on p_i's change
θ_{ij}	:	binary consonance factor of firm i for firm j
θ_i	:	firm i's aggregate consonance factor
$\boldsymbol{\theta}_i$	:	vector of firms' aggregate consonance factors
θ	:	matrix of θ_{ij}
v_{ic}	:	units of product i used in production of a unit of good c
W_{ij}	:	market component for firm i
x_i	:	sales to consumers by firm i
$\mathbf{X}$	:	vector of x_i, $i = 1, 2, \ldots, n$
z_i	:	sales to consumers plus sales to industrial customers by firm i
$\mathbf{Z}$	:	vector of z_i, $i = 1, 2, \ldots, n$

CONTENTS

CHAPTER 3 -- RIVALROUS CONSONANCE: PROGRAMMING CONSIDERATIONS AT THE FIRST LEVEL

CHAPTER 4 -- RIVALROUS CONSONANCE: THEORETICAL CONSIDERATIONS AT THE SECOND LEVEL

CHAPTER 5 -- RIVALROUS CONSONANCE: SIMULATIVE THEORIZING AT THE SECOND LEVEL

CHAPTER 6 -- RIVALROUS CONSONANCE: THEORETICAL CONSIDERATIONS AT THE THIRD LEVEL

CHAPTER 7 -- ISOLATING THE POWER STRUCTURE OF AN OLIGOPOLY

FIGURES

TABLES

CHAPTER 1

THE RIVALROUS CONSONANCE FRAMEWORK FOR OLIGOPOLY ANALYSIS

1. *THE INADEQUACIES OF EXISTING THEORIES*

Oligopoly theory occupies a peculiar position in economic analysis. On the one hand, lavish theoretical attention is bestowed upon it in the form of game-theoretic and bargaining models, entry-barrier theory, and core theory.[1] Yet the ghosts of Cournot, Bertrand, Edgeworth, and Stackelberg process and equilibrium analysis continue to parade through the pages of textbooks, frequently updated to relate them to Nash or core equilibrium concepts.

On the other hand, it is difficult to rid one self of the belief that, despite the intensity of analytical effort, this body of analysis stands apart in antiseptic isolation from the major fields of economists' microeconomic efforts. General equilibrium theory remains almost wholly untouched by it, despite the unchallenged fact that modern industrial economies are permeated with such market structures.[2] Despite conjectures that recent inflation has a microeconomic component in the increased readiness of oligopolistic industries to grant higher wages to labor and pass them on in higher prices, no comparative statics theorems bearing upon such problems have been derived from interdependence theory.

Oligopoly theory has proved unrewarding for several reasons. First, it has aimed at the most general results, seeking to derive theorems of universal applicability to oligopolistic behavior. By its nature, however, each oligopolistic industry is importantly distinctive, with pricing, output, selling cost, innovation, and efficiency outcomes that are heavily impacted by personalities, industry history, and the nature of the product. Existing theoretical approaches are resistant to close tailoring to specific industry analysis and therefore misleading in their treatment of oligopolistic industries in universals.

Second, classical and game-theoretical frameworks are both tied closely to "conjectural" strategies of the "if I, then he" variety. Admittedly, intuitive and experimental support exists for a component of such attitudes in oligopolistic behavior, but, unfortunately, the insight has not proved to be capable of translation in empirical modeling, nor is it an exclusive component. In illustration, although consumer preferences are not, practically speaking, capable of specification, they can be made empirically effective in demand functions. Analogous instruments have been difficult to formulate in other than overly-simple modes (e.g., Cournot) and impossible to isolate empirically.

Third, conjectural schemata are strongly wedded to single-objective modeling, generally the maximization of profit or expected utility. They cannot capture the richness or the plurality of objectives sought by a typical oligopoly.

In recent years the theorist has received welcome guidance from the valuable empirical work done by such investigators as Kaplan, Dirlam, and Lanzillotti [21] in the United States, Fog [12] in Denmark, and Wärneryd in Sweden.[3] From this work has emerged a major theoretical guidepost: the modern oligopolistic firm follows a multiple-objective strategy. In very few cases can any simply-defined profit maximization be discerned; rather, to an almost exclusive degree, the goals sought are a set of mutually constraining and conflicting aims, imperfectly conceived and articulated, uncertainly coordinated, and decentralized in administrative origin and achievement.[4]

The set of goals frequently sought includes some subset of the following:

1. a target rate of return on dedicated capital;[5]
2. maintenance or expansion of market share;
3. maintenance of a profit margin over a standard cost figure;
4. stabilization of prices in the industry;
5. conformance to current antitrust trends;
6. meeting competitors' price leads;
7. minimization of customer inconvenience;
8. exclusion of potential industry entrants;[6]
9. enhancing the welfare of managers.

Another major conclusion emerges implicitly from this recent literature: the preconditions to make formal game-theoretic approaches promising as a general analytical framework for the pricing decision do not exist. The modern corporation is a pluralistic organization with multiple, poorly coordinated, and to some extent, competing, loci of decisionmaking.[7] Within such groups, decisions are arrived at in heuristic, informal, or nebulous manners.[8] Of course, it is possible to use game theory or conjectural frameworks as a formal encapsulation of the informal procedures of rivalrous corporations, but those models are not likely candidates to serve this metaphoric role. Their plausible application requires a clear-cut demonstration of a well-defined locus of decision-making authority with a comprehensive canvas of possibilities, grasp of strategic alternatives, concern with rivals' potential reactions, and constant preoccupation with firm survival or the payoffs implied by the paraphernalia of such theories.

It is difficult, therefore, to accept the war-of-survival paradigm typified by Shubik's early work [41], or, indeed, most of the classical or modern approaches which stress only the individual-firm oriented one-dimensional "reaction function" in one form or another.[9] Rather, the realistic image of rivalrous competition is one which includes competing intrafirm goals and elements of an "organic" subordination of the individual unit's welfare somewhat to the welfare of the whole. That is, there is a definite commitment of the rivalrous firm to the continued peaceful survival of the industry -- a "rivalrous consonance of interests" --even if that implies the foregoing of immediate opportunities by the firm to seek greater benefit through conflict.

In summary, misplaced theoretical ambition, nonobservable variables, and inability to cope with the goal multiplicity and subtlety of the firm in oligopoly, as well as the industry's communitarian aspects have led to a dissatisfaction among economists with existing formal frameworks in this market structure. In their simplicity and generality they serve as often to mislead as to illuminate. We agree with Telser [47] who observes.

> "The formal models often have great mathematical elegance and are fun to play with and teach, but at least from this author's vantage point their existence has had a negligible effect on applied research and policy analysis in the industrial

organization area. General policy prescriptions and uncertainties regarding concentration, price rigidities, barriers to entry, market definition, tacit coordination, etc., seem to exist independently of the formal modeling tradition." (Pp. 213-214)

2. *SOME DESIDERATA*

It would be incorrect to react to such criticism by rejecting formal theory as a means of gaining structural insights into realistic oligopolies. Formal analysis exists to supplement the limitations of the analyst's unaided mind in manipulating more than a small number of interdependent variables. Interdependence of firms' decisions is the very essence of the oligopolistic problem, and we are unlikely to probe very deeply into the implications of hypotheses concerning a specific oligopoly without formal models.

However, we agree with Koopman's assertion[10] that the role of the theorist is to follow the empiricist, not to lead him. Theoretical advance in the social sciences lies in the direction of incorporating, enlightening, and coordinating empirical discoveries. The unrealistic must yield to the realistic postulate unless the simplifying abstraction from reality can be shown to yield more fruitful results through a gain in the ability to manipulate the theory to derive useful insights. Hence, it is always unfortunate for a field when empirical investigator and theorist fail to communicate in continuous fashion, or when the theorists's frameworks are not applicable to the empiricist's tasks.

To be useful, therefore, we shall insist that new theoretical departures conform to a set of requirements that reflect the criticisms in Section 1.1 above.

First, the theory must be operational. Its variables must be observable or derivable from real-world data by practically available -- not merely conceptually feasible -- methods. To the extent valid theoretical concepts are not so translatable, summary or surrogate variables or attributes must be incorporated to capture the impacts.

Second, the theory must accord with general equilibrium frameworks in two senses. Within the industry, it must be tailored to treat the interdependent decision making of the major rivals, retaining their individual identities to incorporate the essence of the oligopoly problem. Moreover, it must be capable of fitting into a larger-scale model that features the interdependence among industries and customers. Otherwise the framework will be incapable of contributing to the analysis of such problems as the transmission of inflationary impacts.

Third, it must be flexible enough to incorporate the richness of realistic variety in rivals' goods (primary and secondary), industry power structures, and attitudes toward competition and cooperation. We reject the notion of a universally applicable theory of oligopolistic behavior, and embrace the need for less ambitious theoretical analyses tailored specifically to given industries.

Within this goal we are most anxious to temper the tendencies to extremes of assumptions concerning rivalrous behavior that the rigid classical and game theory models foster. Conjectural models tend by their nature to incorporate a reactive passivity of firms' expectations to rivals' actions. This is true even for more recent approaches that stress the necessity for consistent conjectures in equilibrium.[11] Conjectures tend -- in more sophisticated models than Cournot's -- to be altered in a time-phased, adaptive fashion in the light of rivals' recent behavior. Such viewpoints also ignore the active signalling to rivals that occurs continuously in realistic mature oligopolistic communities sensitized by years of coexistence. Firms engage actively in the shaping of their rivals' expectations, calming fears of destabilizing the price structure, assuring rivals of a willingness to remain within production ceilings, or, at the other extreme, warning them of contingent intentions to match or outdo rivals' aggressive actions.

Game-theoretic approaches with bargaining and coalition formation implant the analysis in an environment of conflict, ranging from the war-of-survival context to narrow self-interest defined in one-dimensional units of benefit. The competitive overwhelms the cooperative, the latter becoming of interest only if narrow self-interest is served.

Mature oligopolistic industries, in which major rivals have coexisted for extensive periods of time, are much more peaceful *communities* than such frameworks picture. They are blends of the rivalrous and the cooperative, with coexistence generally frankly accepted, and, indeed, with some positive and motivating concern for the image or welfare of the industry. Each rival is solicitous of the impacts of his decisions upon the welfares of each of his major rivals. A great source of this concern, of course, is the fear that if that impact is too painful the rival or rivals will respond with punishing reaction. The desire for a peaceful, stable industry seems a general one in mature industries. "Good citizenship" in the industry implies a recognition of a rivalrous consonance of long-term interests by all participants. Rivalry coexists with strivings for harmonistic existence, in different proportions depending on the industry; live-and-let-live is a characteristic of communitarian life.

In our view, any hope for successful formal analysis of oligopolistic decision making must be based upon the incorporation of these potentials and characteristics. If this work is successful in constructing such analytical frameworks, they will be used to obtain insights into the structure and functioning of the industry. By parametric displacement, it should be possible to illuminate the distribution of benefits and costs that results from the industry's power structure, the consequences of increasing or reducing cooperative tendencies, and the price-output impacts of cost increases.

3. *RIVALROUS CONSONANCE AND CRIPPLED OPTIMIZATION*

To analyze mature oligopoly in a rivalrous consonance context a nonlinear programming approach to firm and industry behavior is formulated in which each rival strives to optimize an objective hobbled by the need to consider other firms' objectives as well as secondary goals of its own. We have termed this framework, together with the algorithm used to solve the system, "crippled optimization".

Because this approach is flexibly tailored to specific industries' cases, it is necessary to present it in exemplifying forms. A specific application of the approach has been made to the Organization of Petroleum Exporting Countries (OPEC) as it functioned in the period 1973-1981 (Kuenne [33]). In this book, however, prototypical but hypothetical cases will be used to formulate the approach in a more controlled manner than realistic research applications permit.

3.1 *Model 1 -- Crippled Profit Maximization: Single Industry*

Let us hypothesize an industry whose firms typically seek to maximize profits within the context of recognized rivalry as a primary objective, subject to the simultaneous striving for a set of secondary objectives. Assume an oligopolistic industry with n firms and associated differentiated products. Rival i (producing product i) strives as a primary objective to maximize "extended profits", E_i:

$$(1) \qquad \underset{p_i}{\text{Max}}\, E_i = \sum_{j=1}^{n} \theta_{ij}(p_j x_j - C_j x_j),$$

where we define:

1. p_i: price of rival i's product;
2. x_i: amount demand by consumers of product i;
3. C_i: average cost, assumed constant, of product i;
4. θ_{ij}: binary consonance factors for firm i relevant to firm j,

   $\theta_{ii} \equiv 1.$

Note that the firm is assumed -- realistically -- to set price rather than quantity of its product. The amount demanded follows from the consumer demand or sales function it faces, which is assumed to be specified linearly:

$$(2) \qquad x_i - a_i + b_{ii}p_i - \sum_{j \neq i} b_{ij}p_j - \mathbf{b_{iq}} \cdot \mathbf{q} = 0,$$

where $\mathbf{q}$ is a vector of variables other than prices of the industry's products affecting sales to consumers.

3.1.1 *The Binary Consonance Factors.* The distinctive term in (1) and the factor that distinguishes the rivalrous consonance model is the presence in rival i's objective function of the profits of all other rivals, each "discounted" by a coefficient, θ_{ij}, where $\theta_{ii} \equiv 1$. The *binary consonance factor*, θ_{ij}, is an element of the n x n consonance matrix θ which defines the industry power structure as well as its specific position on the rivalry-cooperation spectrum.

Specifically, θ_{ij} is the dollar equivalent in rival i's profits at which it values one dollar of rival j's profit or loss. Hence, if $\theta_{ij} = .25$, rival i treats \$1 of profit or loss by rival j as the equivalent of a 25¢ gain or loss to itself. Rival i has n-1 (θ_{ii} is trivially unity) such factors to define its relevant attitudes toward *each* of its rivals. Those coefficients are the behaviorally effective net resultants of rival i's beliefs concerning the ability of rival j to retaliate against it; the effectiveness of rival j's management; the claims rival j has upon its solicitude as a member of the industry; the importance for industry welfare of keeping rival j viable (perhaps for antitrust reasons); and the degree of deference owed rival j on the basis of the mores and folkways of the industry.

Obviously, θ_{ij} need not equal θ_{ji}, and indeed in terms of power structure definition the pair would generally be expected to be inversely related. In any event, they are defined in the consciousness of the relevant rivals' decision makers and therefore need bear no consistent relation to each other. Further, because the elements of θ are binary in their statement, that matrix is a detailed specification of the behaviorally-relevant attributes of the industry.

Of interest, both theoretically and in the empirical determination of the rivalrous consonance structure, is the *aggregate consonance factor*,

$$\theta_i = \Sigma_j \theta_{ij},$$

an element of the vector θ_i. It may be interpreted as firm i's valuation in own-profit dollars of n-1 dollars of profit spread uniformly over its rivals. In a macro sense, it indexes the firm's overall position in the consonance structure of the industry, as determined by its market position, its attitudes towards live-and-let-live strategies, and its feelings of confidence as an industry participant.

The binary consonance factors are related to the aggregate factor by the power structure factors, $k_{ij} \varepsilon \mathbf{K}$, where

$$\theta_{ij} = k_{ij} \theta_i, \quad \Sigma_j k_{ij} = 1.$$

For the industry as a whole the power structure is defined by $\mathbf{K}$, a matrix whose row vectors are the $\mathbf{K}_i$. The k_{ij} describe, for firm i, the specific manner in which its industry solicitude is distributed over *specific* rivals. Hence, $\mathbf{K}$ is a concise and quantitative description of the *relative* power position of each firm in the industry. The binary consonance matrix, θ, converts these positions to absolute terms. The theoretical presentations to follow work largely with θ, but the techniques for the numerical definition of $\mathbf{K}$ and the θ_i as steps toward the isolation of θ will be discussed in Chapter 7.

The binary consonance factors incorporate -- but are more information-inclusive than -- the "conjectures" so dear to the analytical hearts of classical theorists and their modern followers. Moreover, the θ_{ij} are determinate in realistic industrial settings which conjectures are not, and therefore are operational concepts.[12]

In a fully-developed, long-run theory of oligopoly in rivalrous consonance the θ_{ij} would be endogenous to the model, determined by economic, psychological, political, and social variables too complicated in nature to contemplate comfortably. In Chapter 6 θ_i is permitted to become variable ($\mathbf{K}$ fixed) and determined by own-profit maximization considerations in a long-run analysis which attains a generalized Stackelberg solution. Elsewhere, however, θ is treated as fixed in a short-run analysis, and the θ_{ij} are viewed as behavioral parameters that summarize a complex of market and nonmarket forces acting to shape rival i's conduct toward rival j.

When the θ_{ij} are lifted out of the context of constrained optimization and n-firm oligopoly, they may be seen to be related to prior work of other theorists. Within the confines of game-theoretic analysis of unconstrained duopoly, such coefficients have been employed by Robert L. Bishop [5], James W. Friedman [13]-[15], A. Hoggatt [16]-[17], and R.M. Cyert and M.H. De Groot [8]-[9].

3.1.2 *Goal-Defining Constraints.* Firm i's goal profile can be completed by defining a set of constraints that specify other "secondary" goals. These will vary with firm and industry, and the following set will be used as merely illustrative of such secondary goals, although they are believed to have some general applicability in American industry.

First, output must be within the firm's capacity, B_i, to produce:

(3) $C^1 \quad : \quad x_i - B_i \leq 0.$

Second. the firm insists upon retaining a minimum level of sales, M_i, set perhaps by the desire to achieve an expected target market proportion:[13]

(4) $C^2 \quad : \quad M_i - x_i \leq 0.$

Third, the firm sets upper and lower bounds, T_i^+ and T_i^-, on period-by-period price changes, specified as proportions of previous period price, $\bar{p}_i$:

(5) $C^3 \quad : \quad p_i/\bar{p}_i - T_i^+ \leq 0,$

(6) $C^4 \quad : \quad T_i^- - p_i/\bar{p}_i \leq 0.$

Such limits are frequently used to prevent consumer antagonism, antitrust attention, delayed purchases because of customers' expectations of further price falls, and so forth.

Lastly, price is bounded away from a specific lower bound, which we will in further analysis assume is zero, but which may not be:

(7) $C^5 \quad : \quad N_i - p_i \leq 0.$

In this book we will term B_i, M_i, T_i^+, T_i^-, and N_i, as well as parameters of similar function, the *restraints* of the relevant constraints.

3.1.3 *Mathematical Properties.* Crippled optimization models are designed to be numerically specified by econometric or other techniques and to be solved by appropriate algorithms. The solution technique used in our work -- a penalty function nonlinear programming algorithm -- will be discussed in some detail in Chapter 3.3. However, as in the case of most such programming algorithms, convergence of the component problem solutions to global optima and the existence of a dual problem are dependent upon the model's "convexity". At this point, therefore, Model 1 will be examined briefly for this quality.

Effectively, by substitution of expression (2) for x_i in (1), (3), and (4), and of similar expressions for x_j in the like models for firms $j \neq i$ (which models are solved simultaneously as submodels in Model 1), the p_j, $j = 1, 2, \ldots, n$, are the only endogenous variables. Further, since the solution algorithm will solve each firm's constrained maximization problem sequentially, assuming all other firms' prices are held constant at current levels, in the firm's optimization only its own price is variable. Hence, if Model 1 is convex in own-price only all of the subproblems will be convex problems.

Sufficient conditions that each firm's subproblems be convex in the iterations are that (1) its objective function be concave in own-price, and (2) its constraints be convex in own price. Clearly,

(8) $d^2E_i / dp_i^2 = -2b_{ii} < 0,$

since $b_{ii} > 0$, and therefore E_i is (strictly) concave in p_i. Also, constraints (3) and (5)-(7) (with the x_j eliminated by substitution) are linear in own-price and therefore trivially convex. Also, constraint (4) is convex in p_i. Thus, the feasible region will be convex. Therefore, the solutions to Model 1's subproblems (to be explained further in Chapter 3) will be global extended-profit maxima.

3.2 *Model 2 -- Crippled Profit-Maximization: General Equilibrium*

As an illustration of the important potential for crippled optimization modelling to serve as a means of coping with oligopoly in operational general equilibrium systems, let us extend Model 1 into such a context by a few simple adaptations.

Assume that the entire economy contains t firms divided into oligopolistic industries, and that *each* of the firms possesses a constraint set of the type illustrated in (3)-(7). The θ matrix will be a t x t matrix with zero elements for those pairs of firms which have neither rivalrous relations (as in Model 1) nor customer-supplier relationships. That is, we now include the solicitude of a supplier firm for its industrial customers among the consonance factors of the model.

Consumer demands, x_i, remain as defined in (2), where firms j continue to be interpreted as rivals within firm i's industry. However, we now include an industrial demand component in total demand,

(9) $$z_i - \Sigma_c v_{ic} z_c = x_i$$

where we define

1. z_i: total -- consumer plus intermediate -- demand for product i;
2. v_{ic}: units of product i used in the production of a unit of good c.

We will assume a Leontief technology in which the v_{ic} are fixed technical coefficients, that each firm uses one activity to produce its product, and that each activity produces only one product.

Then we may redefine C_i, unit cost, to be

(10) $$C_i - f_i - \Sigma_s v_{si} p_s = 0,$$

where

1. f_i : unit factor cost of firm i's product, assumed constant;
2. p_s : price of a supplier firm's product.

It is then necessary to rewrite firm i's objective function; letting m_j denote firm j's own-profit margin, we define

(11) $$\max_{p_i} E_i = \sum_{j=1}^{q} \theta_{ij}(p_j-C_j)z_j = \sum_{j=1}^{q} \theta_{ij}\, m_j\, z_j\,,$$

and to constrain it with demand functions (2) and (9), unit cost definition (10), and goal functions of the form (3)-(7). These include the constraints

(12) $$p_i \geq N_i\,.$$

Sufficient conditions for the concavity of E_i become a bit more complicated. The Leontief economy can be depicted as

(13)
$$\begin{bmatrix} z_1 \\ z_2 \\ . \\ . \\ . \\ z_t \end{bmatrix} = \begin{bmatrix} 1-v_{11} & -v_{12} & \cdots & -v_{1t} \\ -v_{21} & 1-v_{22} & \cdots & -v_{2t} \\ . & . & \cdots & . \\ . & . & \cdots & . \\ . & . & \cdots & . \\ -v_{t1} & -v_{t2} & \cdots & 1-v_{tt} \end{bmatrix}^{-1} \begin{bmatrix} x_1 \\ x_2 \\ . \\ . \\ . \\ x_t \end{bmatrix}$$

or

(14)
$$\mathbf{Z} = \mathbf{A}^{-1}\,\mathbf{X} = \mathbf{BX}\,.$$

Then, for example,

(15)
$$[dz_1/dp_1, dz_2/dp_1, \ldots, dz_t/dp_1]' = \mathbf{B}[-b_{11}, b_{21}, \ldots, b_{t1}]'\,.$$

E_i is concave in own-price if and only if

(16)
$$d^2E_i\,/\,dp_i^2 = 2[(1-v_{ii})dz_i/dp_i - \sum_{j \neq i} \theta_{ij}\, v_{ij}\, dz_j/dp_i] \leq 0\,.$$

Since **B** in (14) is nonnegative if the Leontief technology is viable, the sign of dz_j/dp_i will depend upon the relative sizes of the elements in the jth row of **B** and the vector of demand function coefficients in (15). If consumers treat all goods as gross substitutes, with $dz_i/dp_i < 0$, $dz_j/dp_i \geq 0$, then, with $\theta_{ij} \varepsilon [0,1]$, the extended profit function will be concave. In general, if the θ_{ij} are small, so the firms do not take rivals' and industrial customers' welfares much into account in their decision making, the probability of (16) holding is also raised, since own-price effects should then dominate.

Model 2, therefore, should yield global optima to each firm's optimization in each iteration of the algorithm. The model incorporates broad decision interdependence among sectors of the economy in manners that are operational. It is viewed, therefore, as a promising beginning to the inbuilding of oligopolistic pricing into general equilibrium models that are realistic and capable of empirical specification.

3.3 *Model 3 -- Crippled Target-Rate-of-Return Optimization -- Single Industry*

As another illustration of the flexibility of the rivalrous consonance framework, suppose the firms in an industry attempt as a primary objective to attain a target rate of return, $\bar{r}_i$, treating shortfalls or overages of the actual rate of return, r_i, as equally undesirable. Moreover, they once more feel constrained to take into account the power structure of the industry as they perceive it. Assume that they strive for a set of subordinate objectives which is, for purposes of this example, the same as the set (3)-(6) in Model 1. Finally, assume each firm has a dedicated capital, K_i, devoted to the production of product i. For simplicity, industrial demand will be ignored as in Model 1.

The matrix, θ, now performs the same function as it did in Models 1 and 2 but must be given a different interpretation. The consonance factor θ_{ij} is simply a weight that reflects the degree of importance rival i accords the attainment of rival j's goal relative to the importance ($\theta_{ii} \equiv 1$) it attaches to attaining its own goal. The factor becomes a pure scaling value without ready interpretation as own-profit translator.

The firm's objective function becomes

$$\text{(17)} \qquad \text{Min } Z_i = \sum_{j=1}^{n} \theta_{ij} \, | \bar{r}_j - r_j |$$

subject to the definitional constraints

$$\text{(18)} \qquad r_j - m_j x_j / k_j = 0 \ ,$$

the definition of the sales function (2), the subordinate goal set (3)-(6), and the lower bound constraints (7).

The objective function (17) is difficult to manipulate mathematically, and, therefore, a more conventional function that retains the symmetry of deviations on both sides of $\bar{r}_j$ and which is convex in p_j is preferable. One acceptable form is simply

$$\text{(19)} \qquad \text{Min } Z_i = \sum_{j=1}^{n} \theta_{ij} (\bar{r}_j - r_j)^2 \ ,$$

but to punish deviations more severely we adopt an exponential form:

$$\text{(20)} \qquad \text{Min ETD}_i = \sum_{j=1}^{n} \theta_{ij} \, e^{s_j^2} \ ,$$

where ETD_i is firm i's *extended target deviation* and $s_i = \bar{r}_i - r_i$ is its *target deviation*. Convexity of this function requires that

$$\text{(21)} \qquad d^2\text{ETD}_i/dp_i^2 = 2 \left[\left[((b_{ii}m_i - x_i)/K_i)^2 (1 + 2s_i^2) + 2b_{ii}s_i/K_i \right] e^{s_i^2} + \sum_{j \neq i} \theta_{ij} \left[(-b_{ji}m_j/K_j)^2 (1 + 2s_j^2) \right] e^{s_j^2} \right]$$

The summation term is obviously positive if any rival is over- or underachieving its target rate. As an adverse case, therefore, assume for $j \neq i$, $\theta_{ij} = 0$. The sign of (21) then hinges upon the sign of s_i. If $s_i \geq 0$, the condition of (21) holds. When $s_i < 0$ it will hold only in neighborhoods of $s_i = 0$, and hence ETD_i will not be convex outside of these neighborhoods. In Figure 1.1.a we illustrate ETD_i for the case where r_i is everywhere greater than or equal to r_i, so that the firm is effectively maximizing profits and convexity rules. On the other hand, Figure 1.1.b illustrates the nonconvexities that occur when r_i lies above $\bar{r}_i$ in domains of p_i. Obviously, in seeking an unconstrained minimum of (19) we run the danger of becoming hung up on a local maximum cusp such as exists at p_i' of Figure 1.1.b rather than achieving the minimum at one of the points of tangency with the horizontal line at p_i'' or p_i''' where $r_i = \bar{r}_i$. Hence, the model will not always be well behaved.

Our reason for striving for a convex programming problem is wholly one of analytical expediency. If a given realistic model specification for an industry is not convex, that fact must be accepted, for it reflects the reality that the industry's decision making leads to the attainment of "good" solutions rather than necessarily globally optimal results. Human decision making, in all likelihood, is more frequently than not of this type. However, although in reality if a firm attains a poor local optimum it will move to improve it, our rigid models are not so flexible intheir goal striving. Hence, aiming for convex nonlinear programming formulations even at the expense of some distortion of reality is to achieve some protection against poor local optima, not an assertion that firms always strive for the very best attainable from their goal set and market setting. If the convexification cannot be obtained without great distortion of reality, it is preferable to embrace the nonconvexity as an important feature of the industry's operation.

3.4 *Hybrid Models and Extensions*

In this book we will remain exclusively with variants of Models 1, 2, and 3 in our illustrations and analyses, with major emphasis on Model 2. However, that should not obscure the great diversity of approach that is possible within the framework. In this section some of this versatility will be illustrated in brief fashion.

It is possible to mix modes of behavior for different firms. Some firms may have as a dominant interest the maximization of profits while others strive toward target rates of return. One can simply use the es_j^2 formulation for all firms j, setting $\bar{r}_j$ to realistic values for rivals who strive for target rates of return and formally defining $\bar{r}_j$ equal to unrealistically high magnitudes for firms that maximize profits, for this will effectively specify that behavior. Hence, es_j^2 is the general functional form that subsumes both types of behavior.

Other motivations are easily formulated. For example, if the industry operates with a dominant firm or firms as leaders, those firms may be depicted as maximizing profits or seeking target rates, with or without positive consonance factors for the like goals of their dominant rival compeers, if any. Followers i may be depicted as having objective functions of the form

$$(23) \qquad \text{Min } Z_i = \Sigma_k \, \theta_{ik} \, e^{(p_i - a_{ik} p_k)} \ ,$$

subject to follower i's other goals as specified in constraints, where firms k are the leaders and θ_{ik} their absolute importance in firm i's view of power structure. Hence, follower i seeks to get as close to the leaders' prices as industry convention permits, subject perhaps to a minimum output or market share constraint, among others. The function (23) is globally convex in p_i which is instrumental for achieving the convexity discussed in Section 3.

Simon's "satisficing" or bounded rationality behavior[14] may be specified in several manners. The parameters which the firm attempts to satisfice are simply forced to lie between constraints that specify upper and lower bounds. Profits, or market share, or sales, or a group of such goal variables can be constrained to lie in such intervals. The objective function may then be taken to contain one goal with perhaps a primary importance for the firm in question in addition to the sum of rivals' objectives as discounted by consonance factors.

The firm's objective function might be specified to minimize firm i's price, for example, taking into account rivals' rates of return:

$$\text{Min } Z_i = p_i + \sum_{j \neq i} \theta_{ij} \, es_j^2 \ ,$$

where the units of i's product for which p_i is stated can be varied to give greater or lesser impact of its minimization on Z_i. If rivals' terms are taken to be profits, presumably p_i will be insignificant in comparison to other-profit impacts on Z_i, and p_i might be eliminated entirely. In conditions of satisficing it presumably is a rather formal inclusion in any event.

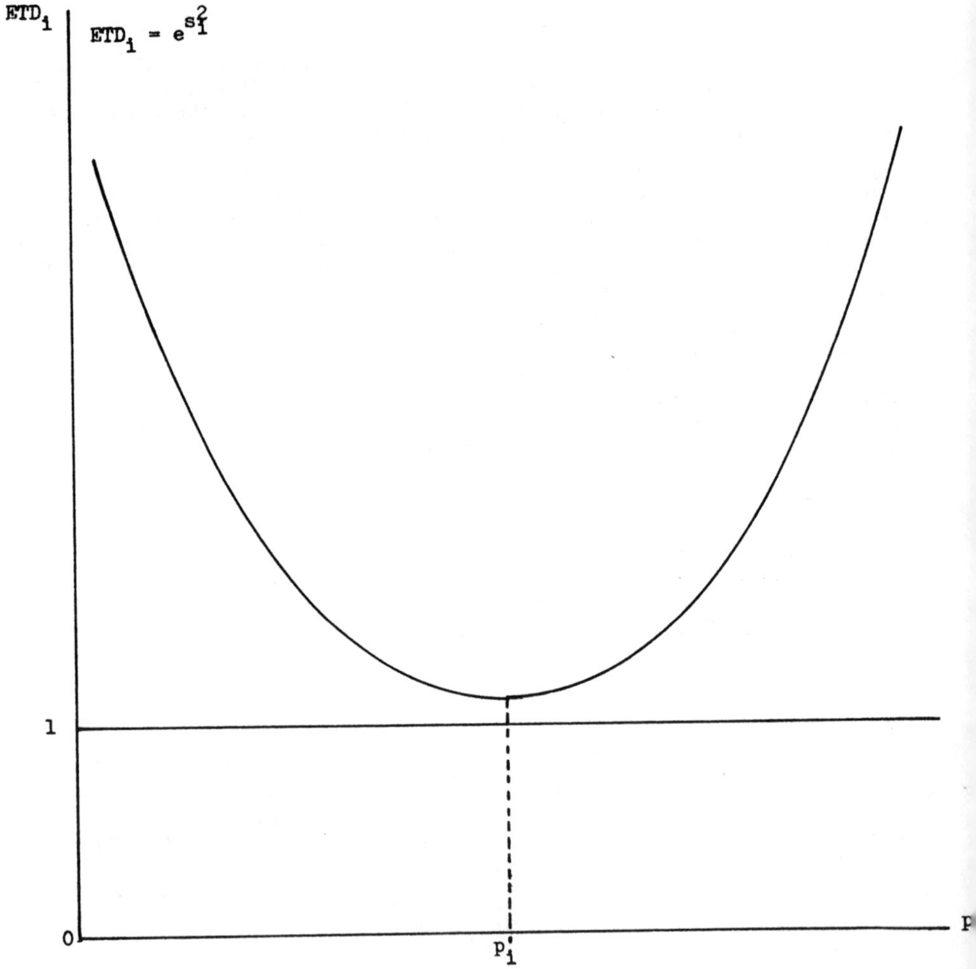

Figure 1.1.a TARGET DEVIATION FUNCTION FOR ISOLATED FIRM i WHEN $r_i < \bar{r}_i$

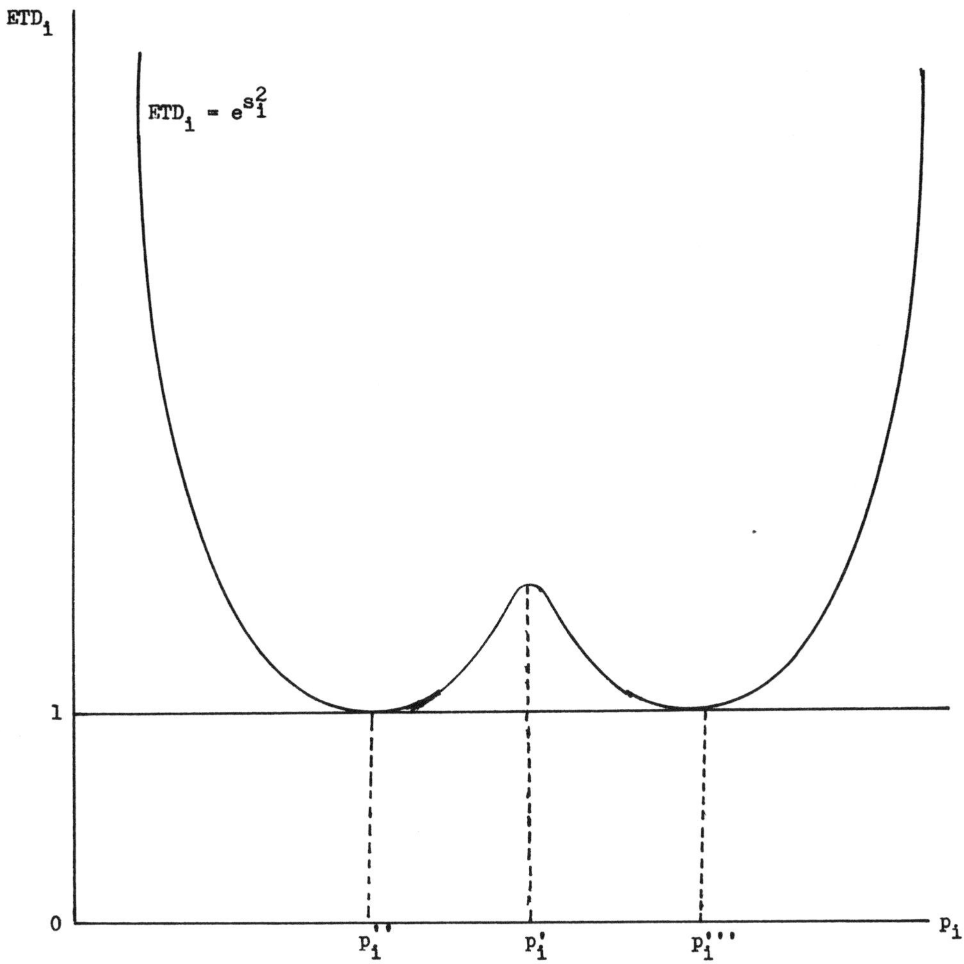

Figure 1.1.b TARGET DEVIATION FUNCTION FOR ISOLATED FIRM i WHEN $r_i > \overline{r}_i$

Satisficing formulations are likely to be nonconvex programming problems where constraints cannot be kept linear or, even if linear, will occur in conjugate pairs that are the negatives of one another. For example, a satisficing goal for profits would be written as

$$m_i x_i \geq U_i$$

$$-m_i x_i \geq -L_i ,$$

where U_i and L_i are upper and lower bounds respectively. If the first constraint in the pair is convex, the second will be concave, and vice versa. Hence, one will violate the sufficiency conditions for a convex program. But the necessity of accepting nonconvexity in general as a condition of the real world applies with even greater force in industries in which satisficing prevails, for "fuzzy" solutions are of the essence of such formulations.

4. *SIMULATIVE THEORIZING WITH RIVALROUS CONSONANCE MODELS*

General economic interdependence models, functionally and numerically unspecified, have yielded few insights into real phenomena. Indeed, nothing is so well-established both in theory and in practice than the proposition that they can *at best* yield few unambiguous theorems,[15] and that in order to reap that meager harvest the most constraining assumptions must be included. Perhaps the best manner of illustrating this failure is to point to the flight of general equilibrium theorists to point set topology away from classic calculus formulations. That movement has reinforced the attachment to pure competition, and has all but made the notion of general equilibrium synonomous with existence and uniqueness of equilibrium proofs. It offers a classic example of the over-theoretization of a field, and the detached sterility that is the fate of a behavioral science that divorces itself from actual behavior. Small wonder that the focus of modern effort is the narcissistic one of constructing models largely for the purpose of proving they have solutions, however unattainable or uninteresting they may be.

Is it not time that the theory community switches its efforts away from the search for the grail of the theorem of universal applicability within the confines of a fantasy world toward the derivation of insights of relevance to specific real-world situations? Should not the generalizations about oligopoly behavior, for example, arise as consistent tendencies in the movements of prices and quantities in models specifically tailored to industries? Is not the lessening of ambition in the face of a rich and complex economic reality that can never be fully understood a need that must be grasped if economic theory is to progress beyond the unattainable fantasies of its youth?

In this spirit I have urged the development of a low-brow theoretical technique called "simulative theorizing" (Kuenne [27]). dIt is concerned with the use of sensitivity or post-optimality analysis of numerically-specified large-scale models to derive insights into the structural and functional characteristics of large-scale systems. In the study of oligopoly, of course, such work is directed to the obtaining of propositions about the implications of the power structure, primary and secondary objectives of rivals, cost changes, and so forth, of specific industries.

What is truly needed is a new "econometrics of simulative parameter displacement" that would develop optimal techniques for designing and using specified models for such purposes. Available techniques at the present are most primitive and ad hoc. Nonetheless, even simple experiments with such oligopoly models are useful to demonstrate the extremely complicated causal pathways that exist and, therefore, the rather formidable tasks that are given ordinary least squares regression in tracing them. Such manipulations will be illustrated for a prototypical Model 2 in Chapter 5. It was also employed to manipulate the GENESYS model of OPEC in [33].

Rivalrous consonance models are well-suited to the purposes of simulative theorizing. Their parameters are selected for both relevance to industry behavior and empirical derivability. Their theoretical structure is simple in basic concept, being composed of functions that depict primary or secondary objectives and definitional relations. They are optimizing models and therefore generally more straightforward in solution than Monte Carlo or expected value simulation models. And, because of their relatively simple structure and optimizing behavior, the search for the driving factors of a solution or the sources of a counterintuitive result is simpler than for more complex models with diffuse motivational modes, as, for example, in pure simulation analyses.

With these features, therefore, the rivalrous consonance model of oligopoly reflects a particular view of the role of theoretical models. Their function is neither to yield propositions of universal validity on the one hand, nor to predict "the" solution for a specific set of parameters describing a single present or future environment. The first, as argued above, do not exist in realistic oligopoly other than as empirical central tendencies derivable from many specific industry studies. The second goal is that of forecasting, and generally is useful only for a degree of quantitative accuracy that is simply not attainable given the limited degree of detail that can be included in theoretical constructions and the limitations of econometric techniques in deriving parameter values.

Rather, the usefulness of theoretical models is to yield primarily qualitative theorems about the structure and functioning of economic entities--theorems that ideally can be tested against the evidence of reality. That usefulness depends upon the practical ability to manipulate the models by parameter displacement to derive insights into the relevant phenomena. Those insights will be deduced of necessity in numerical terms, given the limitations of purely qualitative models, but they should be translated into qualitative or, at best, order-of-magnitude propositions. These structural/functional theorems of imprecise magnitude will be pursued in the theoretical and empirical work that follows. Their deduction constitutes the substance of simulative theorizing.

5. *THE STRUCTURE OF THE ANALYSIS*

The presentation of rivalrous consonance theory is structured at three levels of analysis. The first level is the determination of oligopolistic prices when each firm assumes its rivals' prices are fixed in choosing its optimal price. Models 1, 2, and 3 are analyzed at this simple level in Chapter 2. In Chapter 3 the analysis turns to solution and parametric displacement techniques for the programming formulations of rivalrous consonance at this first level.

The second analytical level concerns itself with the classical short-run oligopoly problem of strategy choice when rivals' policy variables (prices in the present book) are simultaneously determined. Chapter 4 deals at length with the theoretical derivation of theorems under constrained and unconstrained conditions. Then, given the limitations of unspecified models, Chapter 5 presents an extensive illustration of the techniques and power of simulative theorizing at this second level of analysis, using a fictitious Model 2 for its operations. Methods, concepts, and relevant questions are stressed in furtherance of the basic goals of the book.

The third level of analysis is long-run, in that it frees the θ_{ij} to react under the eroding forces of self-interest. This analysis is conducted in Chapter 6, and derives a point of Nash equilibrium which is suggested as a gravitational price vector for rivalrous consonance in mature oligopolies over time.

Finally, in Chapter 7, the theoretical and practical problems of isolating $\mathbf{K}$ and θ_i (hence, θ) are faced, given their crucial importance in rivalrous consonance applications. Methods are developed and tested against the simulative theorizing results of Chapter 5 to suggest their feasibility and the worthwhileness of further experimentation.

1 For surveys of this recent literature see Lester G. Telser [47]; James Friedman [14]; Tun Thin [48]; and William Baumol, John C. Panzar, and Robert D. Willig [4].

2 One recent attempt to integrate oligopoly theory into a general equilibrium framework is Thomas Marschak and Reinhard Selten [37]. Unfortunately, however, it is a very formal analysis which, in the current tradition of general equilibrium theory, equates the latter with proofs of existence of equilibrium. Negishi's [38] classic earlier attempt is really the generalization of monopoly rather than oligopoly in such an interdependent framework.

3 For a general summary of Wärneryd's work, see Johnson [18], Ch. 3.

4 Arthur A. Thompson [49], Ch. 9, contains an excellent summary of the multiobjective nature of the firm's decisionmaking. Carl Kaysen [22] has been a particularly strong advocate of the view that a variety of goals may characterize firms' behaviors.

5 Kaplan, Dirlam, and Lanzillotti [21] found this goal the most frequently stressed by the large firms in their study (p. 130), but it is typical of the poorly coordinated decision making of the corporations that they found it to be of concern at the higher levels of management, the lower rungs of officialdom stressing profit margins on sales (p. 17).

6 This goal is emphasized by Bain [3], Andrews [1], Sylos-Labini [46], and Baumol, Panzer, and Willig [4], among others.

7 For example, cf. Kaplan, Dirlam, and Lanzillotti [21]: "The officials who discussed policy with the interviewers found it difficult to analyze pricing as a separate activity distinct from others entering into company policy. Pricing decisions were made or influenced by executives from production, development, engineering, accounting, finance, sales, and public relations divisions. They were usually considered part of the general strategy for achieving a broadly defined goal." (p. 3) And: "Indeed, top management frequently did not take these decisions and was surprisingly ignorant of the manner in which they were derived -- that is, prices." (p. 5) An excellent presentation of the firm from the viewpoint of organization theory can be found in Oliver Williamson [52], especially 36-37.

8 To quote from Kaplan, Dirlam, and Lanzillotti [21] again: "Economists, legislators, and the public generally would like to see pricing decisions by big companies analyzed in logical fashion, with historical comparisons of competitors' prices, cost factors, and profit margins given consistent and quantitative weight in detailed memoranda of officials involved. Unfortunately for those who would insist on fully ordered business behavior, such strategic memoranda summarizing the considerations at an important conference leading to a price decision are rarely found. Perhaps the presumed formal conference was never held. Even where the people doing the pricing tended to have certain staff information placed before them while making up their minds, whether and just how that information was taken into consideration often remained obscure. There was no document tracing the steps by which the staff information could be said to account for the price decision. Repeatedly, reference was made to the 'art' or 'feel' of pricing rather than observance of a formula". (p. 5).

9 Among modern treatments, Tun Thin's [48] typifies this "monolithic" approach. He identifies two possible motives of the oligopolist: either (1) to seek the maximum payoff for himself regardless of the impact on his rivals, or (2) to wage a price war to kill them off even at the cost of his own short-run profits. This type of "vision" of oligopolistic behavior does not gain support from empirical study.

10 [23], p. (143).

11 See, for example, T. Bresnahan, [6].

12 In R.E. Kuenne [31] θ has been derived for the OPEC cartel in the 1973-1981 time frame. And, again, further techniques for the derivation of power structure and binary consonance factors are presented in Chapter 7.

13 The constraint can be written explicitly as a market share constraint in the following manner:

$$N_i - x_i / \sum_{j \neq i} x_j \leq 0 ,$$

where $N_i = M_i/(1 - M_i)$, and where M_i is minimum acceptance market share. Unfortunately this constraint will not be convex, and hence destroys the convexity of the feasible region and the problem.

14 Herbert Simon [42].

15 See, for example, the implications of Samuelson's theorem of conjugate pairs that the profession has resolutely ignored except in the specific case of the theorem of the second best. P. Samuelson, [40], p. (19), and G.C. Archibald [2].

CHAPTER 2

RIVALROUS CONSONANCE: THEORETICAL CONSIDERATIONS AT THE FIRST LEVEL

Crippled optimization models designed to analyze oligopoly under the rivalrous consonance interpretation, as illustrated in Models 1 - 3 in Chapter 1, are a species of nonlinear programming schemata. Within this context the economic nature of the solutions to these models and some experiments into the parametric displacement of the optima, when *all other rivals' prices and* θ *are treated as parameters*, will be conducted. We term consideration under these conditions *analysis at the first level.*

1. *RIVALROUS CONSONANCE EQUILIBRIUM AND DISPLACEMENT ANALYSIS -- FIRST LEVEL*

1.1 *Model 1 -- Crippled Profit-Maximization: Single Industry*

1.1.1 *Formal Derivation.* The Lagrangean form for rival i's Model 1 formulation (Chapter 1.3.1) may be written (where a_i may be taken as including $\mathbf{b_{iq}\, q}$ of (2) in Chapter 1:

$$(1)\quad \mathcal{L}_i = (a_i - b_{ii}\, p_i + \sum_{j \neq i} b_{ij}\, p_j)m_i + \sum_{j \neq i} \theta_{ij}(a_j - b_{jj}\, p_j + b_{ji}\, p_i + \sum_{k \neq i,j} b_{jk}\, p_k\,)\, m_j - \lambda_1 C_i^1 - \lambda_2 C_i^2 - \lambda_3 C_i^3 - \lambda_4 C_i^4 - \lambda_5 C_i^5\ ,$$

where C_i^1 is the capacity constraint; C_i^2 is the minimum market share requirement; C_i^3 and C_i^4 are maximum and minimum price change constraints; and C_i^5 is the price-bounding (generally, nonnegativity) constraint. (See Chapter 1, (3) - (7) for precise definition.) As in the objective function, sales functions have been substituted for all x_i and x_j in the constraints from (2) in Chapter 1. As indicated in that chapter, $\mathcal{L}_i$ is concave in own-price p_i, with all other prices given in the solution, and therefore the sufficiency condition for a global maximum is met. Finally, we require

$$(2)\quad \lambda_t \geq 0, \quad t = 1, 2, \ldots 5.$$

The Kuhn-Tucker conditions are necessary and sufficient,[1] therefore, to achieve a global maximum:

$$(3)\quad 1.\ \delta\mathcal{L}_i/\delta p_i = [x_i - b_{ii}\, m_i + \sum_{j \neq i} \theta_{ij}\, b_{ji}\, m_j + \lambda_1\, b_{11} - \lambda_2\, b_{11} - \lambda_3/\overline{p}_i + \lambda_4/\overline{p}_i + \lambda_5] \leq 0$$

$$2.\quad p_i(\,[\,.\,]\,) = 0$$

$$3.\quad \delta\mathscr{L}_i/\delta\lambda_t = \overset{t}{C_i} \le 0 \qquad\qquad t = 1, 2, \ldots, 5$$

$$4.\quad \lambda_t(\overset{t}{C_i}) = 0 \quad ,$$

$$5.\quad \lambda_t \ge 0, \qquad\qquad t = 1, 2, \ldots, 5$$

The economic meaning of these first-order conditions for a constrained extended profit (E_i) maximum is straightforward. The λ_t are the dual variables or shadow prices associated with the constraints, and condition (3.4) requires that they be zero if the relevant constraint does not bind in the optimum, or, with (3.5), that they be nonnegative if their relevant constraints are effective there.

To make the economic meaning of (3.1) clearer we rewrite it as a differential:

$$(4)\qquad x_i\, dp_i - b_{ii}\, dp_i\, p_i \le -b_{ii}\, dp_i\, C_i - \sum_{j \ne i} \theta_{ij}\, b_{ji}\, dp_i\, m_j - \lambda_1\, b_{ii}\, dp_i + \lambda_2\, b_{ii}\, dp_i + \lambda_3\, dp_i/\bar{p}_i - \lambda_4\, dp_i/\bar{p}_i - \lambda_5\, dp_i \;.$$

The left-hand side of (4) is recognizable as own marginal revenue with respect to price change (MR_i). (Usually marginal revenue is explicitly related to quantity changes.) The right-hand side, therefore, can be interpreted as "extended marginal cost", with the following terms taken in sequence:

1. Conventional own marginal cost (MC_i);

2. Extended marginal rival profit ($EMRP_i$) impact of firm i's pricing decisions. That is, if $dp_i < 0$, rival j will lose $b_{ji}\, dp_i$ in sales and m_j in profit on each sale. Marginal profit loss is the product of these two terms, and θ_{ij} times this decrement in profit converts the value to its equivalent in rival i's profit. We find it convenient to treat this "other profit impact", summed over all rivals, as a marginal cost under rivalrous consonance -- that is, as a deterrent to firm i's price reduction.

3. The marginal cost of firm i's capacity limitation. If $\overset{1}{C_i}$ binds and λ_1 is positive, it is the marginal impact on extended profits of an increment in capacity B_i. Hence, $\lambda_1 = \delta E_i/\delta B_i$, or the rate at which extended profit changes with respect to an increase in output. The amount of output a fall in price, dp_i, brings about is $b_{ii}\, dp_i$, and hence $\lambda_i\, b_{ii}\, dp_i$ is the marginal cost of the inability to expand beyond B_i in sales. Of course, $\lambda_1 = 0$ if the constraint does not bind, as required by (3.4).

4. The marginal cost of minimum market share. If $\overset{2}{C_i}$ binds and $\lambda_2 > 0$, this implies that p_i is being held "artificially" low to capture marginal sales. If M_i were to fall slightly, so that rival i were less willing to sacrifice extended profit for sales, then p_i could *rise* by dp_i. Sales would fall by $b_{ii}\, dp_i$, extended profits would rise at the rate $\lambda_2 = \delta E_i/\delta M_i$, and hence total extended profits by the product, $\lambda_2\, b_{ii}\, dp_i$.

5. $\overset{+}{T_i}$ is an upper bound on the proportion that price bears to a benchmark. Hence, if $\lambda_3 > 0$, p_i is restrained from moving higher. With a rise in price, the ratio of p_i to the benchmark would rise by $dp_i/\bar{p}_i$, extended profit would expand at the rate $\delta E_i/\delta \overset{+}{T_i} = \lambda_3$, and total extended profit by the increment which is the product of the two.

6. A similar argument to that of 5. holds for T_i^-, the lower bound on $p_i/\bar{p}_i$. If $\lambda_4 > 0$, p_i is forced higher than an unconstrained optimization would bring about. A reduction in T_i^- would allow a price decrease and a fall in $p_i/\bar{p}_i$ by $dp_i/\bar{p}_i$, with a rise in extended profit by $\delta E_i/\delta T_i^- dp_i/\bar{p}_i = \lambda_4 \, dp_i/\bar{p}_i$. Hence, that is the marginal cost of the level T_i^-. Obviously, either λ_3 or λ_4 or both will be zero in the solution: both cannot be positive if $T_i^+ \neq T_i^-$.

7. N_i is a lower bound on price, and if $\lambda_5 > 0$, $p_i = N_i$ is higher than unconstrained maximization desires and thus a cost is inflicted on the firm for adopting it. We will suppose $N_i = 0$ in all analysis to follow.

Thus, (4) is interpreted as requiring own marginal revenue not to exceed own marginal cost plus extended marginal profit impacts on rivals (actual rival profit impacts converted to own profit equivalent) plus the (positive, negative, or zero) own marginal constraint costs. If such extended marginal costs at the optimum exceed marginal revenue, rival i should not produce. If equality rules, output may be (and in general will be) positive by (3.2).

1.1.2 *A Geometrical Interpretation.* The nature of these extended marginal cost components is a contingent one, so that, in general, only one if any of the dual components will be non-zero. The relationships may be depicted graphically in Figure 2.1.[2] In panel a we illustrate an optimum solution for rival i which is not bound by any constraint. The D_i and MR_i curves are the firm's sales function (all p_j, $j \neq i$, and **q** constant) and marginal revenue curve. The curve MC_i is its conventional marginal cost function. The $EMRP_i$ component of firm i's costs is the second term in the right-hand side of (4). For each reduction of p_i, dp_i, with consequent sales expansion, dx_i, firm i inflicts a constant incremental profit loss upon all of its rivals which it translates into an extended profit loss by multiplying by the relevant consonance factors and adding.

The feasible region within which x_i must fall is defined by the requirement that p_i must be nonnegative (on or above the horizontal axis) and the restrictions on sales set explicitly or implicitly by the four primary constraints. Note that two of the constraints vie to set a lower bound (C_i^2 and C_i^3, implying M_i and x_i^+ respectively) and two compete to define the upper bound (C_i^1 and C_i^4, setting B_i and x_i^- respectively). The values x_i^+ and x_i^- are the implied sales limits set by the price bounds $T_i^+ \bar{p}_i$ and $T_i^- \bar{p}_i$ respectively, as drawn in panel a. It follows that if $T_i^+ \bar{p}_i \neq M_i$ and $T_i^- \bar{p}_i \neq B_i$, only one constraint at most can hold at the optimum -- the greatest lower bound or the least upper bound. Hence, one or none of the λ°'s will be positive, where ($^{\circ}$) indicates an optimal value.

In Figure 2.1.a we have illustrated the latter case. Note that as the bounds are drawn, x_i^+ and B_i can never be effective, so that C_i^1 and C_i^3 can be excluded from the model. The feasible region is $x_i^{\circ} \varepsilon [M_i, x_i]$, and in panel a x_i° falls strictly in the interior of this interval so that no constraint binds as an equality. We have, therefore, an effective illustration of a rivalrous consonance partial equilibrium uncomplicated by multiple objectives.

If rival i set all θ_{ij} equal to zero, so that it accorded no consideration to the impacts of its pricing actions on rivals' profits, price would be set at p_i^{o}, where c denotes the Cournot nature of this myopic behavior.[3] Instead, however, rivalrous consonance leads the firm to set the higher price, p_i^{o}, with lower sales x_i^{o}. Not surprisingly, the existence of rivalrous consonance leads the typical rival to a solution with higher price and lower output than it would adopt in a Cournot environment, at least before the reactions of rivals are taken into account at the second analytical level.

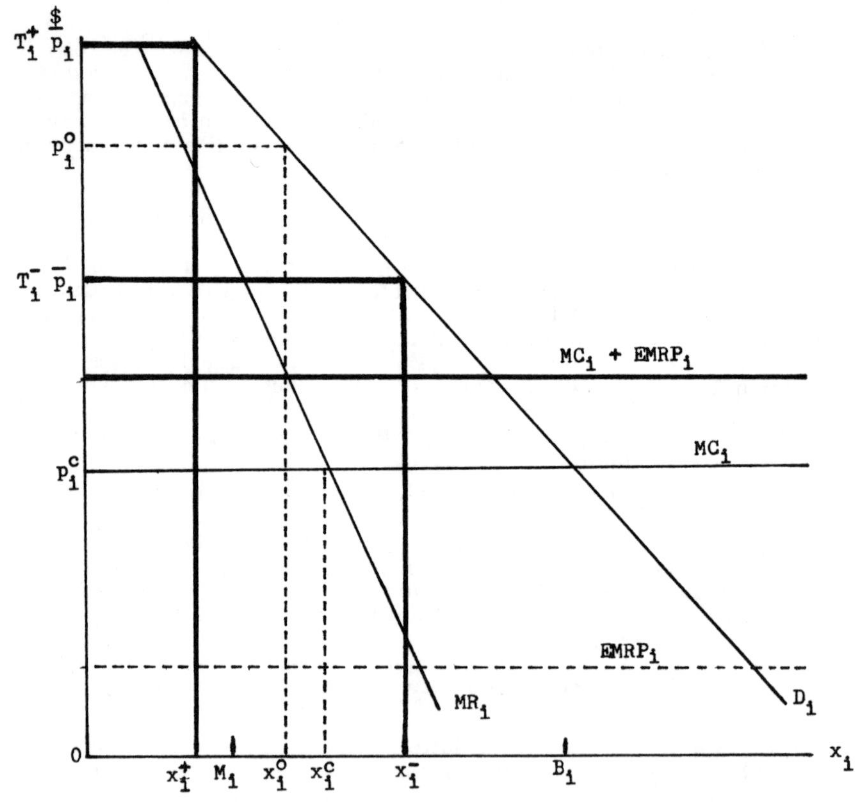

Figure 2.1. CRIPPLED OPTIMIZATION SOLUTIONS TO MODEL 1

a. $\lambda_1^o = \lambda_2^o = \lambda_3^o = \lambda_4^o = 0$

In Figure 2.1.b the case where p_i is constrained by C_i^2 is illustrated. Were price unconstrained, rivalrous consonance would lead to $p_i^!$, determined by the equality of marginal revenue and extended marginal cost (MC_i + $EMRP_i$). But the constraint on minimum allowable sales will not permit this price, and p_i^o is forced to the value that yields M_i in sales instead. The crippled optimization solution interprets this as forcing rival i to subsidize itself by $\lambda_2^o b_{ii}$ for the luxury of maintaining its market position, for that is the marginal imputed value of the goal measured in sacrificed profits. In panel b we have drawn it as a negative marginal cost that lowers the extended marginal cost function. Alternatively, as is clear from (4), we could have added this subsidy to MR_i by shifting the curve up vertically to intersect MC_i + $EMRP_i$ at the solution (p_i^o, x_i^o). Of course, $\lambda_2 \equiv 0$ to the right of $x_i = M_i$, as is shown in panel b, for in this domain the constraint is ineffective.

Had we drawn x_i^+ to the right of M_i on panel a it would be C_i^3 that becomes effective in this type of solution, and the same interpretation of an implied subsidy springing from the marginal benefit to the firm of restraining price rise would be appropriate. It is clear in (4) that both of these constraints contribute positively to the right-hand side, so that when dpi < 0 they become negative costs. We will not, therefore, repeat the similar analysis for this alternative binding of a lower bound constraint on output.

Figure 2.1.c illustrates a constrained optimum at the other end of the sales interval. In the absence of the constraint on price reduction, straightforward extended profit optimization would dictate the price $p_i^!$ with $x_i^!$ in sales. However, at $\overline{x_i}$ the shadow price of maintaining a minimum price becomes positive and, at the particular constellation of circumstances shown in panel c, rises to the value shown. In general, of course, it must be sufficient to raise extended marginal cost to the intersection with MR_i at $x_i^o = \overline{x_i}$. Thus $\lambda_4(1/\overline{p}_i)$ becomes the marginal cost to the firm of maintaining the chosen floor on price. Were B_i -- the limit on production and sales set by capacity or firm policy -- to fall to the left of $\overline{x_i}$ on panel a, C_i^1 would be effective and the marginal cost of inability to boost output would register to raise price to the level permitting B_i to be sold.

1.1.3 *Actual and Imputed Costs and Benefits.* The synthetic or imputed nature of the marginal extended profit function leads to unconventional interpretations of its cost components. In Figure 2.2 we have graphed a typical solution to Model 1 with $\lambda_4^o > 0$, although we continue to present results in conventional fashion with x_i on the horizontal axis. Thus, for example, the curve MC_i is firm i's own marginal cost function, and if the firm set all θ_{ij} to zero and did not restrict the extent to which it could lower price profit would be the rectangle ABCD (we assume average total cost equals marginal cost).

Suppose, now, that firm i adopted a rivalrous consonance attitude in its pricing but repealed self-imposed restrictions on its ability to reduce price. Extended profit -- which includes only own-profits plus extended marginal rival profit ($EMRP_i$) plus MC_i equal marginal revenue (MR_i). This occurs when MR_i rises (as x_i falls) from OD by the increment DN (=GH), the value of $EMRP_i$. By reducing x_i by CH with consequent rise in p_i by EA, own-profit falls by the amount GHC. However, by raising p_i to OE, and thereby lowering x_i by HC, firm i permits its rivals to raise profits, in firm i's valuation, by the equivalent of GRHC, or twice the own-profit loss. Hence, the increment in firm i's extended profit in GHC (=GRC), or loss in own-profit (ABCD - EFHD) plus gain in extended rival profit (GRC).

On the other hand, the marginal cost enhancement introduced by C_i^4 is a fictitious one, necessary to raise price (and reduce sales) to the limit specified. In Figure 2.2 it is added to MC_i + $EMRP_i$ to bring p_i up to OI. Own profits thereby decline a further KGHL. Thus, rivalrous consonance together with the price reduction constraint lower own profit by a total of KCL. However, the rise in p_i necessary to effect the fall of x_i by HL increases extended rival profits by MGHL. Hence, extended profit

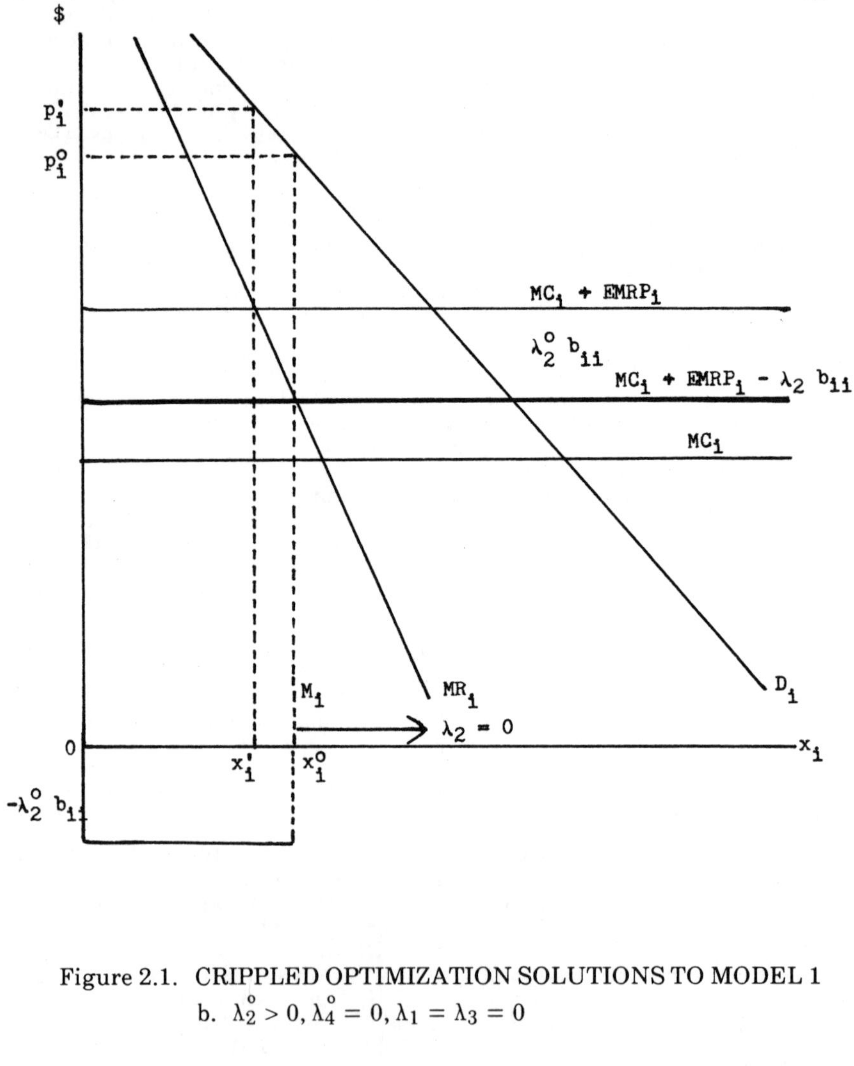

Figure 2.1. CRIPPLED OPTIMIZATION SOLUTIONS TO MODEL 1
b. $\overset{\circ}{\lambda}_2 > 0, \overset{\circ}{\lambda}_4 = 0, \lambda_1 = \lambda_3 = 0$

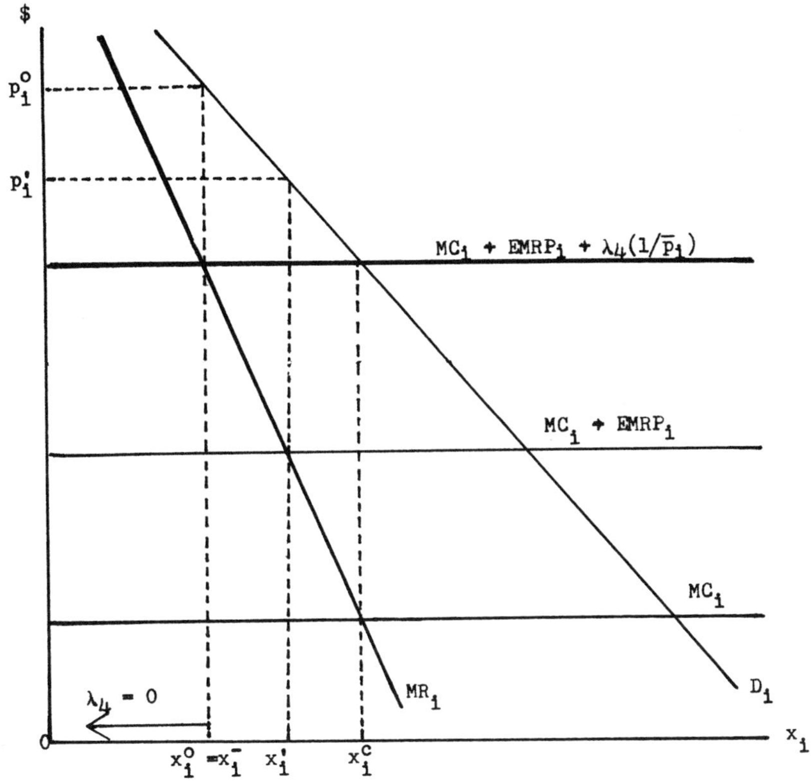

Figure 2.1. CRIPPLED OPTIMIZATION SOLUTIONS TO MODEL 1
c. $\overset{o}{\lambda}_4 > 0, \overset{o}{\lambda}_2 = 0, \lambda_1 = \lambda_3 = 0$

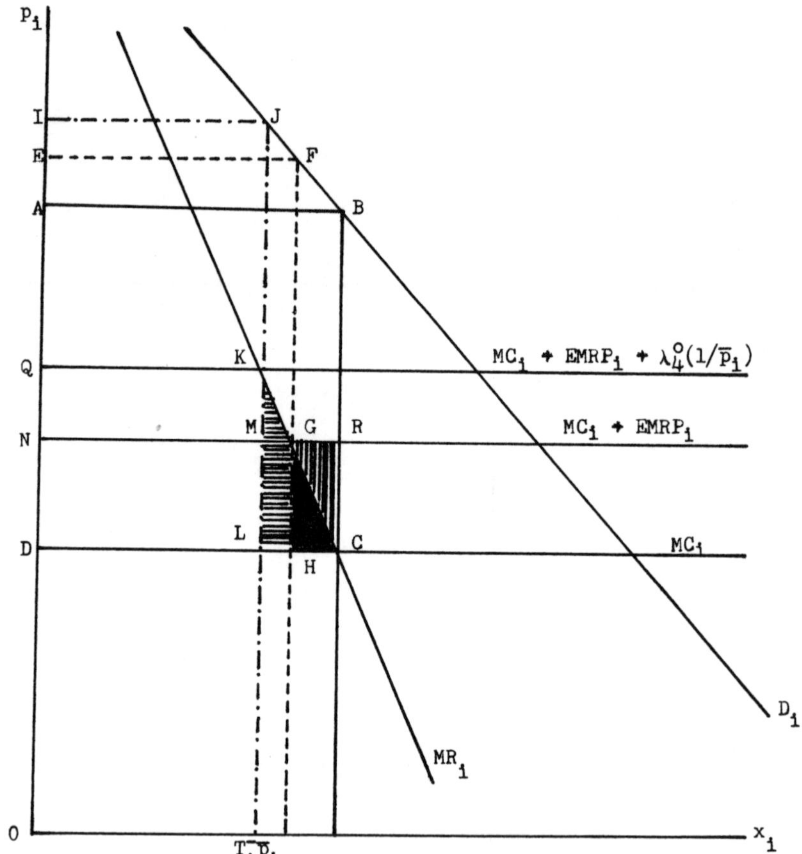

Figure 2.2. AN INTERPRETATION OF FIRM i's OWN AND EXTENDED PROFITS -- LOWER BOUND CONSTRAINT ON p_i

change effected by rivalrous consonance and C_i^4 will be MRCL - GCH - KGM, and the net cost of the constraint in extended (and own) profit will be KMG.

A similar interpretation applies for optima that include synthetic subsidies. Figure 2.3 illustrates the cost and extended profit imputations of a rivalrous consonance solution for firm i when the minimum sales restraint, M_i, is enforced. Once more a myopic firm i neglecting its interdependence with rivals, maximizes its short-term own profits at $p_i = OA$ on the figure. Were extended profits instead adopted as an objective function, unconstrained by other goals, $p_i = OE$ would be set at a cost GCH in firm i's own profits, but with a net gain of GCH (= GRC) in extended profit.

However, $p_i = OE$ must be lowered to OI to permit the minimum sales restraint, M_i, to be attained. Therefore, λ_2^o must be sufficient so that when subtracted from $MC_i + EMRP_i$, price is lowered to OI. Hence, λ_2^o is in the nature of a compensation of lost own-profit per unit of output -- an implied subsidy. As shown in the discussion of Figure 2.2, rivalrous consonance before the imposition of C_i^2 increased extended profit by a net of GRC in Figure 2.3. When λ_2^o becomes positive, $EMRP_i$ falls by GMHL + MRKT, but GHLK of this is recaptured in own-profit. Hence, the net fall in E_i is GMK + MRKT = GKTR, leaving only KTC in incremental E_i above own-profit when C_i^2 is effective.

1.1.4. *Parametric Displacement of First Level Solution.* Because the partial analysis of Model 1 is simple -- with all rival price reactions to firm i's price decisions ignored -- the derivation of qualitative propositions is possible. For the most part, they are trivial, but one of them has an important bearing on rivalrous consonance models.

If any constraint binds in the solution and is assumed to continue to bind when a parameter is changed with no other constraint becoming effective, p_i is unable to change. None of these displacement outcomes is interesting, so we will assume the initial equilibrium is that of Figure 2.1.a in which no constraint binds. We also assume that the parametric shocks are so small that no constraint binds in the new optimum. Then, from (3-1), if we differentiate totally with respect to all prices and marginal costs,

$$(5)\qquad 2b_{ii}\,dp_i = b_{ii}\,dC_i + \sum_{j\neq i} b_{ij}\,dp_j + \sum_{j\neq i} \theta_{ij}\,b_{ji}\,dp_j - \sum_{j\neq i} \theta_{ij}\,b_{ji}\,dC_j\,.$$

Suppose that rival k suffers the misfortune of a rise in unit cost; then

$$(6)\qquad dp_i/dC_k = -.5\,(\theta_{ik}\,b_{ki}/b_{ii}) < 0\,.$$

Thus, in rivalrous consonance, when a rival's profit margin shrinks, other rivals are led at this first level of analysis to *reduce* their prices to take advantage of the discomfiture, not to increase the price protection the affected firm is afforded. Indeed, the greater the solicitude extended firm $k(\theta_{ik})$, the greater the discomfiture inflicted. The reason is clear. A shrinkage in m_k lowers the marginal extended profit term in firm i's necessary condition and shifts the $MC_i + EMRP_i$ curve downward on an unchanged MR_i curve in Figure 3.1.a. Of course, if C_k falls, the firm is afforded more weight in firm i's pricing decision and p_i will rise in consequence. Indeed, changes in the profit margins of rivals under rivalrous consonance are akin to direct changes in power structure perceptions. Thus,

$$(7)\qquad dp_i/d\theta_{ik} = .5(b_{ki}\,m_k/b_{ii}) > 0\,,$$

which substitutes the profit margin as multiplier instead of θ_{ij} in (6) and which, therefore, will be stronger. Nonetheless, the structure and path of the impact

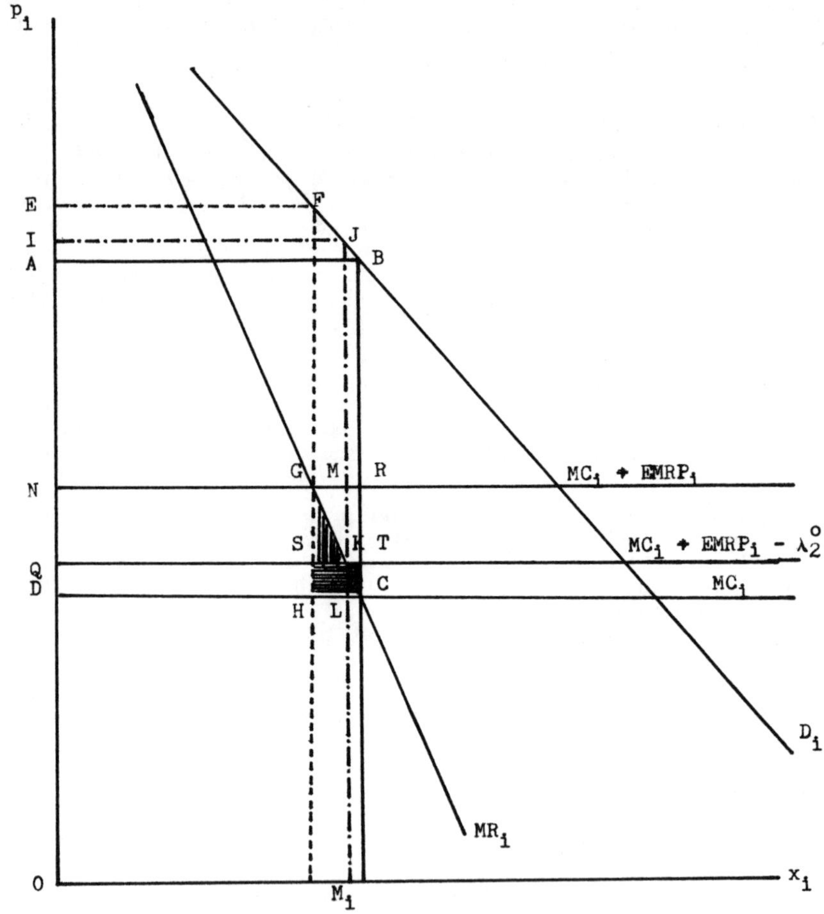

Figure 2.3. AN INTERPRETATION OF FIRM i's OWN AND EXTENDED PROFITS -- UPPER BOUND CONSTRAINT ON p_i

through $EMRP_i$ makes a rise in C_k and a reduction in θ_{ik} similar events in the decision making of rivals.

When we expand our displacement analysis beyond the present partial context into the general analyses, an interesting hypothesis arises. Given a rise in C_k, with p_k held constant, all other rivals should experience some incentive to lower price. Rival k's sales curve should then shift leftward, leading it to lower p_k, shifting rivals' sales curves downward to induce some fall in prices, and so forth, until a new crippled optimization is reached with generally *lower* prices. On symmetrically reasoned grounds, a fall in C_k should put some upward pressure on prices in the industry. Rivalrous consonace yields this somewhat counterintuitive proposition, and it would be interesting to test it against economic reality. Of course, in most instances of historical occurrence of cost inflation *all* rivals will experience the change in costs and the price tendencies in the industry will bear in the same direction as the movement of costs.

We will examine such displacements more rigorously in Chapter 3, but it is interesting to note that the tendency of rivals to lower price and enhance the profit difficulties of a firm when the profit margin is squeezed is not sparked by an atmosphere of price war. That would require that the the θ-terms be negative, and we have ignored that possibility for a mature industry. On the contrary, it occurs in an industry in which active concern for the welfare of rivals is expressed in pricing power. However, because such displacements are most easily analyzed using reaction functions, we will postpone further consideration of the topic until Chapter 6, in which those tools will be used in analyses with all prices and θ-terms variable.

1.2. *Model 2 -- Crippled Profit-Maximization: General Equilibrium at the First Level*

1.2.1. *Formal Derivation.* With the extension of the model to many industries and the additional complication of concern with industrial customers' profits, first-order conditions and their manipulation in unspecified models become clumsy and of limited usefulness. Indeed, we have argued in Chapter 1 that recourse to simulative theorizing is necessary for the derivation of insights from such models. Before we employ such methods for a fictional industry in Chapter 5, however, let us derive the first-order conditions for a small general model, simplified in several dimensions to increase its understandability.

We assume two industries with two rivals each. Firms 1 and 2 form one industry and 3 and 4 the other. Interfirm relations are that firm 1 supplies firm 3, firm 2 supplies firm 4, firm 3 supplies firm 2, and firm 4 supplies firm 1. We have depicted these supplier-customer relations in Figure 2.4.

As discussed in Chapter 1.3.2, total demand consists of consumer plus industrial intermediate demand:

$$(8) \quad \begin{bmatrix} 1 & 0 & -v_{13} & 0 \\ 0 & 1 & 0 & -v_{24} \\ 0 & -v_{32} & 1 & 0 \\ -v_{41} & 0 & 0 & 1 \end{bmatrix} \begin{bmatrix} z_1 \\ z_2 \\ z_3 \\ z_4 \end{bmatrix} = \begin{bmatrix} x_1 \\ x_2 \\ x_3 \\ x_4 \end{bmatrix} \quad \text{(or) } \mathbf{A}\,\mathbf{Z} = \mathbf{X}$$

Then, from (14), Chapter 1,

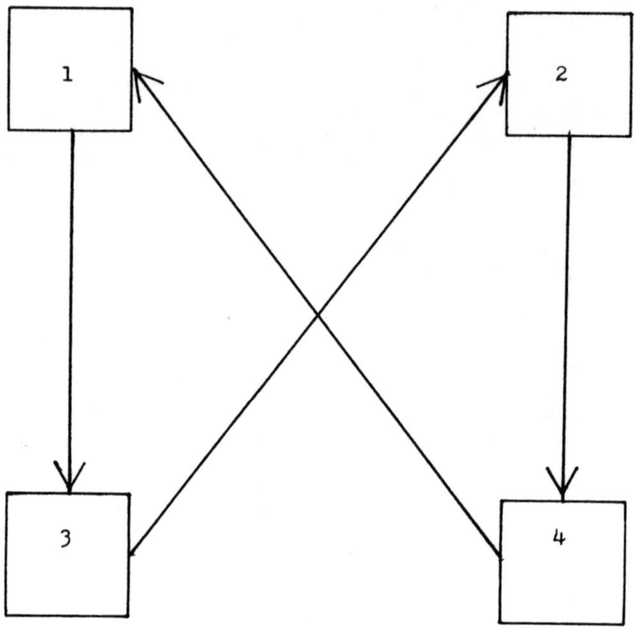

Figure 2.4. INTERFIRM RELATIONS -- MODEL 2 EXAMPLE

$$(9)\quad \mathbf{Z} = \begin{bmatrix} 1/|\mathbf{A}| & v_{13}v_{32}/|\mathbf{A}| & v_{13}/|\mathbf{A}| & v_{13}v_{24}v_{32}/|\mathbf{A}| \\ v_{24}v_{41}/|\mathbf{A}| & 1/|\mathbf{A}| & v_{13}v_{24}v_{41}/|\mathbf{A}| & v_{24}/|\mathbf{A}| \\ v_{24}v_{32}v_{41}/|\mathbf{A}| & v_{32}/|\mathbf{A}| & 1/|\mathbf{A}| & v_{24}v_{32}/|\mathbf{A}| \\ v_{41}/|\mathbf{A}| & v_{13}v_{32}v_{41}/|\mathbf{A}| & v_{13}/v_{41}/|\mathbf{A}| & 1/|\mathbf{A}| \end{bmatrix} \mathbf{X} = \mathbf{BX}.$$

Rival 1's extended profit objective function may then be written

$$(10)\quad \begin{aligned} E_1 &= m_1 z_1 + \theta_{12} m_2 z_2 + \theta_{13} m_3 z_3 \\ &= m_1(\mathbf{B}_1 \mathbf{X}) + \theta_{12} m_2 (\mathbf{B}_2 \mathbf{X}) + \theta_{13} m_3 (\mathbf{B}_3 \mathbf{X}) , \end{aligned}$$

where $\mathbf{B}_i$ is the ith row vector of $\mathbf{B} = \mathbf{A}^{-1}$, and, from (10), Chapter 1, $C_i = f_1 + \Sigma_s v_{si} p_s$. The constraints C_1-C_5 are written straightforwardly with z_1 substituted for x_1 throughout. Because their complications of the first-order necessary conditions have been dealt with extensively in the discussion of Model 1, it will be assumed that none of them binds in the solution and that $z_1^o > 0$.

Then the first-order conditions for firm 1's crippled optimization solution at the first level may be written

$$(11)\quad \delta E_1/\delta p_1 \equiv EMP_1 = [m_1 z_1' + z_1] + [\theta_{12} m_2 z_2'] + [\theta_{13}(-v_{13} z_3 + m_3 z_3')] = 0,$$

where EMP_1 is marginal extended profit, and $z_i' = \delta z_i/\delta p_1$, and (11) may be written, bracketed term by term,

$$(12)\quad EMP_1 = MOP_1 + EMRP_1 + EMCP_1 = 0$$

when we define:

1. MOP_1: marginal own profit of firm 1;
2. $EMRP_1$: extended marginal rival profit of firm 1;
3. $EMCP_1$: extended marginal customer profit of firm 1.

From (11), now, consider MOP_1. The term $z_1' < 0$, and m_1 and z_1 are functions of p_1; further

$$(13)\quad \delta MOP_1/\delta p_1 = 2z_1' = 2(\mathbf{B}_1 \mathbf{X}') = 2(-b_{11} + v_{13} v_{32} b_{21}/|\mathbf{A}|) < 0 .$$

Note that we assume that the household demand curves for each industry's products are unaffected by the prices of the other industry. $EMRP_1$ does not vary with p_1. And,

$$(14)\quad \delta EMCP_1/\delta p_1 = -2\theta_{13} v_{13} z_3' = -2\theta_{13} v_{13} v_{32}((-v_{24}v_{41}b_{11} + b_{21})/|\mathbf{A}|) .$$

Hence, $EMCP_1$ varies linearly with p_1, and its complexity is worth analyzing. We shall begin with the aid of Figure 2.5, which presents a flow chart of the lines of impact of dp_1 upon firm 3's profits.

The first line of impact is a direct path from the change in p_1 on firm 3's profit margin:

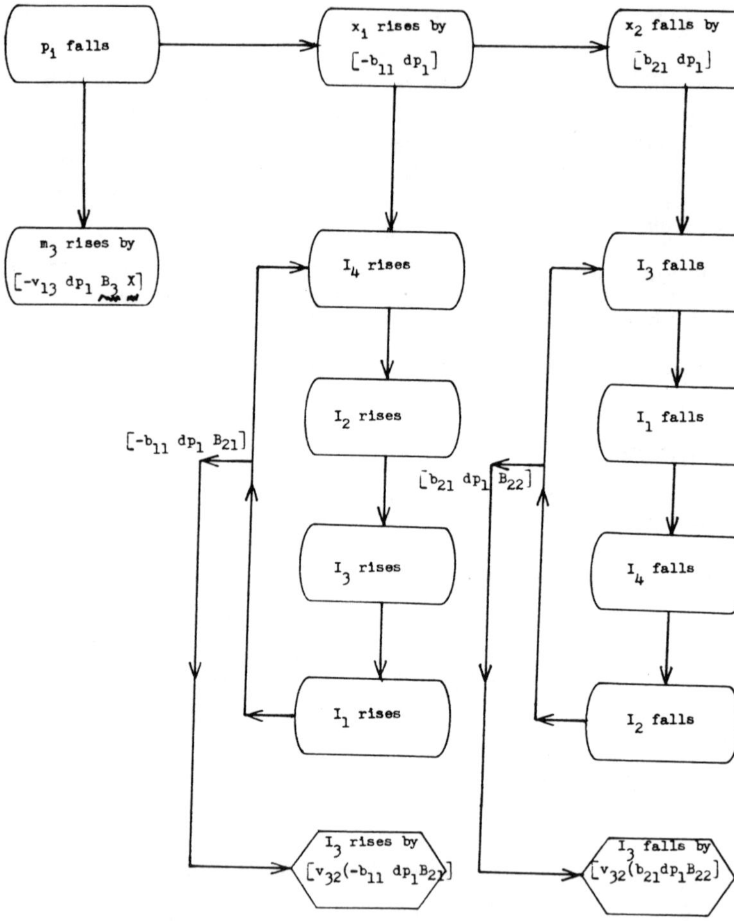

Figure 2.5. FLOW CHART OF CUSTOMER'S PROFIT COMPONENT OF EXTENDED PROFIT

(15) $\delta(p_3 - f_3 - v_{13}\, p_1)/\delta p_1 = -v_{13}$.

This rate of impact will be transmitted to all sales in the initial equilibrium, for a total direct effect of

(16) $-v_{13}\, dp_1\, [\mathbf{B_3\, X}]$.

This total direct effect is shown at the extreme left of Figure 2.5. In the $EMCP_1$ bracket of (11) it is the first term.

We denote industrial demand for a firm's product

(17) $I_i = z_i - x_i$.

The second path of impact is an indirect one upon firm 3's industrial demand arising from the change in firm 1's household sales. When p_1 changes, these will change by $(-b_{11}\, dp_1)$, and alter the demand for firm 4's product as input. However, that in turn changes the industrial demand for firm 2, which alters I_3, which changes I_1, which feeds back to a change in I_4. Hence, a loop from I_4 to itself is set up by the change in x_1. Its importance to the customer's profit component is the total impact it has upon firm 2's industrial sales, and that is given, for each unit of initiating change in x_1, by B_{21}, the total impact on z_2 -- direct and indirect -- of a change in x_1 by one unit. Since x_1 changes by $(-b_{11}\, dp_1)$, the total induced change in z_2 will be $(-b_{11}\, dp_1\, B_{21})$. Since each such unit of firm 2's product requires v_{32} units of firm 3's good as input, it follows that I_3 will change by $-v_{32}(-b_{11}\, dp_1\, B_{21}) = (-b_{11}\, dp_1\, B_{31})$. This line of impact flow is traced in the middle branch of the graph in Figure 2.5.

However, there is a third path of indirect impact which will tend to change I_3 in the opposite direction. This branch is the extreme right line of flow in Figure 2.5, and is initiated by the impact of dp_1 upon rival 2's sales, which will change by $b_{21}\, dp_1$. Since firm 3 is firm 2's supplier, I_3 changes in the same direction, which moves I_1, changing I_4, then changing I_2. The change in I_2 completes the loop back upon I_3, and a converging series of industrial demand impacts is established. It is their total effect upon firm 2's sales that is of interest again, as firm 3 supplies firm 2. The element B_{22} in $\mathbf{B}$ is the direct plus indirect sales impact on firm 2 of a unit change in x_2, and, by reasoning similar to that used in analyzing the second path of causation above, the total impact on z_2 will be $b_{21}\, dp_1\, B_{22}$. Also, in analogous fashion, the industrial sales of firm 3 will be affected to the extent $v_{32}(b_{21}\, dp_1\, B_{22}) = b_{21}\, dp_1\, B_{32}$ shown on Figure 2.5.

The net change in z_3 flowing down these two indirect channels is the sum of the terms: $(-b_{11}\, B_{31} + b_{21}\, B_{32})dp_1$. When this is multiplied by the profit margin, m_3, it is converted to the impact on firm 3's profit from the sales change, and will be found as the second term in the $EMCP_1$ brackets in (11). If we add it to the change in profit accruing from the profit margin change, the total profit impact of dp_1 on firm 3 is obtained, which is $EMCP_1$. It is converted to firm 1's equivalent extended profit by applying θ_{13}.

For $dp_1 < 0$, the profit margin contribution to $EMCP_1$ will be unambiguously positive. On the other hand, the two terms that compose the indirect impacts will be opposite in sign, with the expansion in x_1 giving rise to positive, and the contraction in x_2 to negative effects on sales and hence profits. Normally, $b_{11} > b_{21}$, but $B_{22} > B_{21}$ since B_{22} will include the unit of x_2 that gave rise to the expansion of firm 2's output and B_{21} will not. Thus $b_{11}B_{21} \lesseqgtr b_{21}B_{22}$. However, the profit margin effect will normally outweigh the net resultant of the indirect effects, and we would expect the customer's profit component of extended profit to move in a direction opposite to the sign of dp_1.

Hence, in this expectation the taking into account of customers' welfares acts as a negative extended marginal profit component and *reduces* the degree of price support given rivals. This is made clear in Figure 2.6, which uses a direct interpretation of (11) and (12) and requires an unfamiliar manner of viewing the firm's partial equilibrium.

On Figure 2.6 Firm 1's marginal extended profit components are graphed on the vertical axis against p_1 on the horizontal axis. From (12) there are three components: MOP_1, $EMRP_1$, $EMCP_1$. The latter two, of course, have been translated into firm 1's profit equivalents. It must be recalled in interpreting such figures that all marginal magnitudes are derived from *price* changes, not *quantity* changes.

Firm 1's optimum price, in the absence of a customers' component, would be $p_1^{\prime}$ where $MOP_1 + EMRP_1 = 0$. However, under the assumption that $z_3^{\prime} < 0$, $EMCP_1$ slope upward as drawn (see (14)) and hence will induce $MOP_1 + EMRP_1 + EMCP_1$ -- the extended marginal profit of (11) -- to meet the horizontal axis at an optimum $p_1^{o} < p_1^{\prime}$: rivalrous consonance that includes customers' welfare will dampen oligopolistic price enhancements.

1.2.2 *Second-Order Condition.* Given the linearity of constraints C^1 -- C^5, the convexity of Model 2 depends upon the concavity of the extended profit function (10) in p_1. This requires that $\delta^2 E_1/\delta p_1^2 \leq 0$, which will be true if and only if

$$(18) \qquad z_1^{\prime} - \theta_{13} v_{13} z_3^{\prime} \leq 0 .$$

This condition may or may not hold *a priori*. In practice, however, we expect it to be met in the majority of instances. As discussed in Section 1, $z_1^{\prime} < 0$ and the expectation is that $z_j^{\prime} > 0$ for rivals and suppliers of rivals. But if negative it should be weaker than the $z_1^{\prime}$ term, which reflects direct impacts of own-price changes, and, in addition, is discounted by θ_{13}. This weak negativity should rule for firm i's suppliers.

Our strong expectation, therefore, practically speaking, is that E_1 will be globally concave in p_1, but that cannot be established analytically. In the displacements below, however, we will assume that concavity holds true in all relevant ranges of p_1.

1.2.3. *Some Qualitative Propositions.* All of the theorems we derive in this section will be first level -- partial analytical propositions that hold constant θ and the prices of all firms except that of the firm whose crippled optimization is being considered. They avoid, therefore, the complications of oligopolistic price interdependence, but also thereby sacrifice much of their interest. Moreover, the parametric displacements we investigate have the well-known limitations of classic comparative statics: dependent upon the calculus, they are derived from linearization assumptions that hold only within very small epsilon neighborhoods of the initial optimum. Nonetheless, they yield some interesting insights into crippled optimization.

Consider, for example, the impact on p_1^{o} of a small change in firm 1's factor cost, f_1. From (11), we obtain by differentiation

$$(19) \qquad dp_1^{o}/df_1 = .5(1 - \theta_{13} v_{13} (z_3^{\prime}/z_1^{\prime}))^{-1} .$$

Note first, that if intermediate demand for firm 1's product did not exist ($v_{13} = 0$), or if $\theta_{13} = 0$, this simplifies to

$$(20) \qquad dp_1^{o}/df_1 = .5 ,$$

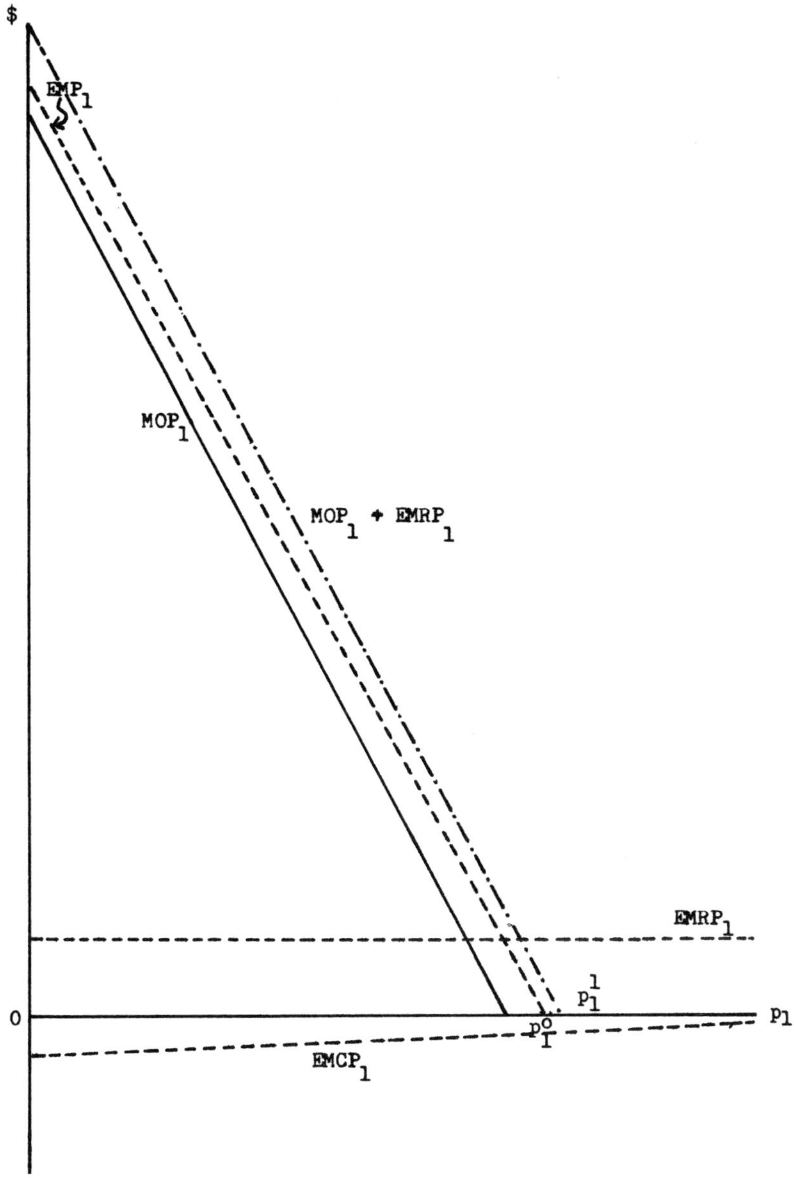

Figure 2.6. EXTENDED PROFIT OPTIMUM FOR FIRM 1 WITH EXTENDED CUSTOMER PROFIT COMPONENT

which is what we would have derived from Model 1 for dp_1^o/dC_1 from (3.1) holding as an equality without binding constraints. Given the linearity of household sales, with marginal revenue linear at half the slope of the sales curve, and with extended *marginal* rival profit constant, optimal price simply rises by half the rise in marginal cost.

The more complicated expression in (19), therefore, is caused wholly by the existence of intermediate demand and firm 1's concern for the profits of its customer. Moreover, the truly complicating factor is that portion of induced industrial demand for firm 1's product that springs indirectly from the impact on rivals' household demand of the change in p_1. For example, in our problem, the total change in z_3 induced by the change in p_1 is

$$(21) \qquad z_3' = B_{31}\,\delta x_1/\delta p_1 + B_{32}\,\delta x_2/\delta p_1 + B_{33}\,\delta x_3/\delta p_1 + B_{34}\,\delta x_4/\delta p_1$$

$$= -b_{11}\,B_{31} + b_{21}\,B_{32} + 0\,B_{33} + 0\,B_{34}$$

$$= v_{32}(-b_{11}\,B_{21} + b_{21}\,B_{22}) = v_{32}\,z_2'.$$

$B_{22} = 1/|\mathbf{A}|$ in $\mathbf{B}$ and, hence, the second term in the last equation is unity larger, but it will be offset by the negativity of the first term, which expanded, is $-b_{11}\,v_{32}\,v_{24}\,v_{41}$, or the expansion in intermediate demand for good 3 set off by the change in consumer demand for good 1 through dp_1, but twice removed from firm 3. Hence, although b_{11} should be larger than b_{21}, because firm 3 is a supplier to firm 1's rivals, we expect $z_3' > 0$, but must recognize that it can be negative for firm i's supplier.

Moreover,

$$(22) \qquad z_1' = -b_{11}\,B_{11} + b_{21}\,B_{12},$$

$$= -b_{11} + b_{21}\,v_{13}\,v_{32} < 0.$$

Hence, from (21), when

1. $z_3' > 0,\ 0 < dp_1^o/df_1 < .5$,
2. $z_3' < 0,\ dp_1^o/df_1 > .5$.[4]

Figure 2.7 illustrates these qualities using the framework of Figure 2.6. Assume $df_1 > 0$. From (11) MOP_1 rises by $-z_1'\,df_1$, which is added vertically to MEP_1 to obtain MEP_2. Then, p_1 rises from p_1^1 to p_1^2 by amounts which are more than one half the change in p_1 that would have occurred in the absence of $EMCP_1$ (p_1^* in Figures 2.7.a and .b) in Figure 2.7.a ($z_3' < 0$) and less than half that amount in Figure 2.7.b ($z_3' > 0$)[5].

When firm 3 is a supplier of firm 1's rivals ($z_3' > 0$) a rise in p_1 increases the sales of firm 3 via an expansion of rivals' output and consequent demand for intermediate inputs, at the same time that it decreases firm 3's profit margin from the rise in cost of its own intermediate input. With p_3 (and all other B_i except p_1) frozen, firm 3's own profit function with respect to p_1 is a parabola rising from a point on the profit axis to a maximum, then falling to the x-axis as p_1 rises. This occurs because as p_1 rises by equal increments, z_3 rises by the same amounts, increasing revenue by fixed increments. However, the profit margin is decreasing, and because it is applied to *all* sales the decreasing revenue from a decreasing profit margin exerts a downward pull that offsets the upward push from increased sales. They attain

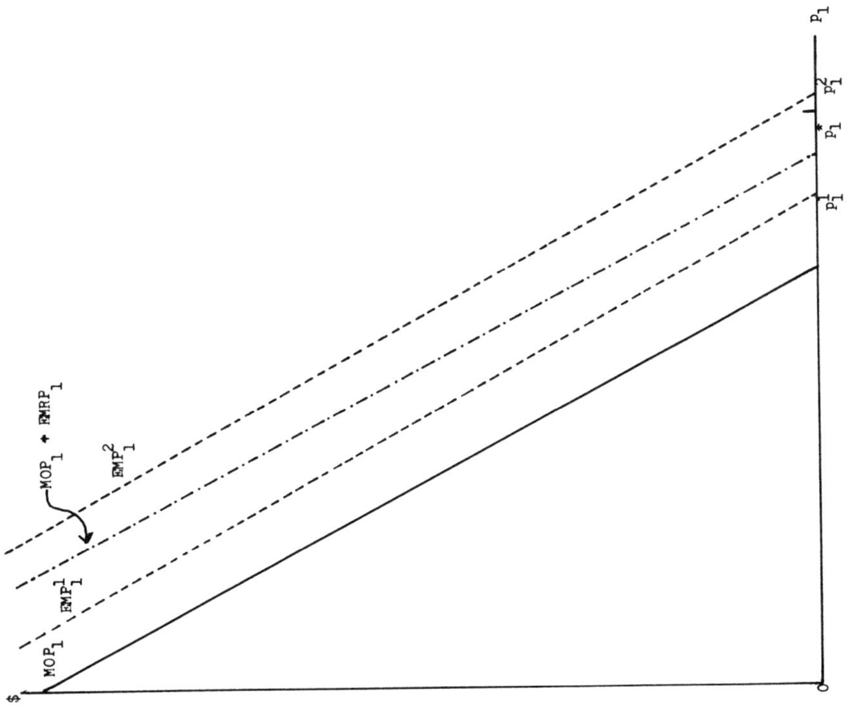

Figure 2.7.a. THE IMPACT OF A RISE IN $f_1, z_3' < 0$

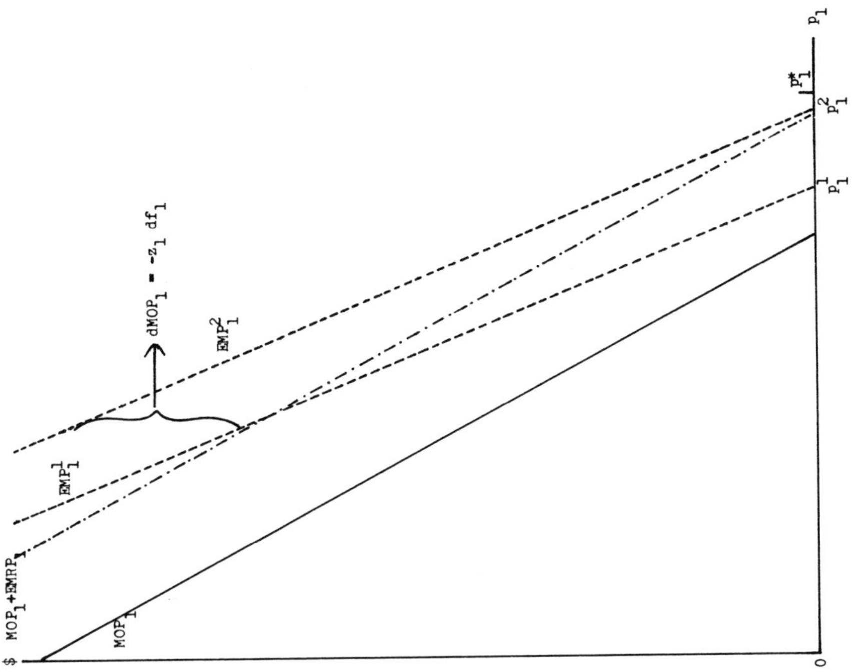

Figure 2.7.b. THE IMPACT OF A RISE IN $f_1, z_3' > 0$

equality at the vertex of the parabola, after which the profit margin force dominates. Hence, when $z_3' > 0$, the $EMCP_1$ is positive at lower p_1, but declines (at a constant rate) to become negative, as drawn on Figure 2.7.b. On that figure, the difference between the $MOP_1 + EMRP_1$ curve and EMP_1' is $EMCP_1$. When f_1 rises, MOP_1 rises by $-z_1' \, df_1$, and p_1 rises from p_1^1 to p_1^2.

The analysis is symmetrical for $z_3' < 0$. The parabolic profit function for firm 3 is U-shaped with respect to p_1 as the negative profit margin decline is ultimately neutralized and then overcome by declining sales as p_1 rises. Hence, $ECMP_1$ is negative in smaller p_1 regions and becomes positive, as drawn in Figure 2.7.a. Interpretation of results is readily adapted from the discussion of Figure 2.7.b above, and need not be repeated.[6]

As first-level analyses, all of these results hinge upon p_2, p_3, and p_4 remaining constant, which cannot be expected. We shall treat these "higher order" displacements in some detail in Chapters 4 and 5. However, the present lower order displacements are useful for insights and conjectures under certain conditions. For example, we would expect that if the steel industry suffered a rise in its marginal cost, and the automotive industry's members could not for competitive reasons raise their prices, the automotive industry's typical z' would be negative. If rivalrous consonance characterized the steel sector and in addition the steel suppliers were sensitive to their customers' welfares, we would conjecture that a sizeable passthrough would result.

But consider the impact on p_1 of a change in rival good p_2. From (11) we obtain

$$(23) \qquad dp_1^o/dp_2 = -.5(z_{12}' + \theta_{12} z_{21}' - \theta_{13} v_{13} z_{32}')/(z_{11}' - \theta_{13} v_{13} z_{31}')$$

where $z_{ij} = dz_i/dp_j$. The first two terms in the numerator will be positive and the last negative, while the second term in the denominator is ambiguous but the first strongly (and, expectantly, dominatingly) negative, yielding a positive numerator. Our expectation, therefore, is that the expression will be positive, with rivalrous consonance increasing the p_1^o response and customer effect dampening it when $z_{31}' > 0$ and increasing it when $z_{31}' < 0$.[7] The interesting insight from (23) is the reinforcing impact of rivalrous consonance. Because the responsive rise in p_1 increases the marginal profit of firm 2, p_1^o is accentuated when p_2 rises exogenously. Price rises in rivalrous consonance, therefore, tend to have a self-reinforcing quality.

1.3. *Model 3 -- Crippled Target-Rate-of-Return Optimization -- Single Industry*

1.3.1. *Formal Derivation.* The extended target deviation objective function for Model 3 is given in Chapter 1, (20), and if the constraint set does not bind, the first-order conditions for a minimum are

$$(24) \qquad \delta ETD_i/\delta p_i = s_i((x_i - b_{ii} m_i)/K_i)e^{s_i^2} + \sum_{j \neq i} \theta_{ij} s_j (b_{ji} m_j/K_j) e^{s_j^2} = 0 .$$

For realistic $\bar{r}_i > 0$, the exponential terms are approximately equal (near unity) and can be neglected in approximation. The condition in (24) then becomes

(25) $$METD_i = s_i((x_i - b_{ii}\, m_i)/K_i) + \sum_{j \neq i} \theta_{ij}\, s_j\, (b_{ji}\, m_j/K_j) = 0$$

$$= s_i\,(MRR_{ii}) + \sum_{j \neq i} \theta_{ij}\, s_j\,(MRR_{ji}) = 0\,,$$

where $MRR_{ki} = \delta r_k/\delta p_i$ is the *marginal rate of return for firm k with respect to* p_i. Hence, the *marginal extended target deviation* ($METD_i$) is composed of own marginal rate and a marginal rival rate component. From (21) in section 3.3 of Chapter 1, ETD_i may not be taken to be everywhere convex, and therefore (24) is not necessarily a global minimum for firm i's extended target deviation.

As a first step in interpreting (25) let us assume tentatively that all $\theta_{ij} = 0$. Let π_i be firm i's profit and $\bar{\pi}_i = \bar{r}_i K_i$ its target profit, and (25) may be simplified to

(26) $$(\pi_i - \pi_i)(d\pi_i/dp_i) = s_i K_i (MOP_i) = 0\,.$$

Then, (26) requires that if the target profit is not achieved, $MOP_i = 0$, but if it is achieved $MOP_i \gtreqless 0$.

The ability to state the condition in terms of target and actual own profits permits us to work with a concave profit function and to present the conditions in Figure 2.8 in terms that are more familiar to most economists than the ETD_i in Figure 1.1.a or 1.1.b. On Figure 2.8 we graph actual profit for firm i as a globally strictly concave function of p_i and depict three alternatives for target profit: $\bar{\pi}_i^1$ is everywhere above achievable π_i; $\bar{\pi}_i^2$ is just achievable when π_i is maximized; and $\bar{\pi}_i^3$ can be under- or overachieved by π_i. Also, MOP_i is graphed as the linear function of price that it is.

For $\bar{\pi}_i^1$ and $\bar{\pi}_i^2$ the profit target deviation $s_i\, K_i = (\bar{\pi}_i - \pi_i)$ is minimized at maximum profit where $MOP_i = 0$ at p_i'. When $\bar{\pi}_i$ intersections with $\pi_i\,(p_i; \bar{p}_j)$ occur, $MOP_i \neq 0$, and (26) requires that $s_i = 0$ at p_i'' or p_i'''.

In the latter cases π_i will equal the area $OABp_i''$ on Figure 2.8 whether p_i is p_i'' or p_i''', because, if the latter rules, positive excess profit $Bp_i'\, p_i''$ must equal the negative excess profit $Cp_i' p_i'''$.[8] The relation between Figures 1.1.a, 1.1.b, and 2.8 should also be made clear at this point. On Figure 1.1.a the relationship to Figure 2.8 is straightforward when $\bar{\pi}_i^1$ holds; and, of course, for $\bar{\pi}_i^2$ the convex target deviation function 1.1.a would merely shift down to tangency with the horizontal line at 1, since $\bar{r}_i$ is attained. The more interesting relationship is with Figure 1.1.b, which is relevant to Figure 2.8 for $\bar{\pi}_i^3$. The target deviation function moves upward from p_i'' to p_i, where it attains a maximum, as is clear from Figure 2.8. The function then falls from p_i' to p_i''', again for reasons that Figure 2.8 reveals.

The danger that we pointed out in the convexity discussion of (24) in Chapter 1.3.3 is that an algorithm that searches out a zero-slope point for the target deviation function will find the local maximum at p_i' rather than the global minima at the tangencies with the horizontal line at 1 on Figure 1.1.b.[9] Note that this point on Figure 2.8 meets the first-order condition (26), for $MOP_i = 0$, although it *maximizes* the target deviation. In practice, therefore, we recommend adding a constraint that requires $(\bar{\pi}_i - \pi_i)$ to equal zero, which will ensure that p_i'' or p_i''' will be attained, unless one or more other constraints bind. In that case the solution should be recalculated with the profit constraint removed. We have found that the SUMT algorithm works well in this latter instance, permitting the equality constraint to depart from equality to allow inequality constraints to bind, rather than rejecting the problem as one with an infeasible constraint set.

Let us now return to (25), retaining the assumption that all $e^{s_k^2} \approx 1$, but permitting θ_{ij} consonance factors to be nonzero, permitting the second term of (25) and

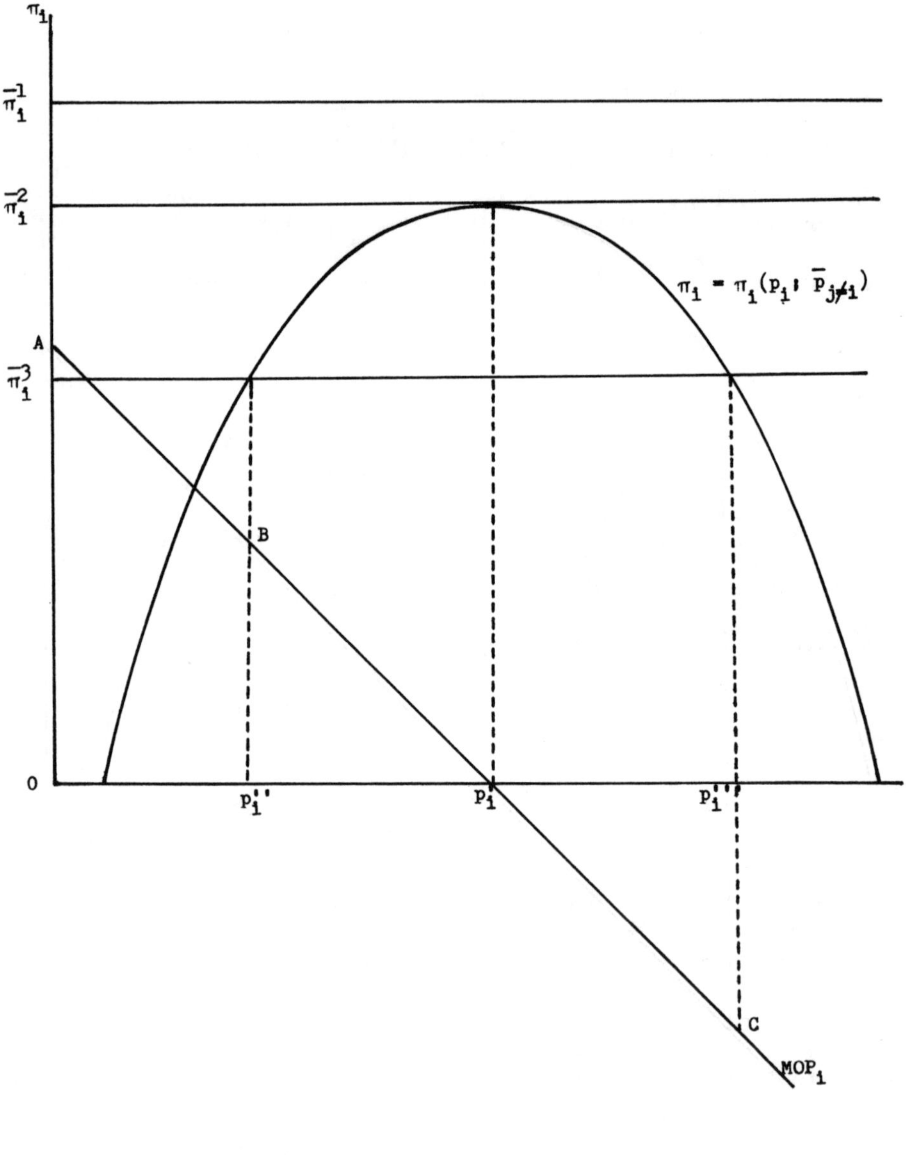

Figure 2.8. THE ISOLATED FIRM i TARGET RATE SOLUTION POSSIBILITIES

rivalrous consonance to enter our analysis. To simplify analysis, let us assume that only one such factor -- θ_{ik} -- is positive, so that firm i deals effectively with only one rival. Then (25) simplifies to

$$\text{(27)} \qquad METD_i = s_i \cdot MRR_{ii} + \theta_{ik} s_k \cdot MRR_{ki} = 0 ,$$

where we also continue to assume that no constraints bind.

It will be recalled that $MRR_{ii} = dr_i/dp_i$ and $MRR_{ki} = dr_k/dp_i$. From the expressions for MRR_{ii} and MRR_{ki} in (25) it follows that $MRR_{ii} \gtreqless 0$, whereas $MRR_{ki} \geq 0$ since rivals' products are all substitutes for that of firm i. In what follows we will assume that $MRR_{ki} > 0$, in which case seven possible solutions are possible, each of which is illustrated in Figure 2.9.a -- 2.9.g, on which RR_k is firm k's rate of return as a function of p_i.

a. $r_i^o = \bar{r}_i$ implies $r_k^o = \bar{r}_k$

b. $r_i^o < \bar{r}_i$ and $MRR_{ii} = 0$ implies $r_k^o = \bar{r}_k$

c. $r_i^o < \bar{r}_i$ and $MRR_{ii} > 0$ implies $r_k^o > \bar{r}_k$

d. $r_i^o < \bar{r}_i$ and $MRR_{ii} < 0$ implies $r_k^o < \bar{r}_k$

e. $r_i^o > \bar{r}_i$ and $MRR_{ii} = 0$ implies $r_k^o = \bar{r}_k$

f. $r_i^o > \bar{r}_i$ and $MRR_{ii} > 0$ implies $r_k^o < \bar{r}_k$

g. $r_i^o > \bar{r}_i$ and $MRR_{ii} < 0$ implies $r_k^o > \bar{r}_k$.

In summary, whenever firm i is operating at its maximum-rate-of-return price or is earning its target rate of return, firm k must also be achieving its target rate. When firm i is underachieving its target rate and $MRR_{ii} \neq 0$, then p_i is at a price where $MRR_{ii} > 0$ or $MRR_{ii} < 0$. In the first case (Figure 2.9.c) a rise in p_i^o to reduce ETD_i should be adopted unless s_k widens, which will happen if $r_k^o < \bar{r}_k$, since MRR_{ki} (not shown in Figure 2.9) slopes positively with respect to p_i. Hence, r_k^o must lie above $\bar{r}_k$. Similarly, when p_i^o lies above profit maximizing price so that $MRR_{ii} < 0$ (Figure 2.9.d) it would be possible to reduce ETD_i by moving leftward (reducing p_i) if this also reduced s_k. But a reduction in s_k would occur only if $r_k^o > \bar{r}_k$, for r_k would fall when p_1 falls. Therefore, if p_i^o is the optimum it must be true that $r_k^o < \bar{r}_k$. Similar interpretations motivate the equilibria when firm i is overachieving (Cases e, f, g and Figures 2.9.e., f., and g.). In all cases, the extents of the deviations of the firms' actual rates from target rates in the equilibrium depend upon the magnitudes of the products of the deviations, the marginal rates of return, and the consonance factors. These magnitudes are not depicted on Figure 2.9.

Case b and e (Figures 2.9.b and e.) are interesting. If Firm i is at its profit maximizing price in equilibrium and underachieving (Figure 2.9.b) or over-achieving (Figure 2.9.e) a slight rise or fall in p_i will have no impact upon firm i's own target rate deviation, and hence a movement either up or down if it closed firm k's target rate deviation would improve ETD_i. If $r_k^o \neq \bar{r}_k$ then in this situation one of these two movements in p_i would be worthwhile, and p_i^o would not have been attained. Therefore, if in fact it has been achieved, it must be true that $r_k^o = \bar{r}_k$, for then slight changes in p_i will have no impact on firm k's target deviation. Finally, this motivation also clarifies Case a (Figure 2.9.a), for if $r_i^o = \bar{r}_i$ at any p_i^o ($MRR_{ii} \gtreqless 0$), first-order movements in p_i right or left will not change own target deviation and therefore will be made in the direction that closes firm k's target deviation. Hence, p_i cannot be optimum unless such movements will not impact firm k's target deviation, and this condition implies that firm k is at a price position analogous to p_i'' or p_i''' in Figure 1.1, where $r_k^o = \bar{r}_k$.

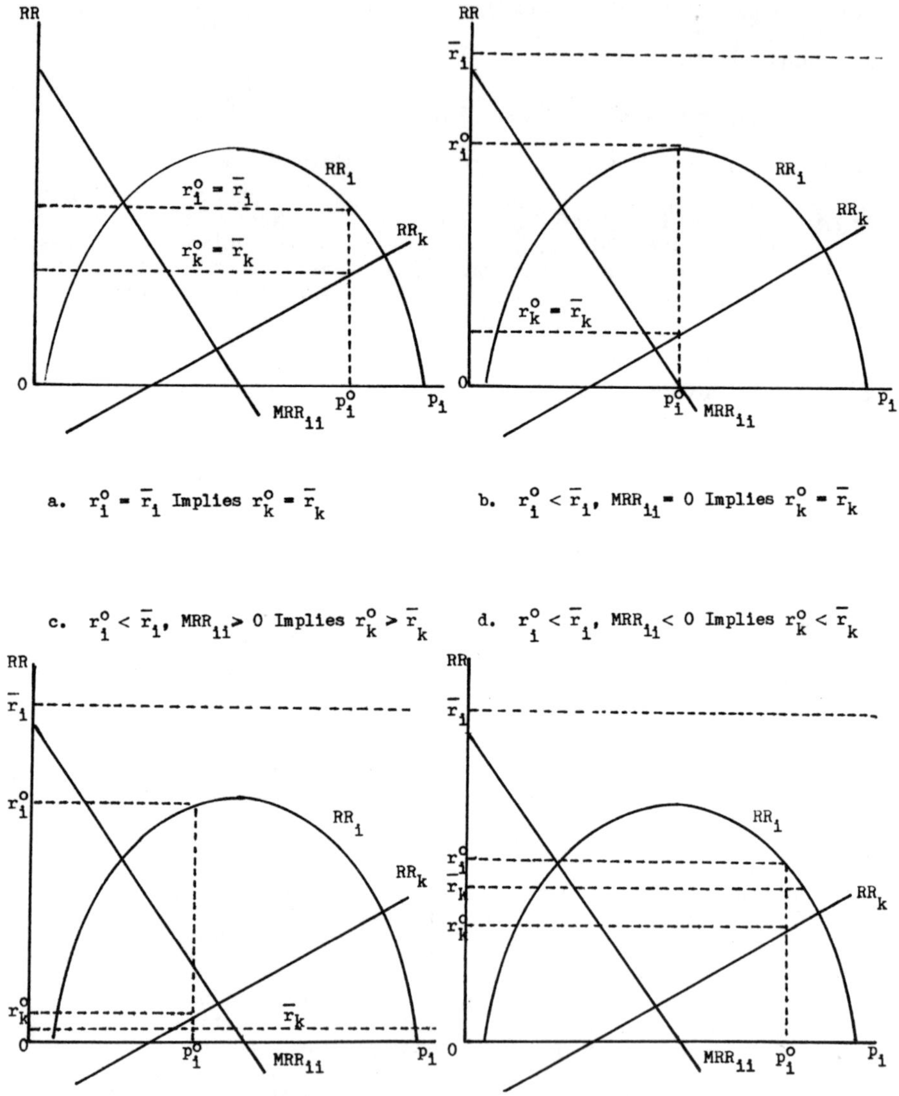

a. $r_i^o = \bar{r}_i$ Implies $r_k^o = \bar{r}_k$

b. $r_i^o < \bar{r}_i$, $MRR_{ii} = 0$ Implies $r_k^o = \bar{r}_k$

c. $r_i^o < \bar{r}_i$, $MRR_{ii} > 0$ Implies $r_k^o > \bar{r}_k$

d. $r_i^o < \bar{r}_i$, $MRR_{ii} < 0$ Implies $r_k^o < \bar{r}_k$

Figure 2.9. FIRM i EXTENDED TARGET DEVIATION ALTERNATIVE SOLUTIONS, ONE RIVAL

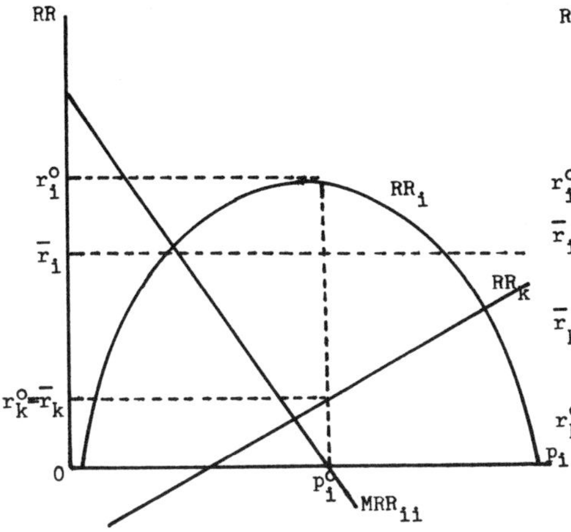

e. $r_i^o > \bar{r}_i$, $MRR_{ii} = 0$ Implies $r_k^o = \bar{r}_k$

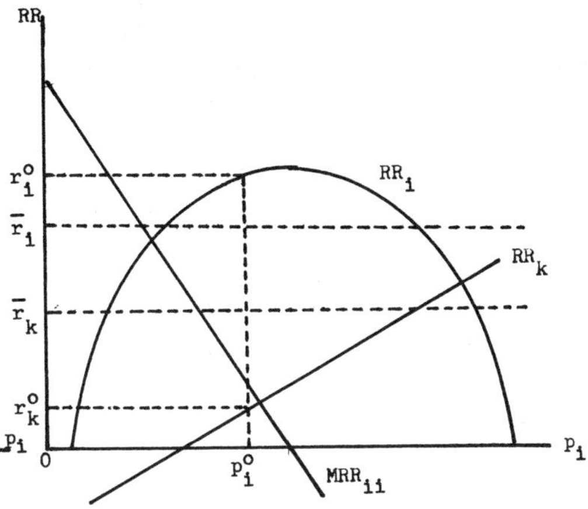

f. $r_i^o > \bar{r}_i$, $MRR_{ii} > 0$ Implies $r_k^o < \bar{r}_k$

g. $r_i^o > \bar{r}_i$, $MRR_{ii} < 0$ Implies $r_k^o > \bar{r}_k$

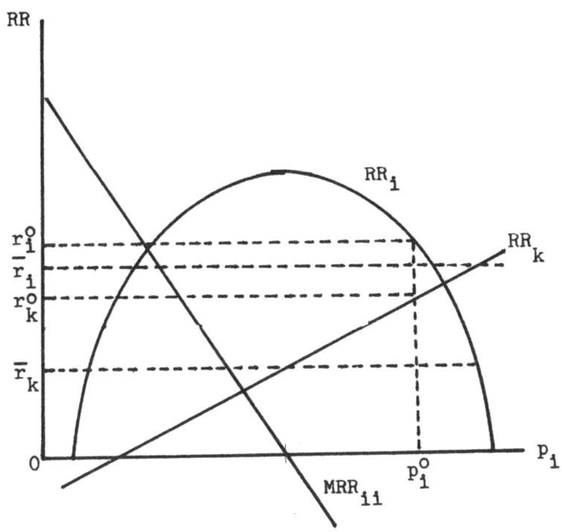

Figure 2.9. FIRM i EXTENDED TARGET DEVIATION ALTERNATIVE SOLUTIONS, ONE RIVAL (continued)

Consider the realistic implications of these propositions. For example, suppose we have a case where, in some initial price configuration:

1. $r_i > \overline{r}_k$, so that rival i is a strong rival or, perhaps, is a satisficer willing to settle for approximations to goal achievements;
2. $r_k < \overline{r}_k$, so firm k is weaker, possibly seeking a larger market share, or perhaps is an overachiever in its goal setting;
3. θ_{ik} is large, in that firm i worries about firm k's willingness to undercut the price structure of the industry;
4. $MRR_{ii} > 0$ and large, so that firm i is operating in a highly elastic own-price region of its sales curve;
5. MRR_{ki} is small, indicating that firm k's sales function has a small cross-elasticity with p_i.

In such a case, as p_i rises past the profit-maximizing price p_i' both firms' target rate deviations close slowly and p_i can be expected to rise into the area where $MRR_{ii} < 0$ and $r_i < \overline{r}_k$, for assumptions 3 and 5 will lead firm i to hold a price umbrella above firm k's head and to thereby underachieve rather than overachieve. The type of equilibrium illustrated in Figure 2.9.d will tend to be approached. A large oligopolist selling a mass-market oriented product, seeking a goal target rate, and worried perhaps about the antitrust implications of its pricing behavior as it relates to a smaller rival selling in a somewhat different market segment, may well hold prices high above what they need to be to achieve its target. Target rate pricing behavior gives its practitioner a low- or high-price option where the target rate is below maximum-profit levels, and its exercise of the high-price option may somewhat paradoxically involve smaller net costs if antitrust considerations outweigh customer antagonism. "Preservation of competition" may bear a high social cost in such cases.

Perhaps an even more frequent case in reality is depicted by the following set of assumptions:

1. $r_i < \overline{r}_i$ and $r_k < \overline{r}_k$, both firms striving toward target rates;
2. $\overline{r}_i \approx \overline{r}_k$, so that both firms share an industry target rate;
3. θ_{ik} is modestly high;
4. $MRR_{ii} > 0$ and is high, own-price elasticity large;
5. MRR_{ki} is moderately high, goods i and k being good substitutes.

Such an initial position cannot continue because if p_i is raised both target rate deviations can be reduced. If, when $r_i = \overline{r}_i$, it is not true that $r_k = \overline{r}_k$, p_i will continue to rise until firm k's extended target rate deviation component in firm i's $METD_i$ counterbalances its own component. If firm k is far below its target in the initial position the equilibrium may occur at a high p_i where $MRR_{ii} < 0$. Once more, rivals' target rate deviations tend to push firms toward the high-price option where target rates are achieved or approached rather than the low-price alternative.

Both of these relatively frequent cases in oligopolistic industries result in prices that are above those that would rule in the absence of consonance, if we assume that firms opt for a low-price option over the high-price option in the latter case. Such a course seems more likely in view of the concerns of firms to avoid customer resentment, avert antitrust suspicions, and to discourage entry into the industry. Under rivalrous consonance in target rate regimes *prices may well go higher than in profit-maximizing regimes* since the firm pays no goal penalties to do so, as is suggested by the cases above.

In a last consideration of the first-order conditions (25) let us drop the assumption that only $\theta_{ik} > 0$. In this case, where all θ-terms are positive, all that we have based upon the firm k component of firm i's ETD_i and $METD_i$ is simply read as the *sum* of those functions over all rivals j. Some rivals may then be over- or underachieving simultaneously with others which are exactly attaining target rates; however, in rival i's equilibrium their θ_{ij}-weighted target deviation components *summed* must equal $s_i \cdot MRR_{ii}$.

1.3.2. *First-Level Comparative Statics Propositions.* Suppose now that the marginal cost C_i of firm i rises slightly. Define:

$$N_1 = x_i MRR_{ii} (1+2s_i^2) + b_{ii} s_i$$
$$D_1 = 2b_{ii} s_i + K_i MRR_{ii}^2 (1+2s_i^2) + K_i [\Sigma j \neq i \, \theta_{ij} MRR_{ji}^2 (1+s_j^2)].$$

Then, by differentiating (24) we obtain (after eliminating the exponential terms in the differential)

$$(28) \qquad dp_i/dC_i = N_1/D_1 .$$

Note that the denominator has all nonnegative terms except for the first, which will be negative when $r_k > \bar{r}_i$. Given the magnitudes of its accompanying terms, however, we will assume that the denominator is always positive, so that the sign of dp_i/dC_i will be determined by its numerator, and, further, given the magnitudes of its second term, that the numerator sign hinges upon the sign of MRR_{ii}. Hence, when

1. $MRR_{ii} > 0, dp_i/dC_i > 0$

2. $MRR_{ii} = 0, dp_i/dC_i \begin{cases} > 0, \text{ if } s_i > 0 \\ = 0, \text{ if } s_i = 0 \\ < 0, \text{ if } s_i < 0 \end{cases}$

3. $MRR_{ii} < 0, dp_i/dC_i < 0.$

To motivate these theorems we will demonstrate several instances in Figure 2.10 for $MRR_{ii} \gtrless 0$, with Case 3 of major interest because it is the counterintuitive result. Under rivalrous consonance in a target rate regime, how can a *rise* in own marginal cost induce a *fall* in price? We deal in turn with two subcases that can occur, depending upon the sign of s_i.

In Figure 2.10.a we present the case where $MRR_{ii} < 0$ and $s_i < 0$. Initial equilibrium for firm i is at p_i^o, at which the firm is overachieving $\bar{r}_i$ at r_i^o at an $MRR_{ii} < 0$. This implies that $\Sigma_{j\neq i}\,\theta_{ij}\, r_j > \Sigma_{j\neq i}\,\theta_{ij}\,\bar{r}_j$ at p_i^o, as shown. When C_i rises, firm i's rate of return at p_i^o falls to r_i'' as the rate of return function shifts downward and to the right. Its MRR_{ii} rises to MRR_{ii}', and, at r_i'', s_i is reduced in absolute amount. Hence, the own target deviation component of (25) -- $s_i\, MRR_{ii}$ -- falls in positive value as both terms become less negative, and it no longer equals an unchanged rivals' target deviation component $\Sigma_{j\neq i}\,\theta_{ij}\, s_j\, MRR_{ji}$. Therefore, p_i must fall to p_i' to induce a simultaneous rise in s_i and fall in the absolute value of the rival target deviation component. Since the rise in s_i is somewhat offset by the fall in MRR_{ii}'s absolute value, the steeper MRR_{ii}' the greater must be the fall in p_i. Equilibrium is reattained at $p_i' < p_i^o$, with implied r_i' and r_j', and with r_i' lower. The aggregate rivals' target deviation term will be lower, which implies that most r_j have fallen.

In Figure 2.10.b, $s_i >$ at p_i^o, implying $\Sigma_{j\neq i}\,\theta_{ij}\, s_j\, MRR_{ji} > 0$. With the rise in C_i the target deviation s_i widens and a fall in p_i must occur to narrow it as well as balance it by widening the rival target deviation component, until $METD_i$ is brought back

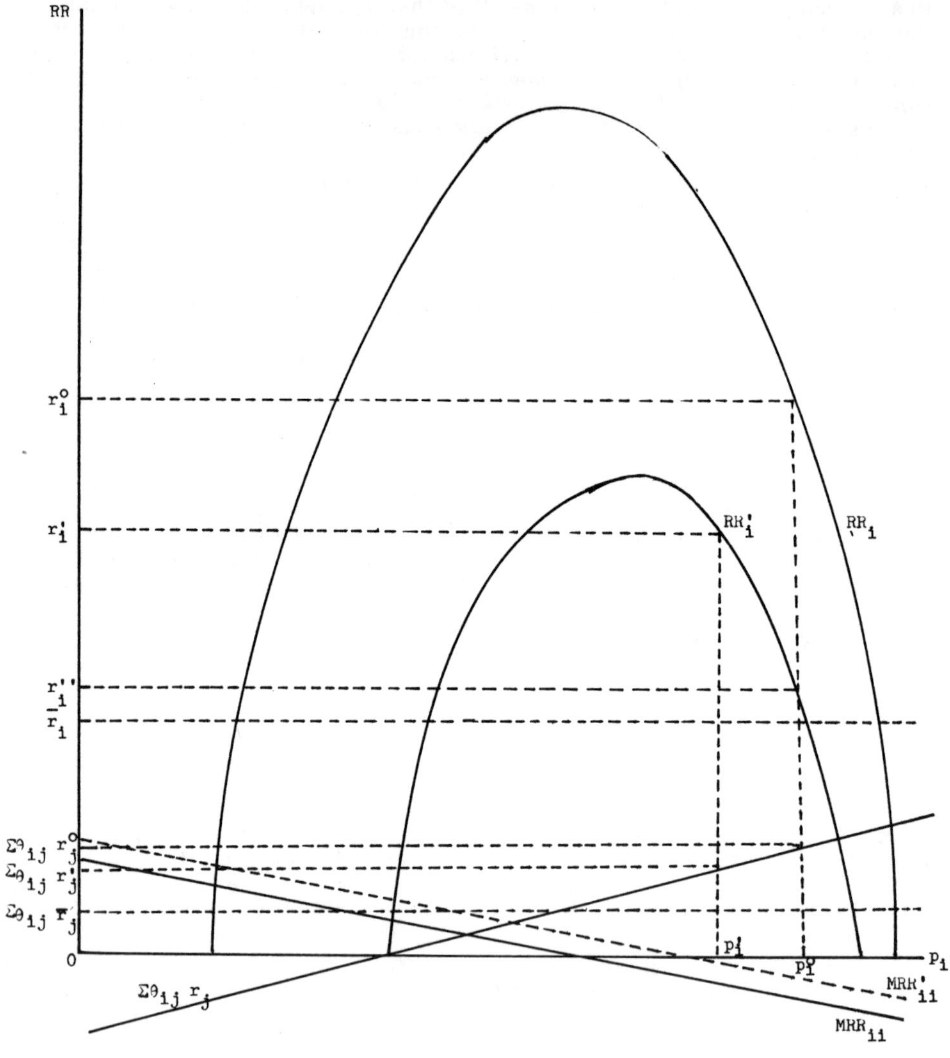

Figure 2.10.a. CHANGE IN p_i WITH RISE IN C_i, $MRR_{ii} < 0$

a. $s_i < 0$ Implies $\Sigma\theta_{ij}\, s_j < 0$

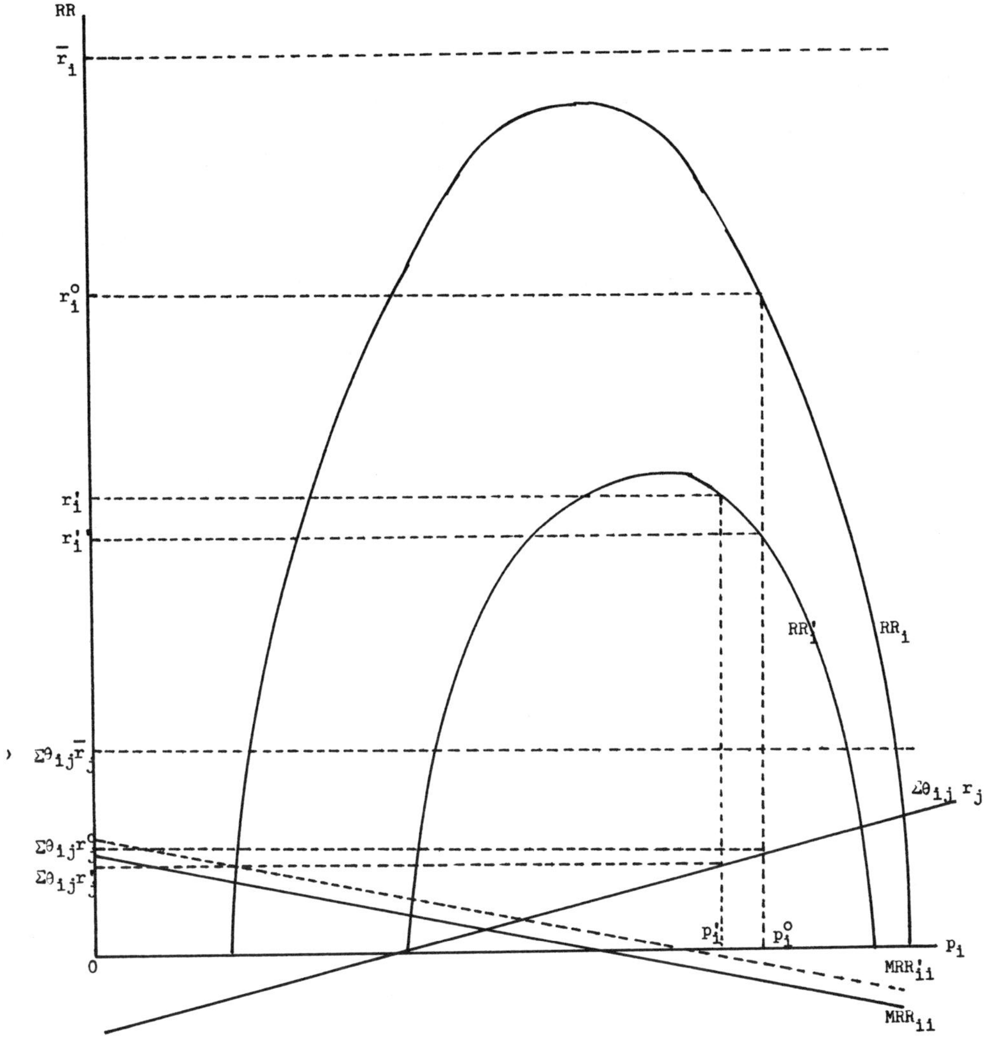

Figure 2.10.b. CHANGE IN p_i WITH RISE IN C_i, $MRR_{ii} < 0$
b. $s_i > 0$ Implies $\Sigma\theta_{ij}\, s_j > 0$

to zero level at p_i. Finally, Figure 2.10.c presents Case 1 where $s_i > 0$ and $MRR_{ii} > 0$, implying $\Sigma_{j \neq i}\, \theta_{ij}\, MRR_{ji} < 0$. A rise in C_i, therefore, lowers r_i and increases s_i. Since $MRR_{ii} > 0$, p_i must rise to elevate r_i, but this in turn induces the rival target deviation component to increase. Price of firm i continues to rise until, at p_i, the rise in s_i and fall in MRR_{ii} are just balanced in the own target deviation component by the rise in the rival target deviation component.

Thus, the interesting theoretical possibility arises that in rivalrous consonance under a target rate of return regime a rise in a firm's marginal cost could lead to cost-induced price *reductions*. When firm i and its rivals are symmetrical in their target rate expectations -- underachieving, overachieving, or exactly achieving -- firm i will be led to operate in the region of negative marginal own profit. Price, therefore, will be above the level that maximizes its rate of return. Under these conditions, a rise in its marginal cost and a decline in its profitability will lead firm i to reduce price self-protectively, although rivalrous consonance will temper that price reduction. On the other hand, under conditions that are most likely to occur when firm i and its rivals are asymmetrical in target rate aspirations, p_i will tend to be at less than profit maximizing levels, and a rise in firm i's cost will lead it to raise p_i, and by less than it would in the absence of rivalrous consonance.

Suppose all $\theta_{ij} = 0$, so that rivalrous consonance is eliminated and the firm operates myopically in a Cournot environment. Then (28) yields three results, depending upon the nature of the initial equilibrium. When $s_i > 0$ and $MRR_{ii} = 0$, so that the initial price is at the maximum profit level, $dp_i/dC_i = .5$, as we have shown in (10) for a myopic profit-maximizing firm. When $s_i = 0$ and $MRR_{ii} \neq 0$, the firm has a choice of selecting p_i below or above the profit-maximizing level. In either case, $dp_i/dC_i = x_i/(K_i\, MRR_{ii})$, which is positive in the first case but negative in the second. Whichever the case firm i opts for, the absolute value of $K_i\, MRR_{ii}$ will be the same, but because x_i is larger when p_i is smaller, the degree of price rise in the first case will be larger absolutely than the degree of price fall in the second.

Assume, now, that rival k raises its price, p_k, for whatever reason. Define:

$$N_2 = K_k\, b_{ik}\, s_i + K_i\, \theta_{ik}\, b_{ki}\, s_k - K_i\, K_k\, \Sigma_{m=i,j,k}\, (\theta_{im}\, .\, MRR_{mi}\, .\, MRR_{mk}\, (1 + 2s_m^2))$$

$$D_2 = 2K_k\, b_{ii}\, s_i + K_i\, K_k\, \Sigma_{m=i,j,k}\, \theta_{im}\, .\, MRR_{mi}^2\, (1 + 2s_m^2)\, .$$

Then, we may write the expression

$$(29) \qquad dp_i/dp_k = N_2/D_2\, .$$

First, assume θij and θik are zero, so that p_k affects pi only through firm i's sales function. Then (20) reduces to

$$(30) \qquad dp_i/dp_k = (b_{ik}\, s_i - K_i\, .MRR_{ii}.MRR_{ik}\, (1 + 2s_i^2))/ (2b_{ii}s_i + K_i.MRR_{ii}^2\, (1 + 2s_i^2)$$

From (25) either $s_i = 0$ and $MRR_{ii} \geq 0$ or $s_i > 0$ and $MRR_{ii} = 0$. In the first case

$$(31) \qquad dp_i/dp_k = -MRR_{ik}/MRR_{ii}.$$

When $MRR_{ii} > 0$, because $MRR_{ik} > 0$ the expression in (31) will be negative; a rise in p_k raises r_i and hence p_i must be reduced to maintain $\bar{r}_i$. In similar fashion, we reason that when $MRR_{ii} < 0$, (31) must be positive, so that when r_i rises with a rise in p_k it will be necessary to raise p_i to reattain $\bar{r}_i$. In the first case target rate of return motivation leads to what appears to be counterintuitive, but what is indeed

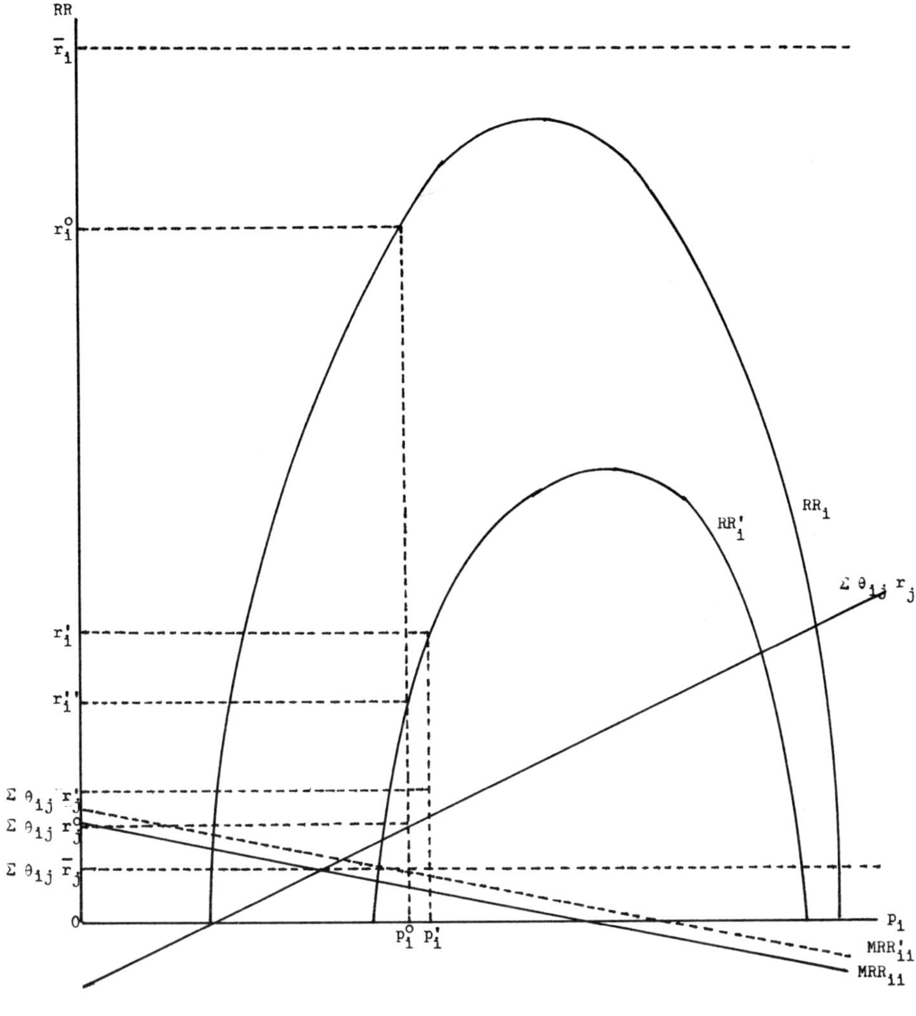

Figure 2.10. CHANGE IN p_i WITH RISE IN C_i, $MRR_{ii} > 0$

c. $s_i > 0$ Implies $\Sigma\ \theta_{ij}\ s_j < 0$

explained readily in terms of this unfamiliar motivation. To add to the complication, of course, in both instances the firm has the option to leap to the opposite side of the profit-maximizing price unless constrained by price change restraints.

When $s_i > 0$ and $MRR_{ii} = 0$, (30) reduces to

$$dp_i/dp_k = .5b_{ik}/b_{ii}. \tag{32}$$

Thus p_i will rise with a rise in p_k at a rate that is directly proportional to the marginal rise in sales caused by the rise in p_k and inversely proportional to the fall in sales occurring from the induced rise in p_i.

When we permit the θ-terms to become positive in (29) the evaluation of the numerator becomes much more complex; however, the sign of the third term is expected to dominate. More specifically, in the summation it seems likely that the element for m = i will outweigh the others and so give a sign to the numerator that is opposite to the sign of MRR_{ii}. Hence, $dp_i/dp_k > 0$ when $MRR_{ii} < 0$ and vice versa, as we would expect from our discussion of (31). However, the other consonance terms in the expression will temper this and may overcompensate, and therefore unambiguous results can be obtained for specific industries only by simulative theorizing.

1.3.3. *The Introduction of Constraints*. The limited capability of classic comparative statics techniques and the recognition of the need for simulative theorizing in oligopoly analysis are even more impressed upon the analyst when the constraint sets C_i^1--C_i^3 are reintroduced into the analysis. General results from parametric nonlinear programming or postoptimality analysis are derivable only from extensions of classic parametric displacement techniques. Infinitesimal changes in parameters are assumed to move equilibrium within ε-neighborhoods of the original equilibrium remaining so in the new. Finite parameter changes with potential changes in the pattern of binding and nonbinding constraints can only be investigated by simulative theorizing techniques.

In this chapter we will limit the treatment of constraints to an indication of the nature of the changes they introduce into the solutions. For the illustration we have used to illuminate target-rate-of-return regimes, the constraint set C_i -- C_i is simple because, as shown in section 1.1, in firm i's solutions either none of the constraints will bind or only one will. We illustrate this in Figure 2.11 in which we have introduced the four constraints into firm i's rate of return diagram. Their interpretation is straightforward. C_i^1 is a capacity constraint upon output, which translates into a p_i below which price cannot fall without stimulating excessive demand from the standpoint of capacity available to satisfy it. Hence, C_i^1 sets a lower bound on price, p_{i1}. C_i^2 defines a minimum acceptable market share for firm i, and therefore, determines an upper bound on p_i at p_{i2}, broaching which would reduce demand below the acceptable level. C_i^3 imposes a direct constraint upon price, setting an upper bound, p_{i3}, on the basis of acceptable price change, and C_i sets a lower bound on the same basis. Hence, C_i^1 and C_i^4 set lower bounds on price and C_i^2 and C_i^3 set upper bounds. Optimal price may, therefore, either (1) be constrained by the least upper bound (arbitrarily, p_{i2} in Figure 2.11) or greatest lower bound (p_{i1} as drawn), not by both, or (2) be unconstrained. Also, p_{i1} and p_{i2} will change positions in a full rivalrous consonance model in which rivals' systems are being solved sequentially, whereas p_{i3} and p_{i4} are fixed in position.

2. *SUMMARY AND CONCLUSIONS*

Theorems about oligopolistic firm behavior under rivalrous consonance must be sought at three ascending levels of complexity. At the first level, equilibria are

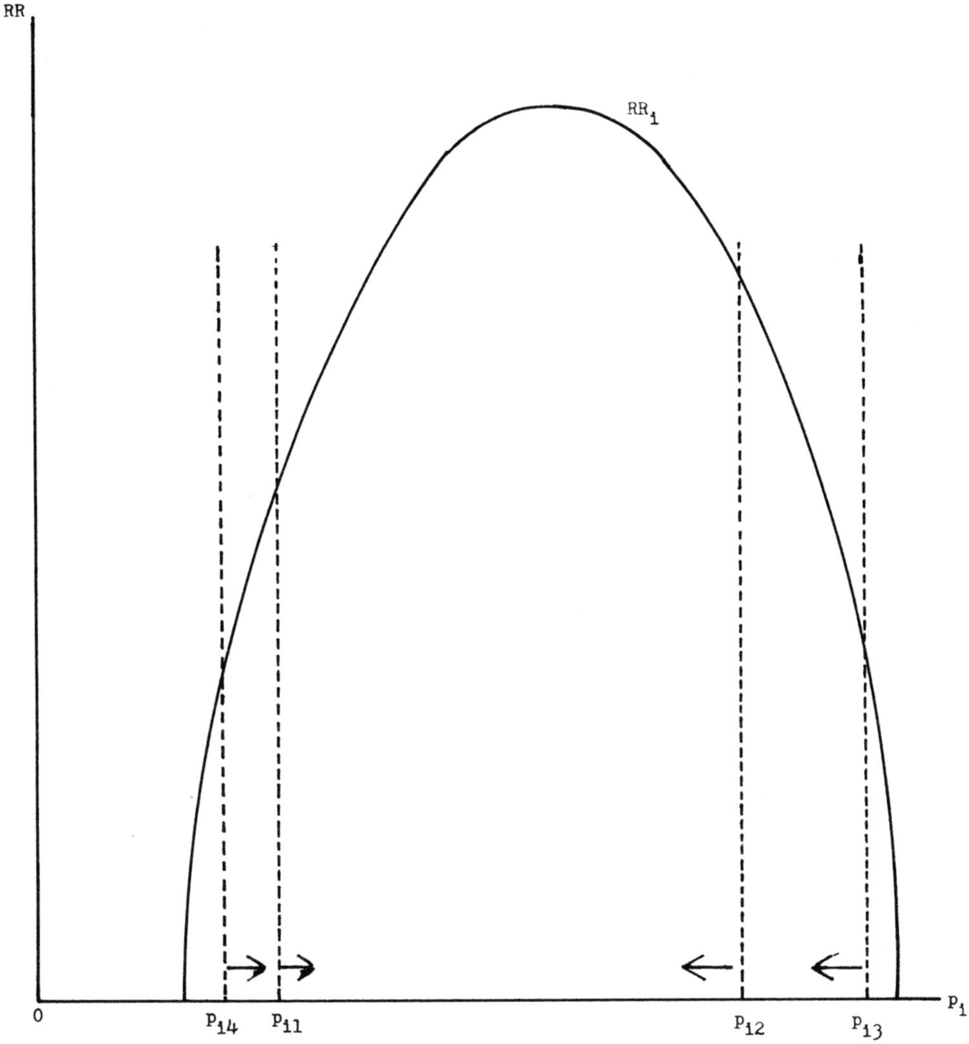

Figure 2.11. THE APPLICATION OF THE CONSTRAINT SET TO FIRM i's RATE OF RETURN FUNCTION

shocked by changing parameters singly, ignoring rival and/or customer reactions. This is standard comparative statics that is properly the domain of purely competitive, monopolistically competitive, and pure monopoly analyses in which the ignoring of competitor reactions can be justified. In this chapter we have limited our consideration to this first level in order to discern some basic patterns that may well be changed by rival and customer reactions at the second and thirdlevels. In the second level these are permitted to register in optimizing price changes, holding consonance factors constant. This context is that of classical oligopoly theory proper, and we present the crippled optimization alternative in Chapters 4 and 5. Finally, in Chapters 6 and 7 we complicate the firms' decision environment further by freeing the binary consonance factors to adapt optimally in a longer run perspective. This is a dimension oligopoly analysis previously has not explored.

At the first level, we have presented first-order conditions for a crippled optimal solution for the firm in rivalrous consonance, using Models 1, 2, and 3. We have interpreted these conditions in economic terms and presented them graphically to deepen insights. In the case of Model 1 we have included the constraint set used for illustration in Chapter 1 for study of the manners in which it affected solutions. We then assumed that all constraints in the initial equilibrium of Models 1, 2, and 3 were ineffective, and that displacements remained in this unconstrained neighborhood, except for brief considerations of constraint complications.

A succession of propositions was derived from the models and interest was focussed upon those that might seem counterintuitive from the viewpoints of conventional theory. In Model 1, a rise in a rival's marginal cost and consequent decline in its profit margin will lead to an impulse for a firm to decrease its price, not increase it. Model 2 includes interindustry customer relationships as well as rivalrous, and with certain expected types of customers' sales reactions to a change in a firm's price we expect that firm's concern for customers' profits to keep price at lower levels. It is, indeed, the complications introduced by this consideration that yields the distinctive differences from Model 1's results. For example, if firm i's marginal cost rises, whether p_i rises by more or less than the rise that would occur in monopoly depends upon certain customers' sales reactions, not upon rivals' experiences. Lastly, dp_i/dp_k is most likely positive, but the degree of change depends upon the relative strength of rivalrous consonance, which tends to increase it, and regard for consumers, which reduces it.

Lastly, Model 3 revealed that target rate of return achievers frequently have an option for lower or higher prices, and that in some important realistic cases we expect the bias toward higher price to be revealed. Which option firms elect is important for the sign of dp_i/dC_i will be negative if the higher price is set and positive if the lower rules. Rivalrous consonance serves to temper these price reactions, however.

Having become familiar with the fundamental mechanisms and impulses of rivalrous consonance in realistically important modelling contexts, we may now take a closer look at first-level comparative statics in a newer programming context.

1 In addition, a regularity condition on the constraints is required to guarantee that the Lagrangean multipliers λ_t exist and are nonnegative at the optimum. A *sufficient* condition to guarantee this *necessary* condition for a local optimum is the independence of the gradient vectors of the binding constraints at the optimum. We assume this condition holds.

2 Note that in Figure 2.1 the marginal functions are graphed conventionally with x_i on the horizontal axis, so that they are explicitly related to quantity variations.

3 We are using "Cournot behavior" in the broader sense of the term: a system of decision making in which each firm assumes its rivals' decision variables (quantity or price) to be constant as it adopts its strategy. In our case of price setting oligopolists, the term "Bertrand behavior" might seem more appropriate, but we believe Cournot's choice of quantity as decision variable was of secondary importance to the mode of conjectural variation he pioneered.

4 When $z_1' < 0$, $z_3' < 0$, then $(\theta_{13} v_{13} z_3')/z_1' < 1$. Assume the contrary, or

$$\theta_{13} v_{13} z_3'/z_1' \geq 1$$

or

$$\theta_{13} v_{13} (-b_{11} v_{32} v_{24} v_{41} + b_{21} v_{32}) \leq -b_{11} + b_{21} v_{13} v_{32}.$$

If $\theta_{13} = 0$, the expression implies $z_1' \geq 0$, which contradicts the hypothesis. If $\theta_{13} = 1$, the expression may be written

$$b_{11} (1 - v_{13} v_{32} v_{24} v_{41}) \leq 0.$$

But $|\mathbf{A}| = 1 - v_{13} v_{32} v_{24} v_{41}$, and by the Hawkins-Simon conditions $|\mathbf{A}| > 0$. Hence, the hypothesis is contradicted at the [0,1] extremes of θ_{13}, and therefore for any θ_{13} in the strict interior of the unit interval.

5 More fully, from (11)

$$dMOP_1 = -z_1' \, df_1 ,$$

and, from (19)

$$dp_1 = -.5(z_1' - \theta_{13} v_{13} z_3')^{-1} \, dMOP_1 .$$

6 Figure 2.7.a permits a relevant observation. It is possible when $z_3' < 0$ that the $EMCP_1$ component can *raise* prices under consonance rather than reduce them. If it were large enough, $EMCP_1$ could move EMP_1 to the right sufficiently to move p_1' to the right of the intersection of $MOP_1 + EMRP_1$ with the p_1 axis. But to do this the slope of $EMCP_1$ must be very steep. From (14), θ_{13} must be large, and/or v_{13} must be large, and/or z_3' must be large. Because customers' consonance factors must be expected to be smaller than rivals', and because z_3' cannot be large in general since firm 3 is not a rival nor a seller to its rivals. Hence, we have assumed $EMCP_1$ reduces p_1 rather than raising it.

7 The motivation of $EMCP_1$'s positive effect on dp_1° when $z_{31}' < 0$ will be developed in Chapter 4.

8 This follows from the nature of π_i as a parabola with vertex over p_i' and with p_i'' and p_i''' equidistant from p_i'.

9 This becomes unlikely when the rival deviation component is included in the ETD_i. When such effects are taken into account, the likelihood of being misled into believing p_i' in Figure 1.1.b, which maximizes ETD_i rather than minimizing it, is the optimum is very small. In the present case this would require the coincidence that at this price it was also true that $r_k = \bar{r}_k$. When more than one rival exists the coincidence becomes even less probable in that all rivals would have to be in this situation for p_i to remain at p_i' when $r_k \geq \bar{r}_i$. Hence, the nonconvexity of own target deviation in this circumstance becomes less worrisome in practice.

CHAPTER 3

RIVALROUS CONSONANCE: PROGRAMMING CONSIDERATIONS AT THE FIRST LEVEL

What we have termed the "second level" of oligopoly analysis is devoted to the classic problem of that market structure: the interaction of rivals' decision making in face of their mutually recognized interdependence. Recognizing the existence of nonmarket or even noneconomic components in the decision environment of the industry community, we seek to capture them along with economic components in the binary consonance factors that define the sector's power structure. In holding these factors constant at the second level, therefore, we limit our consideration to rivals' accommodations to market-transmitted signals. We reserve until Chapter 6 the longer-run adaptations to changes in the industrial environment that affect the structure of θ.

In preparation for this second level analysis to follow in Chapters 4 and 5 we begin in section 1 with an extension of first level crippled optimization theory by discussing the methods of parametric nonlinear programming. This permits us to displace solutions in our models when inequality and/or equality constraints are present. We are then ready to present the Sequential Unconstrained Minimization Technique (SUMT) algorithm which we have modified to yield second-level solutions to the models and, in section 2, to indicate the complications that plague classical displacement analysis and parametric programming for nonspecified models. Finally, in section 3 we briefly summarize results, conclusions, and conjectures in preparation for moving up to second level analysis.

1. *CRIPPLED OPTIMIZATION AS NONLINEAR PROGRAMMING -- FIRST LEVEL*

1.1 *A General Statement of the Crippled Optimization Rivalrous Consonance Model and the Necessary and Sufficient Conditions for Its Solution*

1.1.1 *The Primal Problem.* Let us generalize the three model types of Chapters 1 and 2 to derive a more compact statement of them and of the conditions for their solution, as well as to extend their flexibility. First, let us adopt the convention, as well as to extend their flexibility. First, let us adopt the convention of minimizing the objective function in all cases. It is well known that maximizing a function subject to inequality constraints is equivalent to minimizing the negative of that function when all inequality constraints are multiplied on both sides by -1 and the directions of the inequality signs reversed. Henceforth, therefore, it will be understood that any model which calls for maximizing the objective function will be so converted into a minimization problem.

We assume firm i seeks to minimize its extended objective function subject to q inequality constraints, $g_t(p_i) \geq 0$, $t = 1, 2, \ldots, q$, which include the nonnegativity constraint $p_i \geq 0$. The constraint set may also include pairs that taken together define equality constraints: for example, $g_t(p_i) \geq 0$ and $-g_t(p_i) \geq 0$ imply that $g_t(p_i) = 0$. This permits even greater flexibility in tailoring models to firm and industry specifics.

Firm i seeks to

(1) Minimize $V_i = f_i(p_i; \mathbf{p_r}, \mathbf{p_c}, C_i, \mathbf{Q}, K_i) + \Sigma_r \theta_{ir} f_r(p_i; \mathbf{p_r}, \mathbf{p_c}, C_r, \mathbf{Q}, \mathbf{K_r}) + \Sigma_c \theta_{ic} f_c(p_i; \mathbf{p_r}, \mathbf{p_c}, \mathbf{C_c}, \mathbf{Q}, \mathbf{K_c})$

subject to

(2) $g_t(p_i) \geq 0, \qquad t = 1, 2, \ldots, q,$

where we define:

1. V_i : firm i's extended objective variable
2. f_i : own objective variable component
3. f_r : rival's objective variable component
4. f_c : customer's objective variable component
5. θ_{ir}, θ_{ic}: consonance factors for rivals and customers
6. $p_i, \mathbf{p_r}, \mathbf{p_c}$: own price, rivals' prices, and customers' prices
7. $\mathbf{Q}$: national income and other exogenous sales function variables
8. $C_i, \mathbf{C_r}, \mathbf{C_c}$: own cost, rivals' costs, and customers' costs
9. $K_i, \mathbf{K_r}, \mathbf{K_c}$: own dedicated capital, rivals' dedicated capital, and customers' dedicated capital.

We assume the f_i, f_r, and f_c are convex, the g_t are concave (which implies that all equality constraints in their original form are linear), in p_i. The Lagrangean form

(3) $\mathscr{L}_i = V_i - \Sigma_t \lambda_t g_t(p_i)$

is, therefore, convex in p_i for $\lambda_t \geq 0$.

We assume the following hypotheses to be true:

a. f_i, f_r, f_c and g_t have continuous first derivatives;
b. $\overset{o}{p_i}$ is feasible in that it satisfies (2);
c. at $\overset{o}{p_i}$ the derivatives of $g_t(\overset{i}{p_i})$, g_t, are linearly independent (i.e., no one of them can be derived as a linear combination of the others);
d. the problem functions define a $\mathscr{L}_i$ convex in p_i.

Then:

1. there will exist vectors of dual variables, $\lambda°$, which with p_i satisfy the conditions:
   1. $\overset{i}{V_i} - \Sigma_t \lambda_t \overset{i}{g_t} = 0$
   2. $\lambda_t g_t(p_i) = 0, \qquad t = 1, 2, \ldots, q$
   3. $g_t(p_i) \geq 0, \qquad t = 1, 2, \ldots, q$
   4. $\lambda_t \geq 0; \qquad t = 1, 2, \ldots, q$
2. conditions (4) are necessary conditions for $\overset{o}{p_i}$ to be a local minimum of V_i;

3. given the assumed concavity and convexity of the indicated functions, the problem is convex, and, conditions (4) will be sufficient conditions as well for p_i^o to be a local minimum of V_i;
4. given the convexity of the problem, p_i^o will be a global as well as local minimum of V_i.[1]

1.1.2. *The Dual Problem.* When the primal problem is convex (and only in these conditions) a dual problem to the primal of (1) and (2) exists and may be written (Fiacco and McCormick, [11], p. 92):

(5) Maximize $\mathscr{L}_i(p_i, \lambda) = V_i - \Sigma_t \lambda_t g_t(p_i)$

subject to

(6) 1. $V_i^i - \Sigma_t \lambda_t g_t^i = 0$
2. $\lambda_t \geq 0, t = 1, 2, \ldots, q.$

Note that in the primal problem the objective function V_i is being minimized whereas in the dual problem the Lagrangean is being maximized. A most convenient algorithmic contribution of the dual is that it provides a lower bound on the primal. That is, if p_i is *any* primal feasible value and $[p_i, \lambda]$ is *any* dual feasible vector, then

$$V_i(p_i^*) \geq \mathscr{L}(\tilde{p}_i, \tilde{\lambda}) .$$

For

(7) $V_i(p_i^*) \geq V_i(p_i^*) - \Sigma_t \tilde{\lambda}_t g_t(p_i^*)$,

because where $\tilde{\lambda}_t > 0$ it will multiply a positive $g_t(p_i^*)$ value. Because $\mathscr{L}_i(p_i, \lambda)$ is convex, a tangent hyperplane at $\tilde{p}_i$ must be everywhere on or below it. Therefore,

(8) $V_i(p_i^*) - \Sigma_t \tilde{\lambda}_t g_i(p_i^*) \geq V_i(\tilde{p}_i) - \Sigma_t \tilde{\lambda}_t g_t(\tilde{p}_i) + (p_i^* - \tilde{p}_i)(\tilde{\nabla}_i^i - \Sigma_t \lambda_t \bar{g}_t^i)$,

where $\tilde{V}_i^i$ and $\tilde{g}_t^i$ denote derivatives with respect to p_i at $\tilde{p_i}$. But, by (6.1) and (7), we may rewrite (8) as

(9) $V_i(p_i^*) \geq V_i(\tilde{p}_i) - \Sigma_t \tilde{\lambda}_t g_t(\tilde{p}_i) = \mathscr{L}_i(\tilde{p}_i, \tilde{\lambda})$.

When conditions a. - d. hold and p_i^o is a solution to the primal problem, a solution to the dual exists. Moreover,

(10) $V_i(p_i^o) = \mathscr{L}_i(p_i^o, \lambda^o)$,

from (3) and (4.2). But (p_i^o, λ^o) is then feasible by (4.1) and from (5)

(11) $\mathscr{L}_i(p_i^o, \lambda^o) = V_i(p_i^o) = \text{maximum } \mathscr{L}_i(p_i, \lambda)$

and hence is a solution to the dual.

1.2. *Parametric Programming -- First Level*

It now becomes possible to extend the comparative static analysis of Chapter 2 to incorporate constraints in a general parametric programming approach. We rewrite the general model of (1) and (2) to incorporate shift parameters:

(12) $$\text{Minimize } V_i = f_i(p_i) + \Sigma_r \theta_{ir} f_r(p_i) + \Sigma_c \theta_{ic} f_c(p_i) + \varepsilon_0 \phi_0(p_i)$$

subject to

(13) $$g_t(p_i) + \varepsilon_t \phi_t(p_i), \qquad t = 1, 2, \ldots, q,$$

where ε is a vector of small scalars. Suppose $\overset{o}{p}_i$ is a local minimum of V_i and ε defines a small neighborhood of it. Assume, also:

1. f_i, f_r, f_c, and g_t are twice differentiable;
2. necessary conditions (4) hold at $\overset{o}{p}_i$;
3. at $\overset{o}{p}_i$ the bordered Hessian matrix

$$y^T \nabla^2 \mathcal{L}_i\, y > 0\,,$$

where y is any vector such that $y^T \nabla g_t = 0$ for all t such that $\overset{o}{\lambda}_t > 0$;

4. when $\overset{o}{g}_t = 0$, $\overset{o}{\lambda}_t > 0$, or strict complementarity between dual variables and binding constraints holds.

Under these conditions $[p_i(\varepsilon), \lambda_t(\varepsilon)]$ define a local minimum of V_i, and it follows that, as an approximation[2]

(14) $$\begin{bmatrix} dp_i(0)/d\varepsilon \\ d\lambda_t(0)/d\varepsilon \end{bmatrix} = \begin{bmatrix} \nabla^2 \overset{o}{\mathcal{L}}_i & -\mathbf{G}^\circ \\ \lambda^\circ (\mathbf{G}^\circ)^T & \text{diag}(\overset{o}{g}_t) \end{bmatrix}^{-1} \begin{bmatrix} -\nabla\phi_0 & \lambda^\circ \phi^\circ \\ \mathbf{0} & \text{diag}(-\overset{o}{\lambda}_t \phi_t) \end{bmatrix}$$

where

1. $G^\circ = [\nabla \overset{o}{g}_1, \nabla \overset{o}{g}_2, \ldots, \nabla \overset{o}{g}_q]$
2. λ° is a diagonal matrix of the λ_t
3. diag $(\overset{o}{g}_t)$ is a diagonal matrix of the $\overset{o}{g}_t(p_i)$
4. $\phi^\circ = [\nabla\phi_1, \nabla\phi_2, \ldots, \nabla\phi_q]$.

For example, consider Model 1 as defined in Chapter 1, (1) -- (7), and the case of a rise in the marginal cost of rival k ($\phi_0(p_i) = \theta_{ik}\, \Delta\, C_k\, x_k$), all other $\phi_t(p_i) = 0$. Then the Lagrangean form may be written (with C_j the cost functions and C_i the constraint function in notation)

(15) $$\text{Minimize } \mathcal{L}_i = -x_i m_i - \Sigma_j x_j m_j + \varepsilon_0 \theta_{ik}\, \Delta\, C_k x_k - \sum_{t=1}^{5} \lambda_t C_i$$

and (14) may be specified as

(16)
$$\begin{bmatrix} dp_i(0)/d\varepsilon_0 \\ d\lambda_1(0)/d\varepsilon_0 \\ d\lambda_2(0)/d\varepsilon_0 \\ d\lambda_3(0)/d\varepsilon_0 \\ d\lambda_4(0)/d\varepsilon_0 \\ d\lambda_5(0)/d\varepsilon_0 \end{bmatrix} = \begin{bmatrix} 2(b_{ii} - \lambda_5/p_i^3 & -b_{ii} & b_{ii} & \bar{p}_i^{-1} & -\bar{p}_i^{-1} & -1 \\ \lambda_1 b_{ii} & C_i^1 & 0 & 0 & 0 & 0 \\ -\lambda_2 b_{ii} & 0 & C_i^2 & 0 & 0 & 0 \\ -\lambda_3 \bar{p}_i^{-1} & 0 & 0 & C_i^3 & 0 & 0 \\ \lambda_4 \bar{p}_i^{-1} & 0 & 0 & 0 & C_i^4 & 0 \\ \lambda_5 & 0 & 0 & 0 & 0 & C_i^5 \end{bmatrix}^{-1} \begin{bmatrix} -\theta_{ik}\Delta C_k b_{ki} & 0\,0\,0\,0\,0 \\ 0 & 0\,0\,0\,0\,0 \\ 0 & 0\,0\,0\,0\,0 \\ 0 & 0\,0\,0\,0\,0 \\ 0 & 0\,0\,0\,0\,0 \\ 0 & 0\,0\,0\,0\,0 \end{bmatrix}$$

$$= \mathbf{M}_i^{-1} \mathbf{Q}_i .$$

Of course, by Assumption 4 above, when $\lambda_t > 0$, $C_i^t = 0$, and when $\lambda_t = 0$, $C_i^t > 0$. When all constraints are ineffective ($\lambda° = 0$) at p_i^o, then

(17) $$dp_i(0)/d\varepsilon_0 = -.5\, \theta_{ik}\, b_{ki}\, \Delta\, C_k/b_{ii} ,$$

which duplicates results in (6) of Chapter 2 for $dC_k = \Delta\, C_k\, d\varepsilon_0$. When we allow each constraint to bind *singly*, $dp_i(0)/d\varepsilon_0 = 0$ and

(18)
1. $d\lambda_i(0)/d\varepsilon_0 = \theta_{ik}\, b_{ki}\, \Delta\, C_k/b_{ii}$
2. $d\lambda_2(0)/d\varepsilon_0 = -\theta_{ik}\, b_{ki}\, \Delta\, C_k/b_{ii}$
3. $d\lambda_3(0)/d\varepsilon_0 = -\theta_{ik}\, b_{ki}\, \Delta\, C_k\, \bar{p}_i$
4. $d\lambda_4(0)/d\varepsilon_0 = \theta_{ik}\, b_{ki}\, \Delta\, C_k\, \bar{p}_i$
5. $d\lambda 5(0)/d\varepsilon 0 = \theta_{ik}\, b_{ki}\, \Delta\, C_k$

We use (18.1) and Figure 3.1 to motivate these propositions. Let $\delta Z_i/\delta p_i = Z_i^i$. It is well known that [3]

(19) $$\lambda_1^0 = Z_i^i\, dp_i/dB_i.$$

But

(20) $$Z_i^i = x_i - b_{ii}\, m_i + \Sigma_j\, \theta_{ij}\, b_{ji}\, m_j - \theta_{ik}\, b_{ki}\, \varepsilon_0\, \Delta\, C_k < 0 ,$$

the inequality implied by (20) and $\lambda_1 > 0$, and from C_i^1:

(21) $$dp_i/dB_i = -b_{ii}^{-1} .$$

That is, when $\Delta\, B_i = 1$, sales are permitted to expand by 1 unit, to permit which p_i declines by $-b_{ii}^{-1}$. On Figure 3.1, p_i^o is determined by a binding C_i^1 where $MEP_i < 0$. When B_i rises, p_i^o falls to $-b_{ii}^{-1}\, p_i^o$. Because Z_i^1 is extended marginal profit EMP_i as drawn in the figure, from (19) and (21) it follows that λ_1^o is depicted by the polygon $ADp_i^o p_i^B$. From (19), (20), and

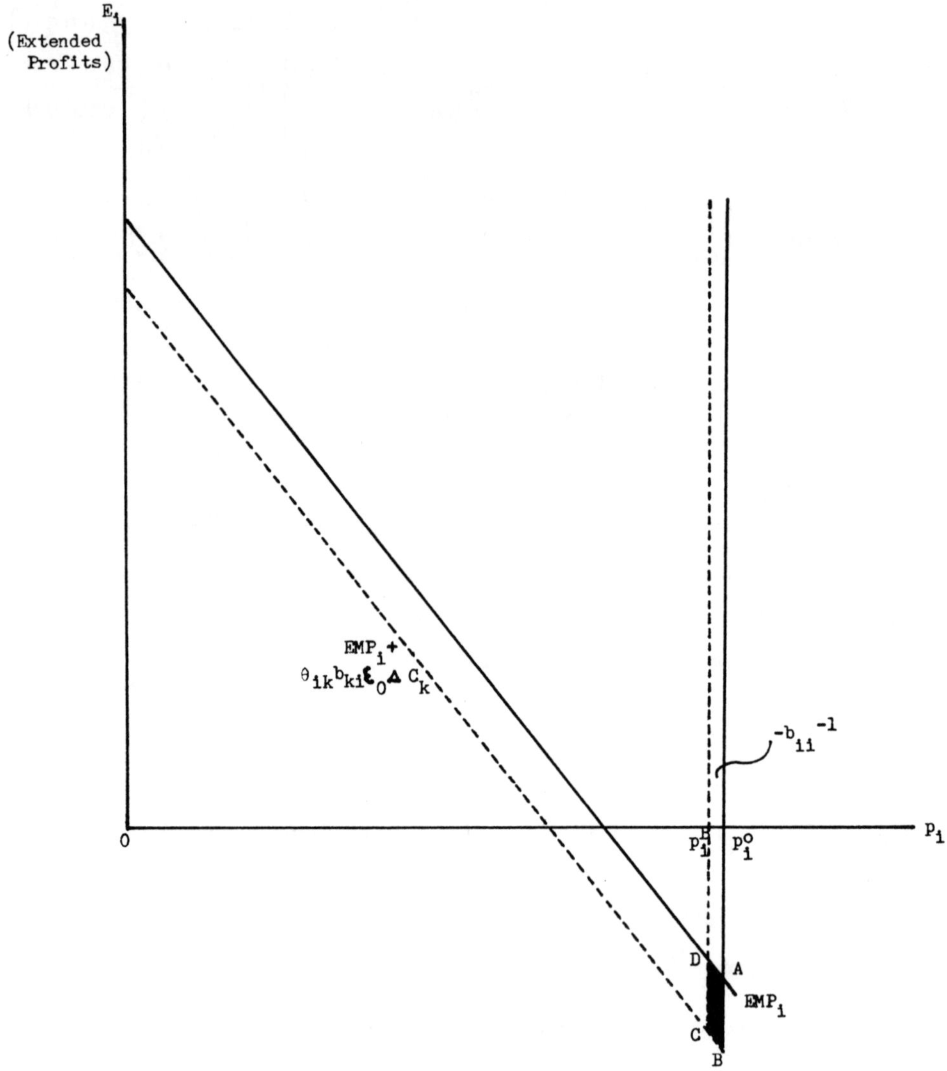

Figure 3.1. MOTIVATION OF THE RATE OF RISE OF $\lambda_1^o > 0$ WHEN C_k RISES

(21):

(22) $d\lambda_1^0/d\varepsilon_0 = d(-Z_i/b_{ii})/d\varepsilon_0 = \theta_{ik}\, b_{ki}\, \Delta\, C_k/b_{ii})$,

which is (18.1).

On Figure 3.1, the last term in (20) is the reduction in EMP_i imposed by $\varepsilon_0\Delta C_k$, depicted as AB. It is multiplied by $-b_{ii}^{-1}$ to yield a positive change in λ_1 when $\varepsilon_0 > 0$ and small. Similar interpretations hold for the other expressions of (18). In general, these interpretations are based upon the directions and amounts of price movement if the restraint of the relevant constraint is relaxed to permit movement in the direction of the $EMP_i = 0$ price.

1.3. *A Penalty Function Algorithm for Solving the Crippled Optimization Model First Level*

We have employed a "penalty function" algorithm to solve such rivalrous consonance models as 1, 2, and 3 at the first level of analysis because it is so readily adaptable to solving at the second level. In this section we will explain the logic of the method briefly, but it must be emphasized that models at the first level of analysis can be solved by any nonlinear programming algorithm.

The Fiacco-McCormick SUMT (Sequential Unconstrained Minimization Technique) ([11]) solves for constrained optima by constructing a sequence of unconstrained minimization problems whose solutions converge (provably for convex problems) to a local solution (global for convex problems) of the original problem. It offers several great computational advantages by approaching boundary optima from the interior of the feasible region, so that the difficulties of moving along boundaries are not confronted and by its ability to solve a sequence of *unconstrained* minimization problems by any number of well-known numerical techniques.

Consider the simple nonlinear programming problem:

Maximize $Z = 2x_1 - .1x_1^2 + 3x_2$

Subject to:

C^1: $x_1^2 + x_2^2 - 25 \leq 0$

(A) C^2: $x_1 + .5x_1^2 + 2x_2 - 12 \leq 0$

C^3, C^4: $x_1, x_2 \geq 0$.

SUMT adopts the minimization convention, and so the first step to use of the algorithm is to multiply both sides of all functions (except the nonnegativity constraints) by (–1):

Minimize $V = -2x_1 + .1x_1^2 + 3x_2$

Subject to:

$$\bar{C}^1: -x_1^2 - x_2^2 + 25 \geq 0$$

(B) $$\bar{C}^2: -x_1 - .5x_1^2 - 2x_2 \geq 0$$

$$\bar{C}^3, \bar{C}^4: \quad x_1, x_2 \geq 0 .$$

The maximization problem is graphed in the lower left corner of Figure 3.2 and its mirror image minimization equivalent in the upper right hand corner.

The algorithm then defines a "penalty function" with a "penalty" or "barrier" term:

(23) $$\text{Minimize } P(x_1, x_2; r_1) = V + r_1 [-\ln \bar{C}^1 - \ln \bar{C}^2 - \ln \bar{C}^3 - \ln \bar{C}^4] ,$$

where r_1 is a positive scalar whose value is set by the analyst. The penalty term is the bracketed expression multiplied by r_1, and its purpose is to prevent the solution of $P(\cdot)$ from reaching the boundary. That is, if one or more constraints bind, its (their) value becomes 0, and $\ln (0) = -\infty$. hence, the $\mathbf{x}$ that minimizes $P( )$ must occur at an interior point (say $\mathbf{x}^1$ on Figure 3.2) of the feasible region.

It may seem paradoxical that we would be interested in the solution to such problems as (23) because in our example, and in most cases, the answers we seek to the original problem will indeed lie on the boundary of the feasible region. As we approach the boundaries from the interior of the region the gradients of $P(\cdot)$ become very steep indeed. However, if we set up a sequence of $P(x_1, x_2; r_j)$ problems where $r_1 > r_2 > r_3 > \ldots 0$ it becomes possible to reduce the penalty term to a value arbitrarily close to zero. Because every solution to $P(x_1, x_2; r_j)$ will be feasible, the sequence of solutions should approach arbitrarily close to the solution to the original problem, without ever quite reaching it.

Note that our original maximization problem A has a concave objective function and convex constraint functions. Therefore, it is a convex programming problem. Multiplying these functions by (–1) merely converts concave to convex functions and vice versa, and hence preserves convexity for the equivalent minimization problem B. Equally important for the solution of the problem, however, is that the penalty term is also a global minimum.

Let us establish that $\ln \bar{C}^k$ is convex in $\mathbf{x}$ when $\bar{C}^k$ is (1) concave in $\mathbf{x}$ and (2) strictly positive. We note that $-\ln \bar{C}^k$ is well defined for $\bar{C}^k > 0$ and that it is a decreasing function of $\bar{C}^k$. Further, $-\ln \bar{C}^k$ is convex in $\bar{C}_k$, i.e., in the value of the constraint when positive, for $-d^2 \ln \bar{C}^k/d(\bar{C}^k)^2 = 1/(\bar{C}^k)^2 > 0$. These conditions are sufficient to make $-\ln \bar{C}^k$ convex in $\mathbf{x}$, as we show below and motivate with Figure 3.3.

Suppose $\bar{C}^k$ is $\sqrt{x} \geq 0$, so that $-\ln \bar{C}^k = -\ln \sqrt{x}$. Note that the latter expression meets the conditions (1) and (2), that it is a decreasing function, and is convex. We have graphed $\bar{C}^k$ on Figure 3.3 as well as its logarithmic transformation. Consider, now, any two values of x for which $\sqrt{x}$ is well-defined, say $x = 1$ and $x = 3$. Then, by the concavity of $\sqrt{x}$ in x

(24) $$\lambda \sqrt{1} + (1 - \lambda) \sqrt{3} \leq \sqrt{\lambda (1) + (1 - \lambda) (3)} , \lambda \varepsilon [0,1] .$$

But, because $-\ln \sqrt{x}$ is a decreasing function of x,

(25) $$-\ln \sqrt{\lambda (1) + (1 - \lambda) (3)} \leq -\ln (\lambda \sqrt{1} + (1 - \lambda) \sqrt{3}).$$

And since $-\ln \sqrt{x}$ is convex in $\sqrt{x}$,

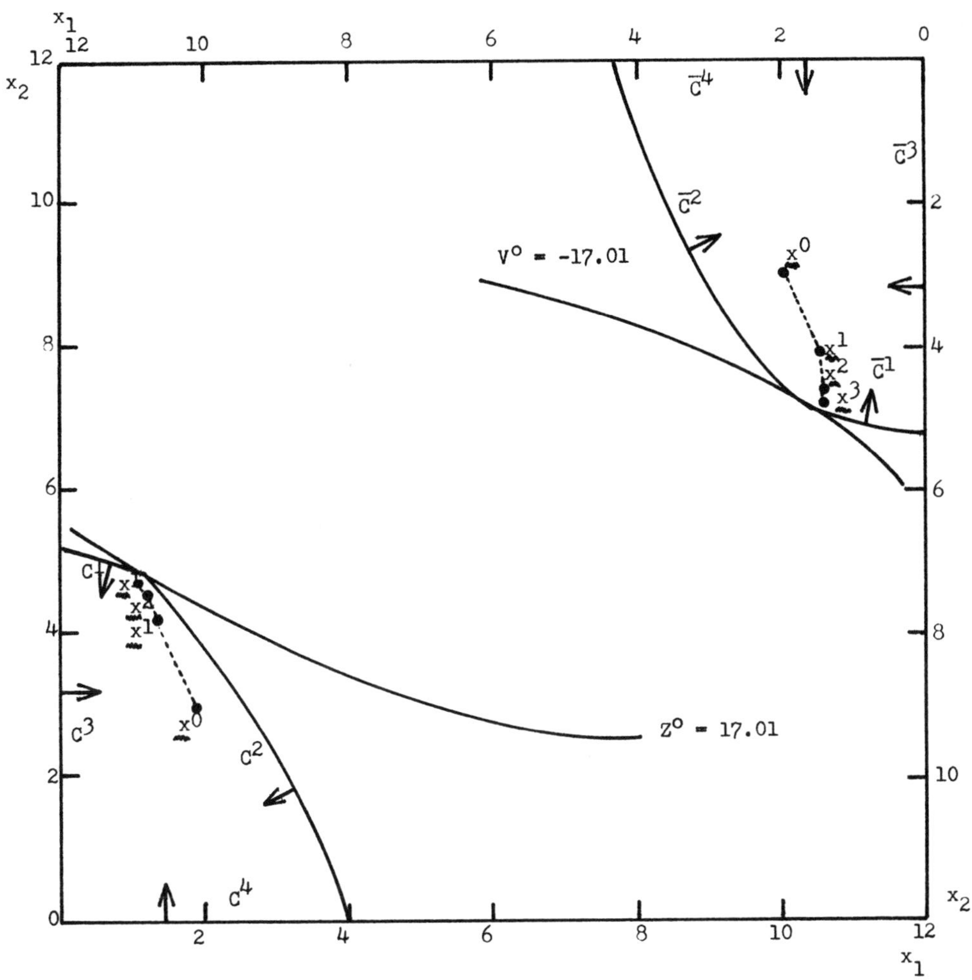

Figure 3.2. A GRAPHIC DEPICTION OF A SUMT SOLUTION TRAJECTORY FOR EXAMPLE

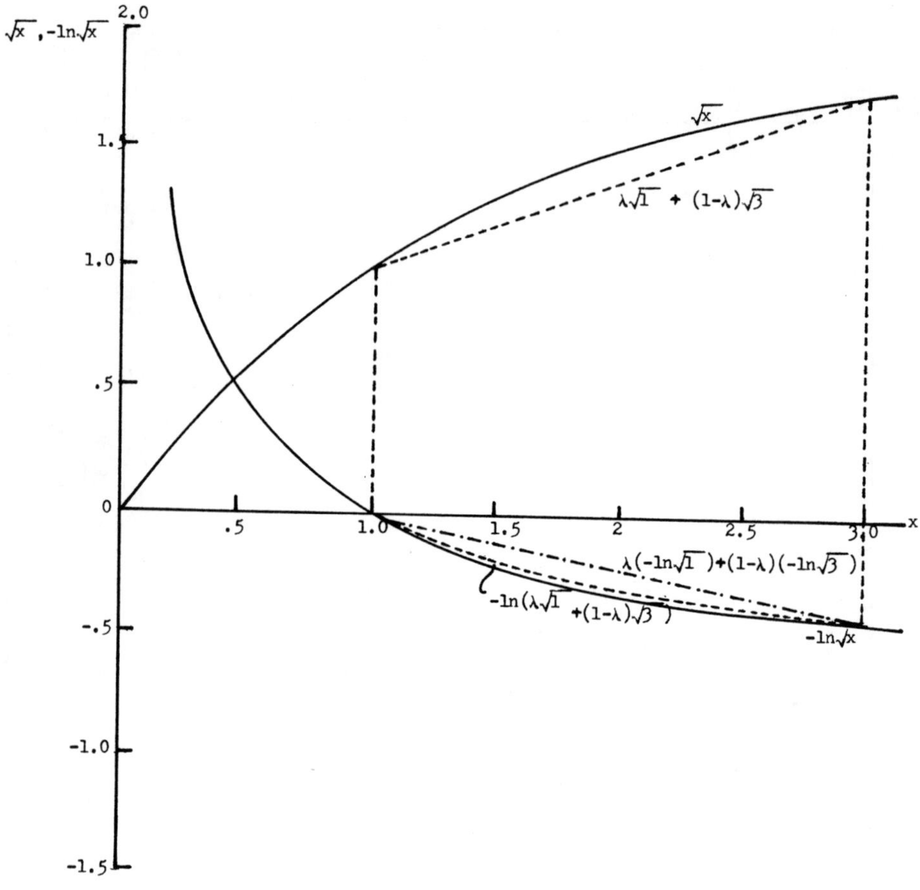

Figure 3.3. DEMONSTRATION OF THE CONVEXITY IN x OF $-\ln(C^k)$

(26) $-\ln(\lambda\sqrt{1} + (1-\lambda)\sqrt{3}) \le \lambda(-\ln\sqrt{1}) + (1-\lambda)(-\ln\sqrt{3})$.

Hence, from (26), $-\ln\sqrt{x}$ is convex in x as well as $\sqrt{x}$, or, in general, $-\ln\bar{C}^k$ is convex in **x** as well as $\bar{C}^k$. Therefore, each $-\ln\bar{C}^k$ function in the penalty term in (23) is convex in **x**, their sum is convex, and, since $r_1 > 0$ and the penalty term is added to V, the convexity of the penalty term in **x** is preserved.

Two convenient properties of (23) are clear: the minimum we seek is an unconstrained minimum and will be a global minimum. Indeed, P(·) is reminiscent of a classic Lagrangean form in which the Lagrangean variable (r_1) has been preset. Given the differentiability and convexity of P(·) in x_1 and x_2, the necessary and sufficient conditions for a global minimum are simply the familiar

(27) $P \equiv V - r_1 \Sigma_t \Delta \bar{C}^t = 0$.

Because the equations of (27) may not be soluble analytically, in the SUMT algorithm a choice of iterative numerical techniques is available to solve them iteratively, beginning from a user-selected original $\mathbf{x}^0$ in the strict interior of the feasible region.

The solution to (27) yields the minimum of $P(\mathbf{x}; r_1)$ which we have graphed on Figure 3.2 as $\mathbf{x}^1$. A new $P(\mathbf{x}; r_2)$ is then specified with a $0 < r_2 < r_1$, $\mathbf{x}^1$ is taken as the new original solution in the numerical iterations for its solution, and $\mathbf{x}^2$ emerges as the solution to $P(\mathbf{x}; r_2)$. This sequence continues with decreasing r, the solutions **x** approaching closer and closer to the true constrained minimum of V, as illustrated in Figure 3.2. Indeed, for a convex problem, a proof exists that the sequence $\{x\}$ does converge on the solution as a limit point.[4]

Two questions arise that warrant answers before we demonstrate the first-level algorithm in solving our example. First, what criterion should be used to decide when to terminate the sequence of penalty function solutions? When has the sequence $\{x_k\}$ approached $\mathbf{x}^o$ sufficiently closely? Second, what is the optimal sequence of r values for the penalty functions?

The first question can be answered neatly *for convex problems* through use of the dual derived in section 1.1.2. For convenience we reproduce it for the current problem:

(28) Maximize $\mathcal{L}(\mathbf{x}, \lambda) = V - \Sigma_t \lambda_t \bar{C}^t$

subject to

(29) 1. $\nabla_x \mathcal{L}(x, \lambda) = 0$

2. $\lambda_t \ge 0, t = 1, 2, \ldots, q$.

But let **x** be any primal feasible value and $\mathbf{x}^*$ any dual feasible value, and we know

(30) $V(\mathbf{x}) \ge \quad (\mathbf{x}^*, \lambda^*) = V(\mathbf{x}^*) - \Sigma_t \lambda_t \bar{C}^t$,

and, of course, for $\mathbf{x}^o$, the optimal solution to the primal,

(31) $V(\mathbf{x}^o) \le V(\mathbf{x})$.

Therefore,

(32) $V(\mathbf{x}^*) - \Sigma_t \lambda_t^* \bar{C}^t \leq V(\mathbf{x}^o) \leq V(\mathbf{x})$,

or the unknown optimal solution to the primal must lie between $\mathscr{L}(\mathbf{x}, \lambda)$ for any dual feasible $[\mathbf{x}^* \; \lambda^*]$ and any primal feasible $\mathbf{x}$.

But consider $\mathbf{x_k}$, or the optimal solution to the penalty function $P(\mathbf{x}; r_k)$. Let us choose it as the primal feasible $\mathbf{x}$ in (31). Once more, let us recall that in the primal problem

(33) $\delta \mathscr{L}/\delta C^t = \delta V/\delta C^t - \lambda_t \, \delta C^t/\delta C^t = 0$

and $\lambda_t = \delta V/\delta C^t$.

Consider once more the penalty function

(34) $P(\mathbf{x}; r_k) = V(\mathbf{x}) - r\, \Sigma_t \ln C^t$,

where

(35) $\delta P(\cdot)/\delta \bar{C}^t = \delta V(\mathbf{x})/\delta \bar{C}^t - r/\bar{C}^t$

Let us assume, by analogy with (32)

(36) $\delta V(x_k)/\delta \bar{C}^t - r_k/\bar{C}^t \approx 0 = \delta V(x_k)/\delta \bar{C}^t - \lambda_t(r_k)$

so that

(37) $\lambda_t(r_k) \approx r_k/\bar{C}^t(\mathbf{x_k})$.

It can be shown (Fiacco and McCormick, [11], pp. 98-99) that the sequence $\{\mathbf{x_k}, \lambda(r_k)\}$ is dual feasible and that its limit points, of which at least one exists, are optimal solutions to the dual. Using (37) we may approximate

(38) $\mathscr{L}(\mathbf{x}^o, \lambda^o) \approx V(\mathbf{x}_k) - \Sigma_t(r_k\, \bar{C}^t(\mathbf{x}_k)/\bar{C}^t(\mathbf{x}_k)) = V(\mathbf{x}_k) - q{\cdot}r_k$.

From (32), therefore, for convex problems there exists for every solution to $P(\mathbf{x}_k; r_k)$ upper and lower bounds on x^o:

(39) $V(\mathbf{x}_k) - q{\cdot}r_k \leq V(\mathbf{x}^o) \leq V(\mathbf{x}_k)$.

At the solution to the very first penalty function, $V(\mathbf{x}^o)$ is known within an error bracket of $q{\cdot}r_k$, and, of course, as r falls toward zero, this bracket narrows. Indeed, as $P(\cdot)$ solutions are encountered it becomes possible to extrapolate $\mathbf{x}^o$. Finally, the analyst may set the absolute value of $q{\cdot}r_k$ he will tolerate as a convergence criterion for terminating penalty function approximations to $\mathbf{x}^o$.

The second question is not so readily answered. Determining the "optimal" $\{r_k\}$ sequence has to this point defied formal solution and must be done heuristically. The tradeoff is that between choosing a sequence that permits rapid approach toward the boundary and $\mathbf{x}^o$ versus the risk of being thrown out of the feasible region by the algorithm's need to cope with the rapidly ascending gradients near the boundaries. The initial value of r is frequently obtained by evaluating the penalty term at the initial assumed solution as well as the objective function and setting r_1 at the quotient of objective function value and the sum of the $-\ln\bar{C}^t$.

Subsequent r-values are typically obtained by dividing the previous value by a constant, for example, as large as 16 for convex problems, perhaps 4 for nonconvex problems.

1.4. *A Computational Example*

As an example of the use and performance of SUMT, consider the simple problem of section 1.3 illustrated in Figure 3.2. Table 3.1 summarizes results of the successive penalty functions. The tolerance criterion is the difference between the primal and dual objective function values that must be reached as a minimum before the last penalty function is accepted as a sufficiently close approximation to the original problem's solution. It was set at .0001 for our use of SUMT. Our initial "guess" about $\mathbf{x}^o$ was set as [2.00, 3.00], deep within the interior of the feasible region, and r_1 was set at 1.00 to be divided by 4 to obtain successive r's.

Table 3.1. SOLUTION BY SUMT OF EXAMPLE PROBLEM

k	Primal		r_k	V	λ_1	λ_2	$\mathscr{L}(\mathbf{x},\lambda)$	Seconds Elapsed	
	x_1	x_2						Cumulative	Increment
0	2.00	3.00	----	-12.60	----	----	----	.166	---
1	1.37	4.23	1.00	-15.24	.191	.813	-19.24	.286	.120
2	1.33	4.69	.25	-16.54	.198	.601	-16.98	.395	.109
3	1.38	4.78	.0625	-16.89	.211	.501	-17.01	.514	.119
4	1.40	4.79	.0156	-16.98	.215	.469	-17.01	.610	.096
5	1.41	4.80	.0039	-17.01	.217	.461	-17.01	.683	.073
6	1.41	4.80	.0010	-17.01	.217	.459	-17.01	.774	.091
7	1.41	4.80	.0002	-17.01	.217	.459	-17.01	.830	.056

Tolerance Criterion = .0001.

The problem was solved in substantially less execution time than 1 second in 7 penalty function approximations; indeed, the primal was solved to two decimal places in 5 iterations. As discussed above, because the problem is convex the first penalty function approximation reveals that the solution we seek lies in the interval [–19.24, –15.24] from our knowledge about $\mathscr{L}(\cdot)$ and V as lower and upper bounds (see (32) above). Indeed, by the second penalty function solution quite tight bounds are set, the dual value being slightly too high due to rounding error.

The value of the penalty term for each iteration is (–17.01 - V), of course, and it must decrease monotonically in absolute terms as r falls. V must also fall monotonically in convex problems, as it does in Table 3.1, but note that x_1 and x_2 need not converge uniformly to their solution values (compare x_1 for iterations 1, 2, and 3). Note that for this small problem, the time for solution of successive penalty functions tends generally to fall. This is not generally the case, for as boundaries are approached gradients become steeper, and larger numbers of iterations of whatever numerical algorithm is being used (Newton-Raphson in our case) to solve them are required.

Because our solution lies at the intersection of the two constraints on Figure 3.2, both dual variables are positive. Their interpretation is the standard one: if $-\bar{C}^1$ were reduced in its restraint from –25 to –26, for example, the objective function value would fall at the rate of $\lambda_1 = .217$ to approximately –17.33, and similarly for $-\bar{C}^2$ and λ_2. The dual variable values for each penalty function permit us to calculate from (37) above the value of the primal constraints for $\mathbf{x}_k$, if such values are desired.

This problem is a simple one, of course, designed for use as an illustration of SUMT as a method, not to be typical of solution problems. Moreover, it is strictly convex, and hence well-behaved. Nonetheless, the rapid convergence to the neighborhood of the solution and the relative speed (for nonlinear programming algorithms) of computation are not atypical for larger problems, as will be seen below.

2. *THE LIMITATIONS OF NONLINEAR PROGRAMMING FOR UNSPECIFIED MODELS*

In this chapter we have at once extended the first-level theoretical basis of Chapter 2 and prepared for the second-level analysis of Chapters 4 and 5. Nonlinear programming has not yet found acceptance in the economics profession as a technique that is more conformant with realistic economic constraints, which occur more frequently as inequalities than equalities, than classical constrained optimization. On the other hand, it shares with the older methodology too many of the familiar limitations with respect to displacement analyses to be viewed as a fundamentally revolutionary development in general equilibrium theory. Such analysis remains heavily dependent upon continuous differentiability, is restricted myopically to infinitesimal movements of parameters and induced microscopic displacements in the neighborhood of an optimum, and additionally, assumes that binding constraints in the initial equilibrium continue to bind and ineffective constraints remain so in the presence of parametric shocks.

Equally damning to both classical and nonlinear programming comparative statics, however, is what Samuelson termed "the law of conjugate pairs".[5] It has never informed economic theory to the extent its importance warrants, and perhaps understandably, for it establishes the narrow potential of large-scale models to yield theorems. The purpose of theoretical models in the social sciences is to derive insights into the causation that underlies economic phenomena -- insights that can be termed "laws" only with the arrogance that springs from envy of the physical sciences. Indeed, even when models are numerically specified their proper usage is not to present the policy maker with "the" answer. They simply are never rich enough in dimensionality, exactitude of interrelationships, or flexibility in regime changes to substitute for their admittedly imperfect but necessary accompaniments: the imagination, experience, and intuition of the policy maker. Ideally, their employment will yield him insights and raise questions for debate that would not have occurred in the absence of the modeller's efforts.

In both cases, the usefulness of the models depends upon the derivation of theorems from the models whose empirical projections must be tested against reality, or at least against the intuition of the user. A model must be manipulable and manipulated, therefore, to fulfill a meaningful role. In theoretical and unspecified models this is done by comparative statics or dynamics or by parametric programming, both of which we have presented for rivalrous consonance models in Chapter 2 and in the present chapter. In numerically specified models, the analogous manipulation techniques are frequently called "sensitivity" or "postoptimality" analysis.

For the case of theoretical unspecified models frequently the only information available for the evaluation of such theorems is the information concerning relationships among variables and in the shapes of functions in the neighborhood of the equilibrium. This information is obtained from first- and second-order necessary and/or sufficient conditions for a constrained extremum, the greater part in restrictions upon the signs of bordered or unbordered Hessian matrices and their principal minors. The law of conjugate pairs asserts that the necessary and sufficient conditions for the unambiguous evaluation of a qualitative theorem involving nonLagrangean variables from an optimization model, using only information obtained from constrained or unconstrained optimization conditions, is that the partial derivatives at the equilibrium be defined, that the parameter whose change displaces the equilibrium enters only that one of the interrelationships among variables define by the first order conditions in whose change we are interested, and that the sign of the partial derivative of this relationship with respect to that parameter be known.

Consider, for example, the simple case of consumer choice among three goods, with utility function

$$U = U(x_1, x_2, x_3), \tag{40}$$

and budget constraint

$$x_1 p_1 + x_2 p_2 + x_3 p_3 = B\,, \tag{41}$$

where **p** and B are parameters. First-order conditions are the well-known interrelationships:

$$\begin{aligned} &1\ \ U^1 - \lambda p_1 = 0 \\ &2.\ U^2 - \lambda p_2 = 0 \\ &3.\ U^3 - \lambda p_3 = 0 \\ &4.\ B - x_1 p_1 - x_2 p_2 - x_3 p_3 = 0\,, \end{aligned} \tag{42}$$

and second-order sufficient conditions for a constrained maximum are that the following bordered Hessian be negative definite:

$$H = \begin{bmatrix} U^{11} & U^{12} & U^{13} & -p_1 \\ U^{12} & U^{22} & U^{23} & -p_2 \\ U^{13} & U^{23} & U^{33} & -p_3 \\ -p_1 & -p_2 & -p_3 & 0 \end{bmatrix} \tag{43}$$

A sufficient condition for the negative definiteness of H is that the nested bordered principal minors alternate in sign negative and positive:

$$\begin{vmatrix} U^{11} & U^{12} & -p_1 \\ U^{12} & U^{22} & -p_2 \\ -p_1 & -p_2 & 0 \end{vmatrix} < 0, |H| > 0\,. \tag{44}$$

Suppose p_1 rises at the equilibrium. Because p_1 appears in both (42.1) and (42.4), the law of conjugate pairs tells us immediately that the sign of dx_1/dp_1 is nonevaluable on the basis of (43) and (44) alone. To derive the expression we differentiate (42) totally to obtain the system:

$$\begin{bmatrix} U^{11} & U^{12} & U^{13} & -p_1 \\ U^{12} & U^{22} & U^{23} & -p_2 \\ U^{13} & U^{23} & U^{33} & -p_3 \\ -p_1 & -p_2 & -p_3 & 0 \end{bmatrix} \begin{bmatrix} dx_1/dp_1 \\ dx_2/dp_1 \\ dx_3/dp_1 \\ d\lambda/dp_1 \end{bmatrix} = \begin{bmatrix} \lambda \\ 0 \\ 0 \\ x_1 \end{bmatrix} \tag{45}$$

Then

$$(46)\qquad dx_1/dp_1 = \frac{\lambda\begin{vmatrix} U^{22} & U^{23} & -p_2 \\ U^{23} & U^{33} & -p_3 \\ -p_2 & -p_3 & 0 \end{vmatrix}}{|H|} - \frac{x_1\begin{vmatrix} U^{12} & U^{13} & -p_1 \\ U^{22} & U^{23} & -p_2 \\ U^{23} & U^{33} & -p_3 \end{vmatrix}}{|H|}$$

$$= \text{S. E.} - \text{I. E},$$

where S. E. denotes the familiar substitution effect of a price change and I. E. the income effect. The S. E. expression involves $\lambda > 0$ for a nonsatiated consumer and a bordered principal minor in the numerator; hence, from (44), it is unambiguously evaluable as nonpositive. The I. E., however, has a nonbordered minor in the numerator and hence is nonevaluable on the basis of (44) alone.

Because dx_2/dp_1 and dx_3/dp_1 also involve nonbordered minors, they are unevaluable, and *any* expression involving $d\lambda$ results in a nonbordered minor and is therefore unevaluable. Also, $d\lambda/dB$ results in the determinant of the Hessian of U in the numerator, whose sign would be determinate if U were concave which is not necessarily true if (43) holds.

The devastating impact of the law of conjugate pairs, therefore, is that use of what is frequently the only information available about the movement potential of endogenous variables limits us to changing only one parameter at a time within a very small neighborhood of the initial equilibrium and can *at best* yield only one unambiguous theorem for each parameter change. In large-scale models with many endogenous variables, therefore, where intuitive notions fail to yield much supplementary help in evaluation, manipulation of theoretical numerically unspecified models is a sterile exercise unless we impose hypotheses designed to drastically simplify the relevant determinants by essentially restricting interdependence. The exercise is self-defeating if the whole purpose of using general equilibrium analysis is to capture such interrelationships.

The use of parametric programming with numerically specified parameters does not possess these limitations, although, of course, one sacrifices the potential for discovering "universal" laws of change in variables as responses to parametric changes. As stated in Chapter 1, with respect to large interdependence models, too much effort is involved in such grail-like searches. Insufficient effort has been devoted to developing frameworks and techniques for efficient "simulative theorizing". By this is meant the abstraction of the most important relationships and parameter values in numerical specification to define a particular body of phenomena with the purpose of gaining structural insights into its underlying causation.

The purpose of the parametric manipulation is not primarily the forecasting of the state of the system for some set of "most likely" parameters to rule in the future. It is, rather, similar to the goals of the pure theorist: to gain structural and behavioral insights. We shall illustrate its uses and implementation in Chapter 5 when we seek to abstract the operational features and parameters of a fictitious general oligopolistic equilibrium example with the purpose of laying bare its power structure and price-setting behavior.

Meanwhile, however, up to this point we have dealt only with first-level analysis that abstracts from interdependence among rivals and our single-firm crippled optimization model contains only one endogenous variable. On both counts the classical displacement analysis of Chapter 2 and parametric programming of this chapter have permitted us to evaluate theorems from unspecified models with some success. That leverage disappears as we move in Chapter 4 to the second level. There it becomes necessary to use simulative theorizing in response to the limitations discussed above.

3. *SUMMARY AND CONCLUSION*

Our construction, manipulation, and presentation of solution methods for typical rivalrous consonance models is now complete for work that is limited to first-level theorem derivation. Again, by first-level we mean analysis that is confined to the oligopolistic rival in an environment that features fixed competitors' and customers' prices and binary consonance factors. In so doing we have introduced the meaning and potential power of the concept of rivalrous consonance, derived some insights into its simpler reactions to parametric changes, indicated its adaptability to operational applications for industrial analysis through nonlinear programming and sensitivity analysis, and, lastly, discussed the theoretical limitations to theorem derivation from large scale interdependence models that are innocent of numerical implementation.

We are now ready, with this background, to confront rivalrous consonance at the second level of analysis, in which consonance factors remain exogenous but rivals fix prices in interdependence cognizance -- the oligopoly problem proper.

1 A full derivation of these theorems and their proofs can be found in Fiacco and McCormick [11], Chapters 2 and 6. Condition c. states a sufficient condition that at p_i^o there is no movement in a feasible neighborhood that reduces V_i. This is a *necessary* condition (with conditions a. and b.) that λ^o and p_i^o exist meeting (4) and that p_i^o is a local minimum. The Kuhn-Tucker Constraint Qualification is sufficient for this quality to characterize the neighborhood of p_i^o, and condition c. is in turn sufficient for the Kuhn-Tucker Constraint Qualification to hold.

One clarification of (4.1) may be helpful. Many readers will be more familiar with the alternative formation

a. $V_i^i - \Sigma_t g_t^i \geq 0$

b. $p_i (V_i^i - \Sigma_t g_t^i) = 0$

c. $\lambda_t, p_i \geq 0$.

This is the form used when the nonnegativity constraint is not included in the constraints. We have included it in the $g_t(p_i)$ set so that c. above does not appear explicitly in system (4). Suppose the nonnegativity is the qth constraint. Then (4.1) may be written

$$V_i^i - \sum_{t=1}^{q-1} \lambda_t g_t^i = \lambda_q ,$$

and in (4.2) will be found

$$\lambda_q (p_i) = 0 .$$

Hence, when $p_i > 0$, $\lambda_q = 0$, and when $p_i = 0$, λ_q is equal to the inequality of a., and, when transposed to the left hand side of (4.1) preserves the equality.

2 The theorem is proved in Fiacco and McCormick, [11], pp. 34-37, by taking total differentials of the necessary conditions that hold as equalities and rearranging terms.

3 Note that for this motivation we are using Z_i (rather than V_i) in a maximization (rather than minimization) context.

4 Fiacco and McCormick, [11], pp. 97-98.

5 See P. Samuelson, [40], p. 19, and, for a fuller demonstration of its devastating consequences for large-scale modelling see G. C. Archibald, [2].

CHAPTER 4

RIVALROUS CONSONANCE: THEORETICAL CONSIDERATIONS AT THE SECOND LEVEL

We begin this second level of analytical effort in section 1 with an extension of crippled optimization to duopoly, ignoring for the sake of simplicity any subgoal constraints on either firm. In section 2 we introduce the constraint subsets of Chapters 2 and 3 into the duopoly model. We then extend Model 1 into simultaneously functioning n-firm pricing in section 3, remaining with the numerically unspecified forms. Finally, in section 4, we summarize the theoretical results. In Chapter 5 we will complete the second level analysis by using simulative theorizing as a tool of investigation.

1. *UNCONSTRAINED DUOPOLY: A CRIPPLED OPTIMIZATION MODEL*

1.1. *A Reinterpretation and Extension of Classic Duopoly Models*

Let us reduce Model 1 to two dimensions: assume only two rivals exist in the industry and neither is constrained from extended profit maximization by subgoals. All other conditions of the model are taken to apply. The objective functions under rivalrous consonance then determine extended profits and each firm seeks a maximum:

$$(1)\qquad \text{Maximize } E_i = x_i m_i + \theta_i x_j m_j, \qquad i = 1, 2, j \neq i,$$

where we drop the second subscript from θ to simplify notation. First-order conditions are then

$$(2)\qquad dE_i/dp_i = x_i - b_{ii} m_i + \theta_i b_{ji} m_j = 0, \; i = 1, 2, j \neq i,$$

which, when solved simultaneously for p_i in terms of p_j, yield the *reaction functions*, R_i:

$$(3)\qquad R_i: \quad p_i^{\circ} = .5b_{ii}^{-1}[(a_i + b_{ii} C_i - \theta_i b_{ji} C_j) + (b_{ij} + \theta_i b_{ji})p_j],$$

$$= .5b_{ii}^{-1}[A_i + (b_{ij} + \theta_i b_{ji})p_j], \quad i = 1, 2, j \neq i.$$

which are linear in prices. These yield, of course, the maximum extended profit price for firm i given $p_j \geq 0$.

Necessary and sufficient conditions for a unique $\mathbf{p}^{\circ}$ to exist are that the matrix

$$(4)\qquad \mathbf{S} = \begin{bmatrix} -2b_{ii} & b_{ij} + \theta_i b_{ji} \\ b_{ji} + \theta_j b_{ij} & -2b_{jj} \end{bmatrix}$$

be nonsingular. Also, for "stability"[1] of $\mathbf{p}^o$, it is necessary when (1) A_i and A_j, the intercepts of the reaction functions, are positive, and (2) the slopes of the functions are positive, that

(5) $(dp_j/dp_i)_i > (dp_j/dp_i)_j$ implying $4b_{ii}\, b_{jj} > (b_{ij} + \theta_i\, b_{ji})(b_{ji} + \theta_j\, b_{ij})$

implying $|\mathbf{S}| > 0$,

or that the slope of rival i's reaction function be greater than the slope of rival j's, both taken with respect to p_i. For the moment, assume $\theta = [1,1]$, so that from (1) each firm maximizes the same function under conditions of joint profit maximization. That common objective function has a Hessian matrix

$$(6) \qquad \mathbf{H} = \begin{bmatrix} -2b_{ii} & b_{ij} + b_{ji} \\ b_{ij} + b_{ji} & -2b_{jj} \end{bmatrix} ,$$

and if $E = E_i = E_j$ is strictly concave in $\mathbf{p}$, we know that $\mathbf{H}$ will in general be negative definite, or

(7) $4b_{ii}\, b_{jj} > (b_{ij} + b_{ji})^2$,

since

(8) $b_{ii} > 0,\ b_{jj} > 0,\ |\mathbf{H}| > 0$.

Broadly speaking, this simply requires that the own-price demand impacts be somewhat stronger -- with a goodly margin to spare -- than other-price impacts. We will assume this is true in rivalrous consonance throughout our analysis, and, indeed, will make an even stronger assumption in Chapter 6. It follows, *a fortiori*, for $\theta_i\ \varepsilon[0,1[$, that (5) will hold and that the reaction functions intersect. The equilibrium p_i^θ for given θ from (3) is

(9) $p_i^\theta = [2b_{jj}\, A_i + (b_{ij} + \theta_i\, b_{ji})\, A_j]/|\mathbf{S}| = N_i/|\mathbf{S}|$, $i = 1,2, i \neq j$.

Thus $\mathbf{p}^\theta$ is the crippled optimization price vector for a given θ where we limit our interest to the unit interval for the consonance factors. Our interest in this book centers upon the mature oligopolistic industry which possesses neither the unrealistic attitudes reflected in $\theta_i > 1$ nor the price warfare inclinations implied by $\theta_i < 0$. It should be noted, however, that rivalrous consonance could be used to analyze such behavior modes.

The upper limit of interest, therefore, for the binary consonance factors is $\theta = [1,1]$, in which case (9) yields joint-profit maximization prices. We shall term $\mathbf{p}^J$ the *Chamberlin solution* in recognition of that economist's featuring of this duopoly result.[2]

On the other hand, if $\theta = [0,0]$, the resulting $\mathbf{p}^C$ is the equilibrium toward which the Cournot process, in which each rival determines his strategy on the assumption his counterpart's strategy will remain fixed, converges. With those strategies concerned with price setting, the mutual myopia will converge upon $\mathbf{p}^C$, and for this reason we refer to this limit of interest as the *Cournot solution*.[3]

We depict the duopoly solutions graphically on Figure 4.1. On the diagram we relate the crippled optimization analyses to the firms' isoprofit curves, the reaction functions (3) derived from them, and the solutions for various θ. We graph p_i and p_j on the axes and only one isoprofit contour -- I_1 and J_1 -- is drawn for each firm. Along the line $x_j = 0$ rival j's price reduces its sales to zero, so that isoprofit contours I become vertical lines above that line of no sales for firm j. Similarly, along the line $x_i = 0$ firm i suffers zero sales and to the right of the line firm j's contours become horizontal lines. The dotted lines C_i and C_j are the given and constant marginal costs of the firms.

Within ABCD -- the region of nonnegative sales and profits for both firms where prices remain relevant -- the joint-profit contours (not drawn) are portions of concentric ellipses which converge with rising joint profits to that center, $\mathbf{p}^J$, the Chamberlin joint-profit maximum price vector. The locus of tangencies of firm i's and firm j's own isoprofit contours, M_iM_j, passes through $\mathbf{p}^J$, touches the lines of no sales at M_i and M_j, and represents a negotiation price set for the firms under collusion, because on that locus one rival's profits can be raised only at the expense of the other's. M_i is firm i's monopoly price and the vertical segment drawn through it is the monopoly profit contour line toward which the isoprofit contours I converge as profits rise. Similarly, M_j is firm j's monopoly price, and the horizontal line its monopoly profit contour. Hence, for each firm, a higher profit level is represented by a move toward M_i and M_j on the isoprofit contour map. The isoprofit functions are hyperbolas before reaching the x_i and $x_j = 0$ lines.

We have drawn the reaction functions defined by (3) for $\theta^o = [0,0]$ and $\theta^1 = [1,1]$. The intersection of the latter on M_iM_j at $\mathbf{p}^J$ reveals the point on the negotiation set where the sum of rivals' profits are maximized -- the joint profit optimum. The θ^o functions are the classic Stackelberg functions, intersecting the I and J isoprofit contours at their minimum points, where they are tangent to horizontal or vertical lines depicting given p_j or p_i respectively. These reaction functions intersect at $\mathbf{p}^C$. The reaction function of θ_i (θ_j) = 1 intersects the joint-profit isocontours where slopes dp_j/dp_i (dp_i/dp_j) are zero.

As noted already at several points in this book, we are interested in interpreting the longer-run pricing behavior in "mature" oligopoly. We therefore assume that neither rival will operate at negative profit levels and that the rivals, while sensitive to industry power structure in their adoption of θ, do not engage in warfare. In the rivalrous consonance framework, firm i is waging war when $\theta_i < 0$, being willing to accept reduced profits or actual losses to inflict reduced profits or losses upon firm j. In my opinion, much too much attention has been paid the pathological behavior potential in duopoly (or oligopoly generally) and too little to the peaceful coexistence aspects of mature duopoly behavior. Therefore, our analyses adopt the unit square for θ as the region of relevance for realistic solutions. If industry mores permit tacit collusion, these limits for θ set the bounding points on M_iM_j within which the solution occurs. But any such point other than $\mathbf{p}^J$ can be attained on M_iM_j only if rival i or j sets a θ value above 1. Hence, on Figure 4.1, our region of admissible solutions is the polygon $\mathbf{p}^J V \mathbf{p}^C T$, with vertices $\mathbf{p}^J$ and $\mathbf{p}^C$.

One of the advantages of a rivalrous consonance framework is that it unifies such diverse analyses as Cournot's and joint profit maximization by showing their equivalence to extended profit maximization with $\theta = [0,0]$ and $[1,1]$ respectively. Indeed, the Cournot equilibrium may seem more plausible in a behavioral sense as the end result of decision making that places no value on rivals' profits than it does when presented in its usual process context wherein both rivals assume against recurring experience that their counterparts will hold strategies fixed.

Beyond these advantages of rivalrous consonance in unifying and rationalizing reaction function theory, it extends the usefulness of these tools by permitting θ-terms to be set in the interior of the unit interval and at different values for the

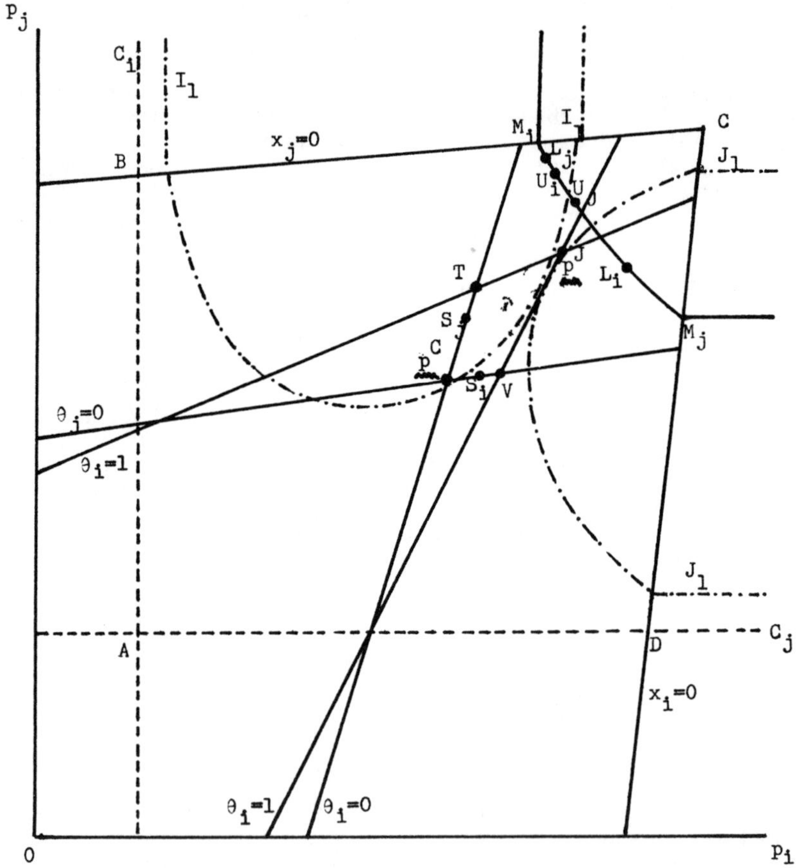

Figure 4.1. ISOPROFIT CONTOURS, REACTION FUNCTIONS, AND SOLUTION REGIONS IN DUOPOLY

duopolists. The vertices T and V of the region of admissible solutions occur, for example, where one firm adopts a θ of 0 and the other of 1. Such solutions cannot be reached by the classical Stackelberg reaction functions.

But suppose that firm j guesses correctly in its judgment of firm i's power-based attitudes and assumes $\theta_i = 0$. Then it can increase its profit by moving to its *Stackelberg point*, S_j, where its profits are maximized (graphically, the reaction function for $\theta_i = 0$ is tangent to a J-contour). However, such behavior is equivalent to maximizing extended profit when θ_j^s is chosen rather than $\theta_j = 0$. Therefore, Stackelberg leadership-followership analysis is seen to be part of the third-level rivalrous consonance theory in which prices *and consonance factors* are variable and optimally determined. It, too, becomes a subcase of rivalrous consonance theory. We will postpone its consideration until Chapter 7.

Where rivalrous consonance theory permits a generalization of classical duopoly theory at the second level of analysis is the formal recognition that θ_i and θ_j need not be *either* 0 or 1; they can assume different values, and values that are intermediate between those limits (in our analysis) or even beyond them. The distinctive nature of our approach consists in the belief that duopolists' (and, more generally, oligopolists') pricing actions are conditioned by a perceived power structure that varies *with each firm*, and that can be closely approximated in the short run by binary consonance factors at which it values others' profits.

It is not necessary, of course, that rival managements actually frame their power considerations in such terms, nor that they literally devise θ estimates. It is sufficient that their attitudes, however determined, can be approximated by such terms in predicting their actions. The treatment of power structure in this disaggregated if unidimensional way has the attraction of being based upon profit considerations -- surely a crucial factor in the firm's strategy -- and permitting all pairwise relations in the oligopolistic pecking order to be included.

We recognize that the wholly rational, full-information basis on which the theory is based (at least ideally) may not conform to realistic duopoly (oligopoly) conditions, and consequently the intersection of reaction functions may occur outside the region of admissible solutions in Figure 4.1. Moreover, we must incorporate other firm objectives in the form of constraints upon price strategies, and we turn to that task in the next section.

1.2. *Introducing Multiple Objectives*

The imposition of constraints C_i^1 -- C_i^5 (Chapter 1, (3) - (6)) serves to truncate the rivals' reaction functions and, when one or more bind, to prevent the attainment of the equilibrium that lies at their intersection. We illustrate the nature of such alternations in Figure 4.2, which should be viewed as the second-level analogue of Figure 2.1.

In the diagram we assume C^2 binds for firm i and C^1 binds for firm j. The conventional reaction functions, R_i and R_j, depict the firms' reactions to rivals' prices under unconstrained extended profit considerations. However, the *constrained* reaction function for firm i is the piecewise linear function $R_i\bar{R}_i$, with the limit price p_i^2 set by C_i^2 truncating R_i as shown by the heavy line in the diagram. Firm j's capacity is completely incapable of supporting the firm's optimal strategies were it not a factor, and therefore R_j at no point becomes part of the constrained function, $\bar{R}_j$ assuming that role for all p_i. The feasible region, therefore, is the shaded area including boundaries , and $\mathbf{p}^o$ the only element in it that is mutually acceptable, for at any $\mathbf{p}$ in the interior of the feasible region each firm is led to alter price in the direction of its R function, and is led to its $\bar{R}$ function. The same will hold for boundary points other than $\mathbf{p}^o$.

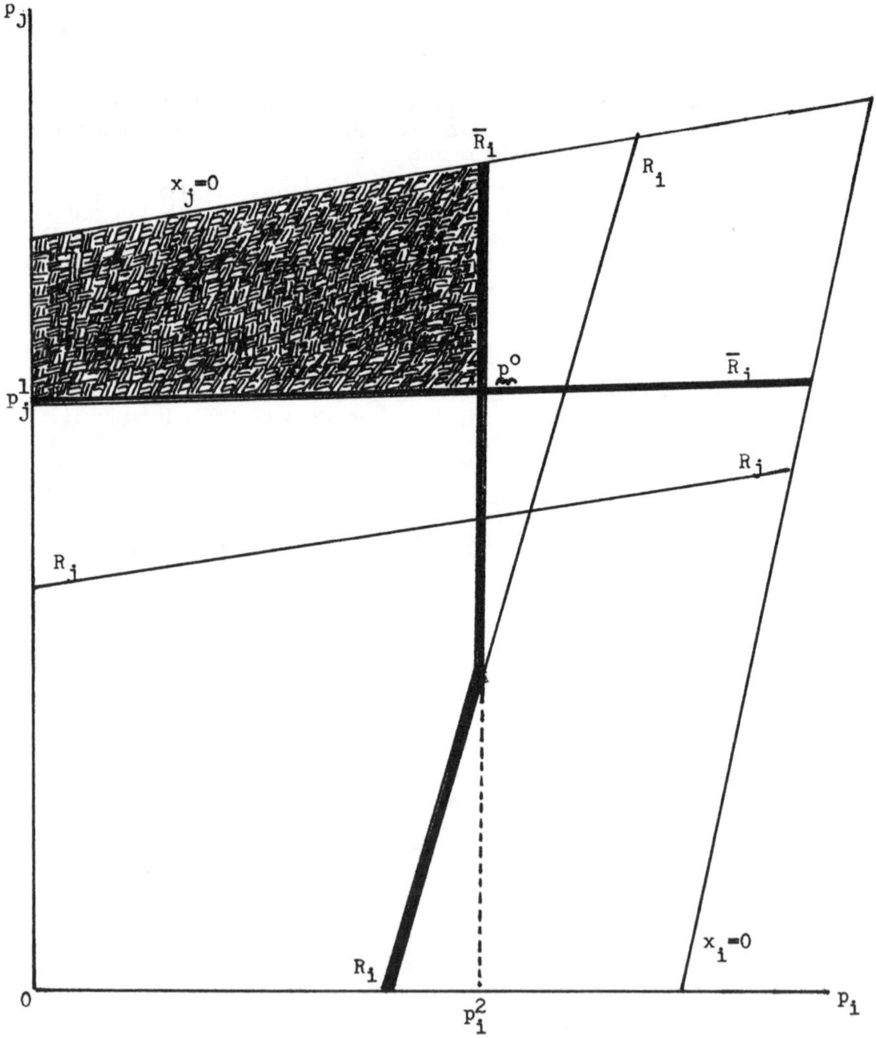

Figure 4.2. CONSTRAINED DUOPOLY REACTION FUNCTIONS WHEN C^2 BINDS FOR FIRM i, C^1 BIND FOR FIRM j

We have investigated the effects of binding constraints extensively in Chapter 2.1.1 and 2.1.2 and in Chapter 3.1.2. With the illustration of Figure 4.2, these discussions illuminate rather completely their implications for second-level analysis. Their realistic implications for oligopolistic decision making are very important and their exclusion from oligopoly analysis constitutes the elimination of solution-determining relationships. Multiple objectives and their constraining impacts upon real-world pricing simply cannot continue to be ignored by theorists in their dedication to unidimensional profit maximization in the name of "rationality" or the "survivor" principle.[4] Consonance shelters rivals from the competitive consequences of a failure to fully exploit short-run profitability considerations to be adopted as corporate policy, enabling the achievement of other goals.

1.3. *Comparative Statics Propositions: Nonbinding Constraints*

For a solution in which C^1 -- C^5 do not bind for either rival, it is clear from Figure 4.1 that a rise in θ_i raises both p_i and p_j. More exactly, if $p_i > C_i$, and b_{ij} and $b_{ji} > 0$, $p_j > C_j$, then $dp_i/d\theta_i$ and $dp_i/d\theta_j$ are positive. From (9),

$$(10) \qquad dp_i/d\theta_i = b_{ji}\,[a_j - b_{jj}\,C_j + \theta_j\,b_{ij}\,m_j + b_{ji}\,p_i]/|\mathbf{S}|\,.$$

The negative definiteness of the quadratic form assumed in section 1.1 for the joint-profit objective function assures that $|\mathbf{S}| > 0$; hence, for (10) to be positive it is necessary and sufficient that

$$(11) \qquad (a_j - b_{jj}\,C_j) + \theta_j\,b_{ij}\,m_j + b_{ji}\,p_i > 0\,,$$

all terms of which will be nonnegative and the first and third positive. Hence, $dp_i/d\theta_i > 0$. Similarly, from

$$(12) \qquad dp_i/d\theta_j = b_{ij}\,(b_{ij} + \theta_i\,b_{ji})\,m_i/|\mathbf{S}|\,,$$

which is positive if and only if $m_i > 0$, as we have assumed.

Not surprisingly, for profitable duopolists, as one or both rivals increase their consonance factors, both prices rise monotonically with positively sloping reaction functions. From Figure 4.1, for θ in the unit square, both firms attain their price maxima at $\mathbf{p}^J$ where $\theta = [1,1]$.

Consider the somewhat less clearcut case of the price impacts of cost increases and their relation to θ. In the second-level analysis of price movements with consonance factor changes we have been able to use the "solution functions" or "reduced forms" derived by solving out the first-order conditions (the reaction functions, R_i and R_j, of (3)) for endogenous as functions of exogenous variables only, and using known signs of Hessians and parameters for evaluation purposes. We must now revert to shocking the system of first-order conditions (2).

To motivate our formal displacement analysis, we first note that the slopes of R_i do not contain cost factors, so that a rise in C_i will result in *shifts* in both firms' reaction functions, with the new functions parallel to the old. Let A_i and A_j be the intercept terms in the original reaction functions. Then, from (3),

$$(13) \qquad 1.\ dA_i/dC_i = 0.5$$

$$\qquad\quad 2.\ dA_j/dC_i = -0.5\theta_j\,b_{ij}/b_{jj}\,.$$

For an own-cost change the reaction function R_i shifts rightward by half the cost increment as shown in Figure 4.3 (a familiar result from our first-level displacement analysis). However, rivalrous consonance shifts R_j down, reducing the rise in p_i that would occur if R_j remained fixed. Before our formal analysis is presented it will be useful to work through the adjustments in **p** informally.

Ignoring rivalrous consonance for the time being, we shift R_i to R_i' on Figure 4.3 with the immediate impact effect of raising p_i^1 to $p^2 \varepsilon \mathbf{p}^2$. But the rise in price shifts firm j's sales function to the right, leading the firm to raise price to $p_j^3 \varepsilon \mathbf{p}^3$, with rivalrous reactions carrying **p** to a new equilibrium at $\mathbf{p}^4$, where $\mathbf{p}^4 > \mathbf{p}^1$. The amounts of price rise in both prices depend upon the slopes of R_j, which from (3), if $\theta_j = 0$, would equal $.5(b_{ji}/b_{jj})$. Rivalrous consonance, however, does have some impact on the slope of R_j in making it steeper by an amount that varies directly with the degree of consideration firm j gives firm i's profits (θ_j) and the sensitivity of x_i to p_j (b_{ij}) and inversely with firm j's own-price sales sensitivity (b_{jj}). Hence, at this partial level, rivalrous consonance acts to raise prices above what they would be in its absence.

However, a second impact of the rivalrous consonance environment now must be taken into account. Firm j now perceives the reason for firm i's pricing initiatives. The rise in C_i when introduced into firm j's extended profit function reduces the extended marginal rival profit ($EMRP_j$) component of firm j's first-order conditions. On Figure 4.3 R_j shifts downward to R_j': it will now react with a lower price to any p_i set. Therefore, $\mathbf{p}^4$ falls initially to $\mathbf{p}^5$, and interactive rivalry carries it to the $\mathbf{p}^7$ new equilibrium. The shift in R_j, being wholly caused by rivalrous consonance, varies directly with θ_j and the sensitivity of x_i to p_i and inversely with its own-price sensitivity. The larger b_{jj} the less the fall in p_j necessary to equate $EMRP_j$ to MC_j.

Therefore, the shift of R_j reflects a *downward* pressure on prices brought about by rivalrous consonance, opposing the *upward* price pressure it exerts via the slopes of fixed reaction functions. A rise in one rival's cost will lead to price changes which include two opposing component forces caused by rivalrous consonance: broadly, a *slope* component which is price-increasing and a *shift* component which is price-decreasing.

The net resultant on **p** is the sum of these forces, and we can depict the outcome in exactly these terms. In Figure 4.4 we reproduce the solution of Figure 4.3 in order to show the components more clearly. In both figures we have magnified the price adjustments for ease of presentation, and, most particularly, the comparison between the extent of the shift in R_j that would be expected has been exaggerated. For p_i, the change from $\mathbf{p}^1$ to $\mathbf{p}^7$ equals the amount of shift in R_i ($\mathbf{p}^1$M), less MN, which is the slope of R_i' times the change in p_j ($\mathbf{p}^1$T). The same reasoning holds for $(p_j^1 - p_j^7)$. We may write

(14) 1. $dp_i = \text{shift of } R_i + \text{slope of } R_i \times dp_j$

2. $dp_j = \text{shift of } R_j + \text{slope of } R_j \times dp_i$.

From (14) and (3)

(15) 1. $dp_i = 0.5dC_i + 0.5\, b_{ii}^{-1} (b_{ij} + \theta_i\, b_{ji})\, dp_j$

2. $dp_j = -0.5\, b_{jj}^{1}\, \theta_j\, b_{ij}\, dC_i + 0.5\, b_{ii}^{-1} (b_{ji} + \theta_j\, b_{ij})\, dp_i$,

or

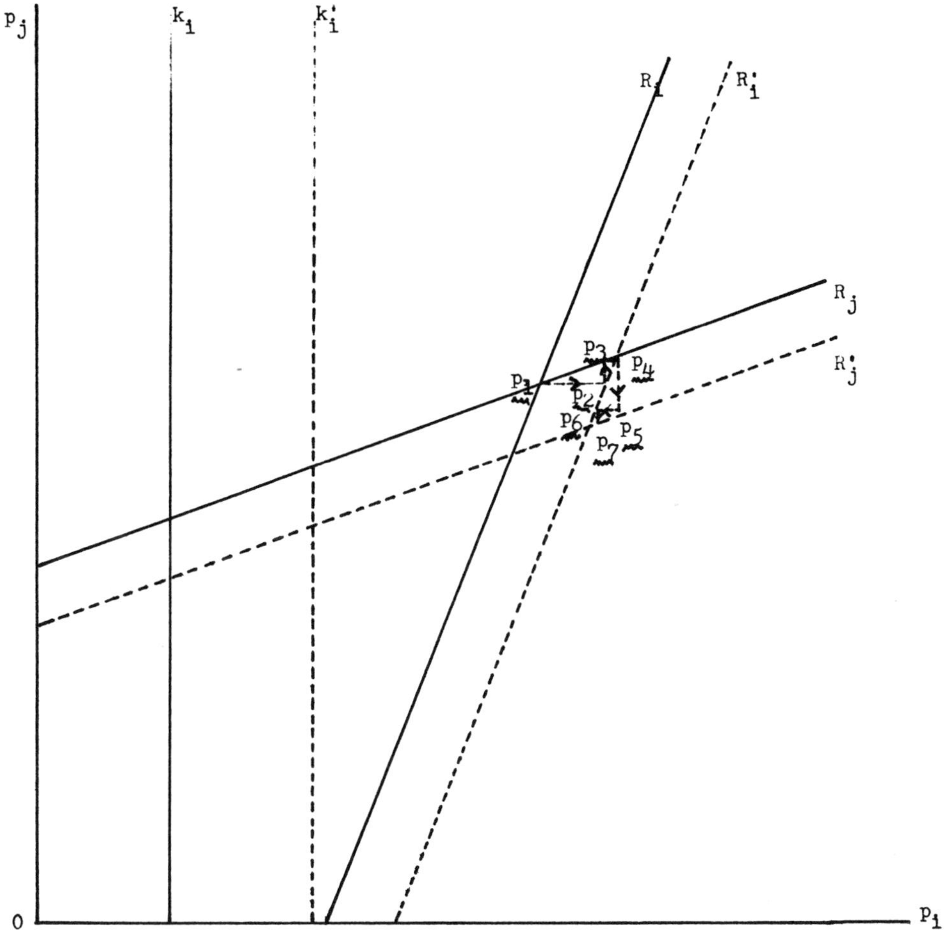

Figure 4.3. COMPARATIVE STATICS OF A PRICE CHANGE

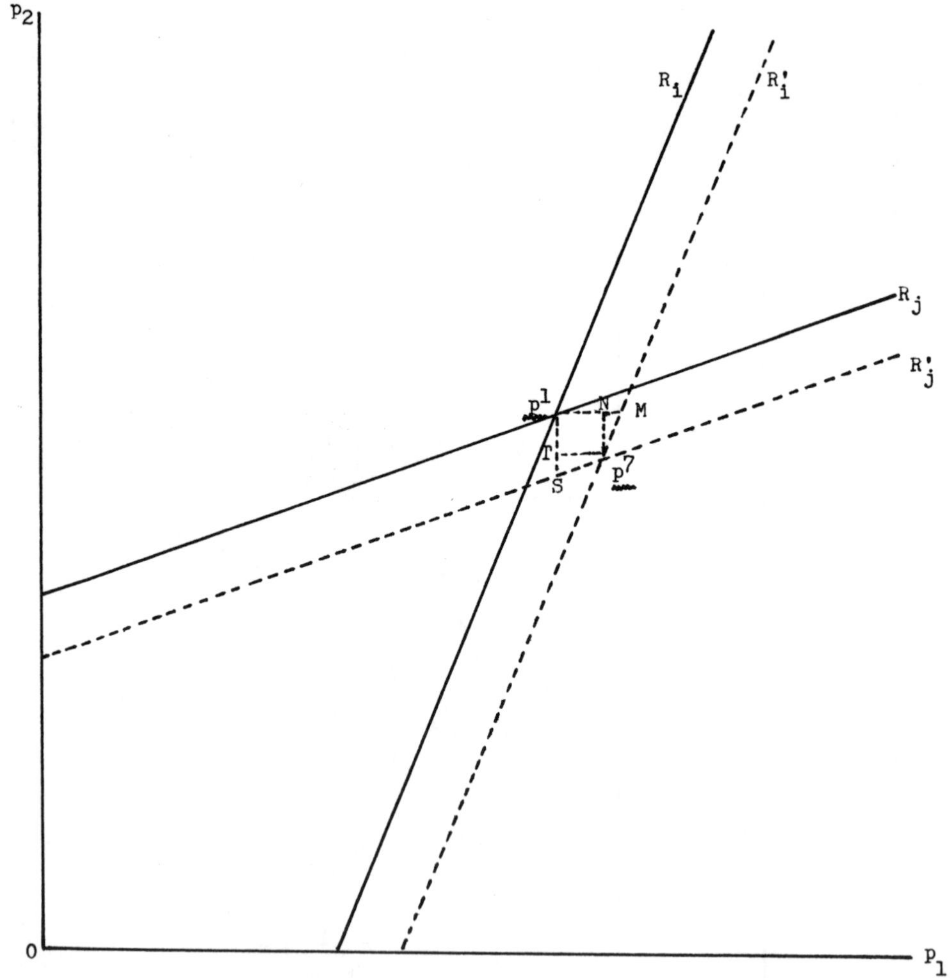

Figure 4.4. THE SHIFT-AND-SLOPE ANALYSIS OF PRICE CHANGE

$$(16)\quad \begin{bmatrix} 1 & -0.5\, b_{ii}^{-1} (b_{ij} + \theta_i b_{ji}) \\ -0.5\, b_{jj}^{-1} (b_{ji} + \theta_j b_{ij}) & 1 \end{bmatrix} \begin{bmatrix} dp_i/dC_i \\ dp_j/dC_i \end{bmatrix} = \begin{bmatrix} .5 \\ -0.5\, b_{jj}^{-1} \theta_j b_{ij} \end{bmatrix}$$

which is the displacement system if no constraints bind obtained by differentiating (3) totally. Therefore,

$$(17)\quad \begin{aligned} &1.\ dp_i/dC_i = (2b_{ii} b_{jj} - \theta_j b_{ij}^2 - \theta_i \theta_j b_{ij} b_{ji})/|\mathbf{S}| \\ &2.\ dp_j/dC_i = b_{ii} (b_{ji} - \theta_j b_{ij})/|\mathbf{S}| . \end{aligned}$$

These expressions could be obtained directly by differentiating the reduced forms (9), but the method we have used better illuminates the relationships implied by rivalrous consonance.

Because the denominators $|\mathbf{S}|$ of (17) are positive by our assumption of negative definiteness in section 1.1 above, the signs of the expressions depend upon the signs of the numerators. Can rivalrous consonance ever lead to the perverse case where $dp_i/dC_i < 0$? This expression will be negative if and only if

$$(18)\quad \theta_j b_{ij} (b_{ij} + \theta_i b_{ji}) > 2b_{ii} b_{jj} .$$

But strict concavity implies

$$(19)\quad 2b_{ii} b_{jj} > .5(b_{ij} + \theta_i b_{ji}) (b_{ji} + \theta_j b_{ij}) .$$

Taken together, (18) and (19) imply that in the perverse case

$$(20)\quad \theta_j b_{ij} > b_{ji} ,$$

or that the sensitivity of x_i to p_j, even when discounted by $\theta_j \,\varepsilon\, [0,1]$, is greater than the sensitivity of x_j to p_i. From (17.2) it is seen that (20) is also the condition that $dp_j/dC_i < 0$, so that the prices of both firms are always changed in the same direction. Also, from (20), since $\theta_j \,\varepsilon\, [0,1]$, it is implied in perversity that $b_{ij} > b_{ji}$.

We shall show that the perverse case is possible, but only under unusual and improbable circumstances. First, let us define α_i and α_j:

$$(21)\quad \begin{aligned} &1.\ \alpha_i = b_{ij}/b_{ii} , \\ &2.\ \alpha_j = b_{ji}/b_{jj} , \end{aligned}$$

and from (18)

$$(22)\quad \theta_j b_{jj}^{-1} \alpha_i^2 b_{ii} > 2 - \theta_i \theta_j \alpha_i \alpha_j .$$

The second term on the right-hand side, as the product of two to four decimals, will realistically approach zero, so we can approximate as a necessary and sufficient condition for $dp_i/dC_i < 0$

$$(23)\quad b_{ii}/b_{jj} > 2/\theta_j \alpha_i^2 .$$

Because $\theta_j\, a_i^2$ should be very small, the right-hand side of (23) should be very large. For perversity to affect p_i, therefore, b_{ii} must be *much* larger than b_{jj}.

This condition is highly improbable in a closed duopoly system of rivals with near parity of sales and close substitute products. Suppose $\theta_i = \theta_j = 1$ -- a most-favorable assumption for perverse price movement. Then (18) becomes

$$(24) \qquad 2b_{ii}\, b_{jj} < b_{ij}\,(b_{ij} + b_{ji}).$$

If $b_{ii} = b_{jj} = b_1$, then (24) is written

$$(25) \qquad 2b_1^2 < b_{ij}\,(b_{ij} + b_{ji})\,.$$

But, from (19) and concavity, $b_1^2 > b_{ij}\,(b_{ij} + b_{ji})$, which assures that (25) cannot occur. Therefore, improbable departures from size and substitution parity must characterize the duopoly for perversity of this type to arise.

Thus, our second-level analysis assures us that if $dp_i/dC_i < 0$ so will $dp_j/dC_i < 0$, but leads us to expect this joint happening only in improbable situations. In terms of Figures 4.3 and 4.4, we expect the shift in R_i to outweigh the shift in R_j. But nonetheless we denote in rivalrous consonance an interesting price effect that other oligopoly theories have not isolated. A definite tendency exists to damp down price increases due to cost rises and price decreases due to cost reductions. Oligopolistic pricing tends to moderate price changes in both directions, making them "stickier" than they would be in the absence of rivalrous consonance.

1.4. *Comparative Statics Propositions: Binding Constraints*

When the constraint sets are built into the problem we fall back once more upon the four hypotheses stated in Chapter 3.1.3 in our previous parametric programming model. For each duopolist, then, at the initial equilibrium, it is true that

$$(26) \qquad \begin{aligned}
&1.\ \nabla_{p_k} \mathscr{A}_k = 0,\ k = i, j \\
&2.\ \lambda_{1,k}\,(B_k - x_k) = 0 \\
&3.\ \lambda_{2,k}\,(x_k - M_k) = 0 \\
&4.\ \lambda_{3,k}\,(T_k^{+} - p_k/\bar{p}_k) = 0 \\
&5.\ \lambda_{4,k}\, p_k/\bar{p}_k - T_k^{-}) = 0 \\
&6.\ \lambda_{5,k}\,(p_k - N_k) = 0
\end{aligned}$$

It will be recalled that we assume in this initial position that λ_k elements are nonnegative and remain so when the system is shocked.

If we differentiate this system to tally with respect to **p**, λ, **C**, and constraint parameters, we may employ the prior analysis summarized in (16) of Chapter 3 to write the system compactly:

$$(27) \qquad \begin{bmatrix} dp_i \\ d\lambda_i \\ \\ dp_j \\ d\lambda_j \end{bmatrix} = \begin{bmatrix} \mathbf{M_i} & \mathbf{0} \\ & \\ & \\ \mathbf{0} & \mathbf{M_j} \end{bmatrix}^{-1} \begin{bmatrix} \mathbf{A_i} & \mathbf{B_{ij}} \\ & \\ & \\ \mathbf{B_{ji}} & \mathbf{A_j} \end{bmatrix} \begin{bmatrix} dC_i \\ d\mathbf{V_i} \\ \\ dC_j \\ d\mathbf{V_j} \end{bmatrix}$$

where $\mathbf{M_i}$ is a 6 x 6 matrix defined in (16) of Chapter 3; $\mathbf{A_i}$ is a 6 x 6 diagonal matrix with main diagonal $[b_{ii}, -\lambda_{1i}, \lambda_{2i}, -\lambda_{3i}, \lambda_{4i}, \lambda_{5i}]$; and $\mathbf{B_{ij}}$ is a 6 x 6 matrix with $-\theta_i b_{ji}$ as row 1, column 1 element and zeroes elsewhere. The vector $\mathbf{dV_k}$ is the set of firm k's restraint differentials. Of course, $\mathbf{M_j}$, $\mathbf{A_j}$ and $\mathbf{B_{ji}}$ are analogously defined.

Despite the nondense nature and the block-diagonal structure of the matrices, evaluation of such systems as (27) can become cumbrous because two objective functions and constraint sets are involved rather than one, and interdependence makes the system indecomposable. For unconstrained systems we have already derived and discussed dp_i/dC_i and dp_j/dC_i indicating the possible but improbable ambiguity of sign that results.

One fortunate feature of rivalrous consonance frameworks is that multi-objective function problems become single objective function problems when all $\theta_{ij} = 1$. As we have seen in section 1.1, if we assume that the single function formed by adding firms' profit functions is strictly concave in *all* prices, and if *all* $\theta_{ij} \leq 1$, then $|\mathbf{S}|$ in (4) and (9) will be expected to be positive. If we solve (27) for a single parameter change by Cramer's method, this information can be valuable (as we have seen in (17) above), so that information derivative from maximization second-order conditions will be useful. Hence, the sign of such expressions will be determined by their numerators only, easing but not eliminating our problem of theorem evaluation (again, as shown in (17)).

But the theorem of conjugate pairs is of further help, for if we study the noninverted matrix that pre-multiplies the parameter vector on the right-hand side of (27) it will be seen that both C_i and C_j enter two of the twelve displacement equations, so that (as we have seen) we expect ambiguous theorems if only maximization information is available. On the other hand, the restraints enter only one equation, and their partial derivatives in those equations are unambiguously signed λ's. Hence, we expect that changes in such restraints will yield at least one evaluable theorem each.

Finally, the matrices of (27) are so non-dense (i.e., contain so many zeroes) that some signs can be derived from simple additional assumptions. For example, consider dp_i/dB_i and dp_j/dB_i. On the basis of the law of conjugate pairs the evaluation determinants do not include principal minors of the Hessian of the joint profit function and cannot be evaluated with second-order information only. However, one expression reduces to

$$(28) \qquad dp_i/dB_i = -1/b_{ii},$$

which is immediately determinate from knowledge of sales curve coefficients' signs. Also,

$$(29) \qquad dp_j/dB_i = -(0.5(b_{ji} + \theta_j b_{ij}))/b_{ii} b_{jj},$$

which, if we accept that $(b_{ji} + \theta_j b_{ij}) > 0$, implies that the expression is negative. Hence, if a firm increases its scarce capacity, both prices will fall in duopoly to accommodate the incremental profit. This is clear from Figure 4.2 if $\bar{R}_i$ shifts left along R_j. Similar theorems for the other restraints could be derived, but they too would be obvious from depicting the relevant binding constraints on Figure 4.2 and shifting the effecting reaction function right or left as appropriate. We shall not pursue the displacement analysis, therefore.

2. *DIFFERENTIATED OLIGOPOLY: A CRIPPLED OPTIMIZATION MODEL*

2.1. *The Extension to N-Firm Models*

Because of the additive nature of the firms' objective and demand functions, as well as the add-on nature of the constraint sets, the duopoly model generalizes in straightforward fashion to n-firm oligopoly. For example in the n-firm unconstrained model the reaction functions (3) generalize for (say) firm 1 to

$$(30 \qquad p_1 = 0.5\, b_{11}^{-1} [A_1 + \sum_{j=2}^{n} (b_{1j} + \theta_{1j} b_{j1}) p_j] ,$$

where $A_1 = a_1 + b_{11} C_1 - \sum_{j=2}^{n}(\theta_{1j} b_{j1} C_j)$. Hence, the functions become hyperplanes in price space. The matrix **S** in (4) generalizes straightforwardly to

$$(31) \qquad \mathbf{S} = \begin{bmatrix} -2b_{11} & b_{12} + \theta_{12} b_{21} & \cdots & b_{1n} + \theta_{1n} b_{n1} \\ b_{21} + \theta_{21} b_{12} & -2b_{22} & \cdots & b_{2n} + \theta_{2n} b_{n2} \\ \cdot & \cdot & \cdots & \cdot \\ \cdot & \cdot & \cdots & \cdot \\ \cdot & \cdot & \cdots & \cdot \\ b_{n1} + \theta_{n1} b_{1n} & b_{n2} + \theta_{n2} b_{2n} & \cdots & -2b_{nn} \end{bmatrix}$$

and, with $\theta_{ij} \varepsilon [0,1]$, both the existence of a solution and its "stability"[6] will be guaranteed if the joint profit function formed by summing all own-profit functions has a second-order differential that is negative definite in all prices. A sufficient condition for strict concavity is that each profit function be jointly strictly concave in all prices, which simply implies marginal profits decline as any price or group of prices is raised, all other prices constant. We will assume this latter condition holds, and that the second-order differential is negative definite, in which case **S** can be assumed to be negative definite.

In a fully constrained rivalrous consonance system with n rivals, the analogue of the duopoly displacement system of (27) is

$$(32) \qquad \begin{bmatrix} dp_1 \\ d\lambda_1 \\ dp_2 \\ d\lambda_2 \\ \cdot \\ \cdot \\ \cdot \\ d\lambda_n \end{bmatrix} = \begin{bmatrix} \mathbf{M}_1 & 0 & 0 & \cdots & 0 \\ 0 & \mathbf{M}_2 & 0 & \cdots & 0 \\ \cdot & \cdot & \cdot & \cdots & \cdot \\ \cdot & \cdot & \cdot & \cdots & \cdot \\ \cdot & \cdot & \cdot & \cdots & \cdot \\ 0 & 0 & 0 & \cdots & \mathbf{M}_n \end{bmatrix}^{-1} \begin{bmatrix} \mathbf{A}_1 & \mathbf{B}_{12} & \mathbf{B}_{13} & \cdots & \mathbf{B}_{1n} \\ \mathbf{B}_{21} & \mathbf{A}_2 & \mathbf{B}_{23} & \cdots & \mathbf{B}_{2n} \\ \cdot & \cdot & \cdot & \cdots & \cdot \\ \cdot & \cdot & \cdot & \cdots & \cdot \\ \cdot & \cdot & \cdot & \cdots & \cdot \\ \mathbf{B}_{n1} & \mathbf{B}_{n2} & \mathbf{B}_{n3} & \cdots & \mathbf{A}_n \end{bmatrix} \begin{bmatrix} dC_1 \\ dV_1 \\ dC_2 \\ dV_2 \\ \cdot \\ dV_n \end{bmatrix}$$

(or)

$$\mathbf{dX} = \mathbf{M}^{-1}\, \mathbf{A}\, \mathbf{dE} .$$

In real-world systems all $\lambda_{5i} = 0$ and, as we have seen in section 1.2 of Chapter 2, at most only one of the nonnegativity constraints will bind (with one non-zero λ) for each firm unless constraints coincide and become redundant. Hence, the **M** and **A** of

(32) will be simpler in structure than they might appear from our definitions above. Moreover, unless these conditions $|\mathbf{M}_i|$ will always be evaluable as to sign from the implied strict concavity of each profit function and the nonnegativity of the λ terms and the constraint values C_k^t. By virtue of the block-diagonal structure of the first right-hand side matrix in (32) its determinant will be the product of the $|\mathbf{M}_i|$ and hence also evaluable as to sign. Thus, in a Cramer method solution for a displacement expression, the denominator determinant will be unambiguously signed and the sign of the expression will be determined by the numerator determinant.

What with the many combinations of potential constraints among firms that might bind, it is not fruitful at this level of analysis to attempt an evaluation of the relevant numerator terms. But two general observations are in order, both of which stress the richness in potential to yield qualitative theorems of rivalrous consonance models. Two types of parameter are found in the displacement system (32). The first is the cost term, C_k, whose relevant columns in **A** contain only n (of 6n) nonzero elements of which one is b_{kk} and the others $-\theta_{kj}\,b_{jk}$. Hence, these nonzero terms are sign-determined, and therefore, when the relevant column is substituted for a column in **M** to solve for a displacement result by Cramer's method the simple structure of **M** is not disturbed and unambiguously signed expressions or expressions that can be signed with simple additional hypotheses will result. The second type is relevant to changes in the restraints; of course, most of the relevant columns in **A** will be null vectors because their constraints do not bind. For binding constraints, the relevant column vectors will contain only one element -- a positive or negative λ term -- and thus evaluable displacement theorems should be readily forthcoming.

Within the terms of theorem derivation by parameter displacement in large-scale interdependence systems, rivalrous consonance frameworks have structures that are quite rich, at least for convex models and linear constraints. But as we discussed in Chapter 1, such theorems are limited in their ability to yield realistic insights by the restrictions of the methodology: infinitesimal parameter and variable movements, changes limited to a single parameter, and the inescapable ties to convex or otherwise well-behaved systems. The derivation of structural insights into realistic oligopolistic competition by rivalrous consonance modelling and manipulation demands methods that do not depend wholly on these conditions of usage. We present supplementary techniques in Chapter 5.

3. *SUMMARY AND CONCLUSION*

The generalization and enrichment of classic duopoly reaction function analysis that rivalrous consonance permits allows us to derive new theorems about the source of price stickiness in periods of cost inflation and deflation. A potential perverse price movement case can also be examined fruitfully.

The extension of these displacement systems to n-firm cases under constraints is straightforward and results in simple linear structures. They permit some unambiguous -- if frequently trivial -- theorems to be derived under the severe restrictions of classic displacement methods. More useful results must be sought by manipulative procedures which we term simulative theorizing. We turn to them in Chapter 5.

1 We are reluctant to use the term "stability" in the absence of an explicit dynamic model depicting the manner of rivals' price adjustments over time when p_i^o and p_j^o do not rule. We are falling back upon Marshallian intuitive quasi-dyanamics in a Cournot-type adjustment process of the familiar type of moving from one reaction function to another with each rival setting its optimal price for a given rival price.

2 See E. H. Chamberlin, [7], pp. 50-51, 54.

3 We are again referring to Cournot behavior in the broader sense (see fn. 3, Chapter 2). Our characterization permits us a clearer insight into the nature of joint-profit maximization vs. Cournot behavior than Chamberlin's classic interpretation and terminology gives (Chamberlin, [7], Chapter 3). The distinction is not that of recognizing or ignoring mutual interdependence: the presence of b_{ij} and C_j in (3) for any θ guarantees this interdependence is present. It is rather the valuation attached to rivals' adverse profit experiences, i.e., θ, that is the crucial difference.

4 A counter-example is provided by Corwin D. Edwards, [10].

5 This type of "unconstrained" perversity will be distinguished in Chapter 7 from perverse price movements that occur because of price constraints.

6 See fn. 1 of this chapter.

CHAPTER 5

RIVALROUS CONSONANCE: SIMULATIVE THEORIZING AT THE SECOND LEVEL

Simulative theorizing, as defined and defended in Chapter 1.4, is the alternative methodology to classic parametric programming or displacement. Its greatest disadvantage, of course, is the need to sacrifice generality by specifying explicit models with specific numerical parameter values. Insights are inescapably associated with such specifics, and rather than stated as neatly-delimited theorems must be presented as tendencies and conjectures about a specific oligopoly's structure and performance. That is not as intellectually satisfying, admittedly, as neat theorem-proof sequences, but at least it yields information that can be pieced into an understanding of the industry that is operationally testable under stated conditions. And, it must also be recalled, the generalizability of those crisp theorems is frequently severely limited by the set of hypotheses that constrains them. The sacrifice in extent of applicability, therefore, may be substantially less than might appear at the surface.

1. *SIMULATIVE THEORIZING: AN EXAMPLE*

At this stage of the presentation of rivalrous consonance it will be useful to construct fictitious industries with which to demonstrate the potential usefulness of the technique for obtaining insights. To this end let us assume two industries are conjoined in a Model 2 general equilibrium context as joint suppliers to each other as well as sellers to the external sectors of the economy. Table 5.1 summarizes the base case parameters and the functions of the firms, which are assumed to be maximizing extended profits subject to constraints C^1 -- C^5.

To judge from their market share aspirations, firms 1 and 2 are dominant in industry 1, with firm 3 limiting itself to a minor portion of the market. Firms 2 and 3 essentially treat their rivals equally at the same absolute levels in terms of rivalrous consonance, while firm 1 defers substantially less (but about even-handedly) to its rivals. Moreover, firm 1 has the most ungenerous attitude of any firm to its only industrial customer, firm 5, compared with firm 2's deference to customer 4. Firm 3 is unique among the five firms in that it has no industrial customers, hence no sales on intermediate good account.

Firm 1's relative slighting of rivals' and customers' welfares is reflected in its *consonance indices*, which are the ratios of the aggregate consonance factors (the amount of consideration given) obtained by summing row elements of θ_1 to the sum of consonance consideration received obtained by summing column elements of θ_1. Its *rivals' consonance index* (RCI) is .59 and its *customers' consonance index* (CCI) is .43, with a *total consonance* index (TCI), summing over rivals and customers, of .54. Note that firm 1 is the only net receiver of consonance in either industry. Firm 2's index values are [1.13, .80, 1.03] respectively, and Firm 3's are [1.43, 0, 1.15]. Rival 2 especially is showing a much more generous attitude toward customers than its rivals, and in total consonance is about at par in giving and receiving. Rival 3 is by this measure markedly most sensitive to the profit implications of its price changes for its rivals and firm 1 by far the least sensitive in the industry. Firm 3, of course,

Table 5.1. BASE CASE PARAMETERS AND FUNCTIONS

Firm and Product	Restraints:					Consonance Factors (θ):				
	B_i	M_i	$\bar{P}_i$	T_i^+	T_i^-	1	2	3	4	5
Industry 1										
1	32,000	.40	1,000	1.10	.90	1.00	.09	.07	0	.03
2	28,000	.30	950	1.08	.92	.13	1.00	.14	.08	0
3	20,000	.10	950	1.15	.85	.15	.15	1.00	0	0
Industry 2										
4	18,000	.50	1,100	1.13	.75	.07	0	.05	1.00	.17
5	10,000	.12	1,500	1.12	.88	0	.10	0	.19	1.00

<u>Sales Functions: Consumer Plus (Intermediate) Demand:</u>

$$\left.\begin{aligned} z_1 &= 45{,}000 - 53.00p_1 + 9.35p_2 + 8.97p_3 + (.21z_5) \\ z_2 &= 34{,}000 + 11.85p_1 - 55.00p_2 + 12.18p_3 + (.10z_4) \\ z_3 &= 29{,}515 + 8.38p_1 + 8.99p_2 - 42.00p_3 \\ z_4 &= 26{,}910 - 32.00p_4 + 3.55p_5 + (.20z_1 + .21z_3) \\ z_5 &= 15{,}500 + 3.62p_4 - 12.00p_5 + (.27z_2) \end{aligned}\right\} = \mathbf{Z} = \mathbf{X} + \mathbf{I}$$

<u>Sales Function Reduced Forms:</u>

$$\begin{aligned} z_1 &= 50{,}428 - 52.38p_1 + 6.25p_2 + 9.62p_3 + .58p_4 - 2.50p_5 \\ z_2 &= 38{,}321 + 10.98p_1 - 54.69p_2 + 11.49p_3 - 3.19p_4 + .31p_5 \\ z_3 &= 29{,}515 + 8.38p_1 + 8.99p_2 - 42.00p_3 \\ z_4 &= 43{,}194 - 8.72p_1 + 3.14p_2 - 6.90p_3 - 31.88p_4 + 3.05p_5 \\ z_5 &= 25{,}847 + 2.96p_1 - 14.77p_2 + 3.10p_3 + 2.76p_4 - 11.92p_5 \end{aligned}$$

<u>Sales Functions (Related to Consumer Demand):</u>

$$\mathbf{Z} = \mathbf{B}\,\mathbf{X} = \begin{bmatrix} 1.001 & .057 & .001 & .006 & .210 \\ .020 & 1.001 & .021 & .100 & .004 \\ 0 & 0 & 1.000 & 0 & 0 \\ .200 & .011 & .210 & 1.001 & .042 \\ .005 & .270 & .006 & .027 & 1.001 \end{bmatrix} \mathbf{X}$$

<u>Cost Functions:</u>

$$\begin{aligned} C_1 &= 525 + .20p_4 \\ C_2 &= 318 + .27p_5 \\ C_3 &= 582 + .21p_4 \\ C_4 &= 652 + .10p_2 \\ C_5 &= 1{,}175 + .21p_1 \end{aligned}$$

is a special case with respect to its CCI, and once more firm 1 reveals the lesser sensitivity of either actual industry 1 supplier. Firm 3 is the largest net giver of total consonance in its industry.

The reduced forms, of course, summarize the net price impacts, direct and indirect, including those flowing from consumer and intermediate sectors, upon sales. We will be able to gauge elasticities in the base case solution once we present it, but in absolute sales responsiveness to prices the three firms seem well matched in terms of sensitivity to rivals' prices. Firm 1 has a bit more independence, and its lower consonance values have some basis in its demand structure. Firms 1 and 2 are about equally sensitive to own price but substantially more so that firm 3 in absolute values. Firm 2 is the most responsive in Industry 1 to rival and customer prices. It stands, therefore, to gain most from the price effects of consonance.

On the other hand from **B** firm 1 is surprisingly sensitive to firm 2's household sales via the customer relations of firm 5 to firm 2 and firm 1 to firm 5. Firm 2 is equally sensitive to its rivals' household sales, but at a rate about half that of firm 1 to firm 2. Firm 3, of course, is not affected by any other firm's sales. Some notion of the importance of these effects can be obtained by the following computations. From Firm 2's household sales function, a lowering of its price by about 1.8¢ will increase sales by 1 unit of good 2. This price decrease will reduce firm 1's sales by .17 unit. However, the indirect effect via customer relations will increase sales of good 1 by .05, reducing firm 1's sales loss by 29 percent to .12 unit. Following the same rules of computation we find a p_1 reduction of 1.9¢ reduces x_2 by .22, with only a .02, or 9 percent, customer relation offset. Lastly, a 2.4¢ reduction in p_3 leads to a unit increase in x_3 by .29 unit with only a .02 unit offset, a 7 percent offset. Firm 2 is relatively unaffected by indirect customer effects set off by rivals' price actions.

In terms of cost structure, firm 2 seems by far to be the lowest cost rival, barring an extraordinary differential in p_5 above p_2, and firm 3 the high cost producer. Note that firm 4 supplies both 1 and 3, and hence has a substantial customer interest in the industry, whereas firm 5 supplies 2.

From the data the industry profile seems to display the following form. Industry 1 is led by firm 1, which seems confident of its ability to set price in relative disregard of rivals and customers' profits, based to some degree on the success of its product differentiation, which seems to imply less sensitivity of product 1 to competing products than its rivals, as well as to customer prices. Moreover, it is somewhat buffered by indirect customer sales from firm 2's price competition. Its largest rival is firm 2 which gives firm 1 and firm 3 about equal deference and is equally sensitive to both firms' products both directly and indirectly. Its greatest potential advantage is a substantially lower cost structure. Firm 3 gives evidence of being a high-cost producer aiming for a small segment of the consumer market in strong competition with more favored rivals.

Industry 2 presents the tableau of a high-cost firm 5 with low own-price and cross-price sensitivity but with high customer-price sensitivity competing for a small slice of a market with a more advantageously placed firm 4. The latter is moderately sensitive to own price and its customers' prices, selling a cheaper product than its rival and aiming for a mass market. Firm 4 has consonance indices of [.89, 1.50, 1.07], which reflect its great sensitivity to customers and a feeling of greater strength than its rival, but, perhaps through fear of antitrust violation as an attitude of live-and-let live, is a bit more ready to defer to that rival than the objective parameters warrant. Firm 2's sensitivity to its customers is well-founded in its demand patterns. The sales function reveals the direct dependence through the large sizes of b_{41} and b_{43}, and B_4 shows a quite large indirect dependence via rivalrous relationships. An 8¢ reduction in p_5 to obtain a unit rise in x_5 reduces x_4 by about .3 unit, but .04, or about 14 percent, of this is neutralized by indirect customer effects.

Firm 5 has consonance indices of [1.12, 3.33, 1.45], which properly reflect its necessary deference to its rival and, more importantly, its dependence upon customer firm 2. Its total sales function reveals a larger coefficient for p_2 than for own-price, indicating its almost complete dependence upon intermediate demand. Its high cost, low market share aspirations, and small penetration into the consumer market lead us to expect it will be the smaller factor by far in its industry.

In terms of rival consonance, firms 4 and 5 treat each other with nearly equal deference -- a deference greater than that afforded by Industry 1 to rivals. Both firms, but especially firm 5, are much more deferential to customers than industry 1 counterparts, being net givers by far. Indeed, firm 5's posture is the most deferential in total consonance of any of the five, but firm 4, rather surprisingly given its dependence upon two customers' demands has a TCI about equal to those of firms 2 and 3.

1.2. *The Base Case Solution*

The SUMT algorithm was used to solve the first-order conditions with an additional constraint to force such marginal extended profit terms to zero for each firm. SUMT has the practical advantage of permitting these constraints to depart from equality when one of the four original constraints binds and, in the relatively few cases this occurred in the base case and displacement solutions, this feature proved quite convenient.

In Table 5.2 the base case solution is presented in full. The results are fairly close to the expectations that were grounded in the industry profiles. Firms 1 and 4 do in

Table 5.2. BASE CASE SOLUTION

Variable /Firm	1	2	3	4	5	Ind. 1	Ind. 2
p_i	947.02	894.34	937.82	933.71	1,560.38	928.57*	1,102.91*
z_i	12,075	8,089	6,103	6,266	2,325	26,266	8,591
x_i	11,582	7,457	6,103	2,571	155		
I_i	493	632	0	3,695	2,170		
C_i	711.74	739.30	778.08	741.43	1,373.87		
m_i	235.28	155.04	159.74	192.27	186.51		
m_i/p_i	24.8%	17.3%	17.0%	20.6%	12.0%		
Profit (π_i)	2,841,027	1,254,036	974,854	1,204,744	433,688	5,069,917	1,638,432
E_i	3,035,141	1,856,229	1,589,113	1,526,086	787,993	6,480,483	2,314,078
$(E_i-\pi_i)/\pi_i$	.07	.48	.63	.27	.82	.28	.41
Market Share	.46	.31	.23	.73	.27		

*Sales - weighted average.

fact dominate their respective industries in sales, profits, and profit margins. Moreover, the extended profit indices, measured as the ratio of the surplus of extended profits above own profit to own profit, are markedly lower for these dominant firms than for their rivals. They are much more deferred to than deferring. In Industry 1, the larger extended profit index of firm 3 compared with that of firm 2 is somewhat unanticipated given their near symmetry in rival consonance factors. It is explained, of course, by the absence of customers for whom consonance would dictate lower prices and lessened extended profit. It gives a gross and uncertain index of the importance of customer consonance to the price solution of firms 1 and 2. The explanation is reinforced by the large discrepancy in these values for firms 4 and 5 and their quite divergent customers' consonance coefficients.

The subordinate importance of intermediate sales to industry 1's total sales contrasts greatly to their dominance in industry 2's sales. On the basis of sales functions only, we would expect the rival price consonance effect (which exerts positive impacts on firms' prices) to dominate customer price consonance effects (which exert *negative* price forces) in industry 1, and the opposite situation in industry 2. Rivalrous consonance acting via sales functions lifts prices in industry 1 above what would occur in its absence, but reduces industry 2 prices.

Costs in industry 1 are not in line with our expectations gleaned from the cost functions. Firm 2's factor cost advantage is largely neutralized by the high cost of its intermediate input 5, and firm 1 emerges as the lowest cost firm. This contributes to the large profit margin it enjoys, in support of the great deference it received via consonance effects. This cost neutralization also helps to explain why firm 3 does better in terms of market share and sales than its high factor cost and low minimum market share led us to believe it would. Despite the high price which its rivals' consonance effects force upon it, its sales and profit margin are sustained by rival 2's similar costs and rival 1's high price, as well as the lack of extended customer consonance noted above.

It is now possible to determine price elasticities of sales in the neighborhood of the base case solution. In Table 5.3 we record these *total* elasticities derived from the sales function reduced forms. The own- and cross-elasticities of row firm sales with respect to column firm prices are displayed.

Table 5.3. TOTAL SALES FUNCTION PRICE ELASTICITIES AT THE BASE CASE SOLUTION

Firm i/ Firm j	1	2	(ε_{ij}) 3	4	5
1	-4.11	.46	.75	.04^{s}	-.32^{c}
2	1.50	-6.50	1.33	-.37^{c}	.06^{s}
3	1.30	1.32	-6.45	0	0
4	-1.32^{c}	.45^{s}	-1.03^{c}	-4.75	.76
5	1.21^{s}	-5.68^{c}	1.25	1.11	-8.00
s : supplier	of row firm				
c : customer	of row firm				

Firm 1's own-price elasticity, like all others, is large, yet the smallest of all firms'. More significantly, its rivals' price cross-elasticities are quite small, and hence it is insulated from these rivals' price actions to a greater degree than we suspected from the sales functions alone. On the other hand, from column 1 of Table 5.3, firm 1 has large impacts upon all other firms' sales, and hence the basis for large consonance effects, especially rivals', exists. Firm 2 and firm 3 reveal much more sensitivity to rivals' prices, and the symmetry of the firms in their relations with rivals that we denoted from their sales functions and consonance factors is repeated here. Finally, industry 1's sales insensitivity to customers' prices persists in the elasticities.

Industry 2 does reveal very much higher customer price elasticities and, indeed, even for the prices of industry 1 firms that are not customers of the supplier firms. These latter effects indicate that when a noncustomer price rises, customers' sales rise, with substantial increases in the supplier sales. The impression we derived of industry 2 as extremely dependent on industrial demand is strengthed by Table 5.3. Rival elasticities are greatest for firm 5, as is own-price elasticity, so that it is very punishing in terms of own-profits to keep its price as high as the base case value. Note, interestingly, from the last column of the table, that firm 5's price does not have a large cross-elasticity with any other firm; hence, it is the most isolated firm of the five from the viewpoint of its price actions' impacting others' profits directly via demand. On the other hand, with its small amount of sales it feels the effects of all other firms' price actions quite sensitively.

In other respects the base case solution offers some interesting insights. The power structure encapsulated in θ in Table 5.1 leads to substantial other-profit components in the five firms' optimal extended profits. The extended profit index is .32 for the total of 5 firms. A substantial amount of consideration of others' welfares is reflected in the final price outcome. Industry 2, at .41, is far more deferential than industry 1 at .28, as we expect from our analyses of θ, the reduced form sales functions, and elasticities. However, one unexpected result is the rather low firm 4 extended profit index when compared with firm 2, although both firms have roughly equal total consonance indices. The probable explanation is the much greater sensitivity of firms to p_2 compared with p_4. Once more, firm 2 reveals itself to be the most highly interconnected firm of either industry.

We have also concluded that the major beneficiaries of industry 2's deferential policies will be industry 1 customers for its intermediate inputs, so that its weighted price of $1,102.91 is *lower* than it would be in the absence of customer consonance. On the other hand, industry 1's rivals' consonance component should be larger than its customer consonance component, so its weighted price of $928.57 should be *higher* than it would be in a nonconsonance framework. Of course, one cannot be positive of these conjectures because in the absence of consonance the entire price solution will change with complex effects in both industries, and the net resultants will be uncertain in their final price implications. However, in section 1.3's structural displacement analysis it will be possible to get more precise measures of these consonance components.

If the extended profit indices can be taken at this stage as crude measures of relative benefit and sacrifice for the firms in rivalrous consonance -- and we shall be able to address this question also more exactly in section 1.3 -- then, in industry 1, firm 1 benefits most (or sacrifices least), with firm 3 the smallest beneficiary and firm 2 intermediate in benefit but much closer to 3 than 1. In industry 2, firm 4 is the major beneficiary (smaller sacrificer), showing greater benefits than firms 2 and 3 as well, and firm 5 the smaller beneficiary (greater sacrificer) of any of the five firms. However, since industry 2's probable reaction to consonance is to lower prices, and because its sales functions are own-price elastic, these expectations may be revised when we analyze these factors more closely. Section 1.3 will provide better answers.

The effective consonance received by a firm from a rival or supplier is an amalgam of two factors: 1) the sensitivity of the firm's sales to the rival's or supplier's price, and 2) the binary consonance factor of the rival or supplier for the firm's profits. To get a better measure of these two factors acting together, we multiply θ_{ij} by ε_{ji} and display the results columnwise in Table 5.4. In the matrix, element (i,j) is the

Table 5.4. EFFECTIVE CONSONANCE FACTORS, BASE CASE SOLUTION

Firm i/ Firm j	1	2	3	4	5	Sum
1	---	.14	.09	0	.04	.27
2	.06	---	.18	.04	0	.28
3	.11	.20	---	0	0	.31
4	.01	0	0	---	.19	.20
5	0	.01	0	.14	---	.15
Sum	.18	.35	.27	.18	.23	

product $\theta_{ij}\ \varepsilon_{ji}$ from the data in Tables 5.3 and 5.1, and denotes the effective consonance given firm i by firm j. Hence, column sums index firm i's receipt of effective consonance and row sums index firm i's rendering of such aid. The total effective consonance index is the ratio of row to column sums for each firm, and effective rival and customer consonance indices are the ratios of relevant row items summed over relevant column items summed. In Table 5.5 we contrast the rival, customer, and total consonance indices previously computed for θ only with their respective effective consonance index counterparts.

The theory behind these effective consonance indices is that a firm's effective rival or customer support increases as its binary consonance factor for that customer or rival rises, or as the relative impact of its price upon that other firm's sales rises. The concept, therefore, is a quite different one from the consonance indices listed in Table 5.5 based solely on the first of these influences. Their juxtaposition in that table should not lead us to interpret them as alternative measures of the same concept.

Table 5.5. CONSONANCE AND EFFECTIVE CONSONANCE INDICES

Firm/ Index	Rival		Customer		Total	
	ERCI	RCI	ECCI	CCI	ECI	CI
1	1.35	.59	4.00	.43	1.50	.54
2	.71	1.13	4.00	.80	.80	1.03
3	1.15	1.43	0	0	1.15	1.15
4	1.36	.89	.25	1.50	1.11	1.07
5	.74	1.12	.25	3.33	.65	1.45

In terms of extended price aid to rivals, the ERCI show firms 1, 3, and 4 as net givers of such relief, with firms 1 and 4 about equal in that regard. Firms 2 and 5 are net recipients of such sensitivity. On customer consonance account firms 1 and 2 are much more important givers, and firms 4 and 5 large net receivers of such consideration. Firm 3, of course, is neither giver nor receiver. Finally, in terms of total effective consonance, Firm 1 is the largest net giver, firms 3 and 4 about equal in their small net giver balances, and firms 2 and 5 share a position of net receivership.

These effective consonance measures, being constructed with base case elasticities, are of undetermined meaning beyond the neighborhood of that solution. It remains to be seen if they contribute any worthwhile insights when solutions are some distance from the base case.

In summary, the base case solution serves to reinforce and sharpen the profiles of the firms and industries gained from parameters and functions. Industry 1 is a consumer-oriented industry with small interest in its intermediate good industrial customers. Consonance concerns, therefore, revolve about interrival relations, even though it effectively has a powerful impact upon its customers. In these rival relations, firm 1 stands apart as dominant firm benefiting directly from its rivals' concern for its profits, but given its importance in their sales dispensing a great deal of aid to them. Firms 2 and 3 are weaker, with firm 3 showing the greater tendency to defer to the other two rivals. Firm 2's weaker impacts on firm 1 render it a net recipient of aid from rivals. Although all three industry 1 firms are nominally benefitted by industry 2's large binary consonance factors for customers, this aid is severely attenuated by the small relative influence of industry 2 prices on industry 1 sales. Rivalrous consonance is not absent from industry 2, with firm 4 receiving the greater benefit as the dominant firm, but customer consonance poses a conundrum. Although nominal consonance factors are large, the degree of impact upon industry 1 profits may be small because of low cross-price elasticities on industry 1 sales. However, another aspect of this benefit accrues through the effects on profit margins, and our measures ignore these.

Consumer demand is important to firm 4 but outweighed by industrial; in firm 5's case, consumer demand is negligible. In both industries the weakest rival is also the high cost producer and, in the case of firm 5, by a large amount.

But these insights are limited in scope, not exhaustive in converage, are ambiguous in some features, and are in the nature of conjectures. As noted in Chapter 1, we view the role of modelling and of simulative theorizing as an efficient extraction of insights derived imaginatively from a set of well-designed parameter displacements. In sections 1.3 and 1.4 we shall attempt to validate and extend the insights into the anatomy and physiology of the two industries. Our purpose is to illustrate for one specific case techniques that of necessity must be flexible and tailored to plumb insights and conjectures as they arise in preliminary study of parameters, functions, and base case solution and in the simulative theorizing dynamic.

In consonance frameworks we divide parametric displacements into two types: 1) *structural* displacements, that aim to lay bare the structure of benefits and losses from rivalrous and customer consonance in the industries, and to better discern the effective implications of power structure; and 2) *functional* displacements, that have the goal of revealing the responsiveness of the policy or state variables to changes in firms' operating environments exclusive of power structure. We will illustrate the use of each type successively below.

1.3. *Structural Displacements*

In this section we will violate the rules of second-order analysis to permit θ to change, but only to limiting values. In the first case -- the Cournot case -- θ is taken as the 5 x 5 identity matrix, so that each firm determines price in myopic disregard of the welfares of rivals and customers. The equilibrium achieved is the price counterpart of the famous Cournot equilibrium, where each firm is happy with the status quo only where it has achieved a price that maximizes its profit at prices at which all other firms are doing the same. All parameters in the base case except θ are unchanged in deriving this Cournot solution.

The Cournot solution permits us to study the prices and profits that would occur in the base case were rival and customer consonance nonexistent. Hence, a measure of the impacts of the consonance environment and its implied power structure upon firms' prices and profits -- the total consonance effect -- is obtained by subtracting the Cournot values of these variables from the base case counterparts.

We may decompose the total consonance effect (TCE) into a rival consonance effect (RCE) and a customer consonance effect (CCE) by two further displacements. First, we introduce into an otherwise unchanged base case parameter set a θ in which binary customer consonance factors are set equal to 0, and rival consonance factors retain their base case values. The solution to this displacement case yields the profits and prices that would have occurred had only rival consonance been operative. Hence, the RCE is measured as the rivals-only solution value of a variable minus the Cournot solution value.

Lastly, to capture the CCE we again alter θ to eliminate all binary rival consonance and preserve only customer consonance factors. The solution reveals the values the base case solution would have taken if only customer consonance were operative. These solution values less the corresponding Cournot solution values yield the customer effect. Then,

(1) (Base case variable value - Cournot case variable value) =

(Pure rival consonance case variable value - Cournot case variable value) + (Pure customer consonance case variable value - Cournot case variable value) + (Residual)

or

(2) Total consonance effect (TEC) = Rival consonance effect (RCE) + Customer consonance effect (CCE) + Residual (R)

1.3.1 *Profit Effects of Rivalrous Consonance.* In Table 5.6 we list the Cournot solution profits and the total, rival, and customer consonance effects for profits, with the residuals.

Table 5.6. DECOMPOSITION OF BASE CASE CONSONANCE EFFECTS: PROFITS

Firm	Cournot Case Profits	TCE		RCE		CCE		Residual	
		Value	Percent	Value	Percent	Value	Percent	Value	Percent
1	2,807,833	+33,194	+1.17	+21,754	+.76	+11,212	+.40	+128	---
2	1,223,003	+31,033	+2.47	+11,113	+.89	+19,888	+1.59	+32	---
3	963,245	+11,609	+1.19	+8,272	+.85	+3,363	+.33	+75	---
4	1,223,718	-18,974	-1.57	-15,667	-1.30	-4,414	-.37	+1,107	+.09
5	442,217	-8,529	-1.97	-9,520	-2.20	+18	---	+973	+.22

The broad pattern of benefits and costs is what in fact our analysis in sections 1.1 and 1.2 led us to expect. Industry 2 is a net profits loser and industry 1 a net profits gainer from the patterns of consonance existent in the economy. But the consonance and effective consonance factors -- taking into account only direct effects -- fail as reliable predictors in crucial important respects. Most of industry 2's profit sacrifices were due to rivalrous consonance not customer consonance, a result that ECCI and ERCI predict but not CCI nor RI. Moreover, firm 5 is a slight net gainer from customer consonance, an occurrence that was projected by its ECCI.

On the other hand, industry 1's experience has been rather reliably predicted by the consonance indices, but not the effective consonance indices. The rival consonance effects in absolute terms are ranked in the order of RCI, but the percent-of-base-case profits rankings are better projected by ERCI. Essentially, all firms are about equally benefitted in relative terms by rivalrous consonance. The customer effects are quite strong, and firm 2 a large beneficiary as projected by its CCI but not its ECCI. Moreover, firm 3, which must give no consideration to industrial customers, having none, does quite well on this account, a result which, as the consequence of indirect factors, cannot be projected by either index. Indeed, in general it is the indirect effects of firms' price actions that so alter the direct effects as to lead us to treat the consonance indices based solely on θ and the effective consonance indices based on price elasticities and θ as disappointing indicators of profit implications except in the broadest terms.

In more detail, the consonance effect profile firm by firm is the following. Firm 1 benefits by about 1.17 percent of base case profits from consonance, about two-thirds of which springs from the direct and indirect effects of the rival consonance component. The relatively large customer consonance effect results from the very low regard it gives its customer and, most importantly, the heavy dependence of firm 4 upon both firms 1 and 3. A strong force exists to keep p_4 low, therefore, and both industry 1 customers benefit from larger profit margins.

Relatively, firm 2 is the largest beneficiary from consonance of any firm in either industry, to the extent of about 2.47 percent of base case profits. Most of this -- about two-thirds -- arises from customer consonance. As we shall see in the price decomposition to follow, firm 5, supplier to firm 2, reduces price about \$9.00 because of customer consonance, in turn saving firm 2 \$2.42 in cost. This increment applied to Cournot case solution sales of 8,178 amounts to \$19,791, or almost the whole of the customer effect. It must be offset by the loss of profit sustained by the reduction of p_2 inspired by the extension of consonance aid to firm 4, its customer, an amount of price reduction unrelated to the fall in cost and subsequent profit-maximizing price fall. But we know that in the absence of consonance the firm will maximize profits by reducing price by one-half the fall in marginal cost, or, in the present case, by \$1.21. Hence, the extension of aid to firm 4 is small, or \$.03. This reduces profit by about $.03 \times 8,178 = \$245$ -- the Cournot case solution z_2 -- offset by the profit margin times the small rise in z_2 a change of \$.03 would bring about, which we will ignore. Hence, our crude estimate of the customer consonance effect is \$19,546, which is very close to the estimate of Table 5.6. Thus, firm 2 is a large net beneficiary from customer consonance -- a direct effect of that profit margin force both ECCI and CCI simply failed to project.

Industry 1 firms benefit about equally in relative terms from the rival consonance effect profits. Firms 2 and 3 exhibit that rivalrous symmetry we have identified in sections 1.1 and 1.2 in their closely corresponding relative gains, and firm 1 is a bit less the beneficiary in these terms. Almost none of industry 1's increased profit margins are diminished by cost increases on intermediate inputs because of rival effect price increases in industry 2. Since the three firms' costs rise very little, the rise in profit margins is almost wholly induced by the urge to protect rivals which turns out to have the effect of a tacit collusion that benefits each member of the industry. Rivalrous consonance in this instance is a pattern of cooperation perhaps evolving through changes in the power structure over some period of time, a long-term adjustment to be discussed in Chapter 6.

We have discussed industry 2's light penalties or positive gains on customer effect account that can be explained by joint price reduction under high own-price elasticity conditions. The high penalties paid by both firms in the rival effect component are a compound of the high own-price elasticities they face coupled with the induced price rises in their products, and, more importantly, the extremely high cross elasticities with their customers' prices (see Table 5.3). That is, the high penalties are more the indirect effects via the rival consonance induced price increases of their customers with consequent output reductions than the result of their own price actions. More specifically, p_4 rises only .08 percent although sales fall 1.34 percent between the rival effect only and Cournot case solutions, and p_5 falls .22 percent with sales reduction of 3.53 percent. Hence, a seeming paradox arises: industry 2's great dependence on industrial demand does not penalize it greatly through deference to customers but rather because rival consonance price effects in industry 1 reduce demand for its products on intermediate good account.

1.3.2. *Price Effects of Rivalrous Consonance.* But what of the price effects of rivalrous consonance? In table 5.7 we have decomposed total price effects of the structural displacements into rival and customer consonance effects using the same methodology employed in our profits analysis and displayed in (1).

Table 5.7. DECOMPOSITION OF BASE CASE CONSONANCE EFFECTS: PRICES

Firm	Cournot Case Prices	TCE		RCE		CCE		Residual	
		Value	Percent*	Value	Percent*	Value	Percent*	Value	Percent*
1	943.92	+3.10	.33	+3.40	.36	-.33	-.03	+.03	---
2	890.32	+4.02	.45	+5.23	.58	-1.24	-.14	+.03	---
3	930.20	+7.62	.81	+8.17	.87	-.59	-.06	+.04	---
4	936.95	-3.24	-.35	+.78	.08	-4.01	-.43	-.01	---
5	1,565.83	-5.45	-.35	+3.46	.22	-8.99	-.58	+.08	---

*Percent of base case price.

In general, relative price changes in both industries on all accounts are quite small, despite what we feel are at least moderately high consonance factors. The total effect of consonance is to *reduce* the prices of industry 2 because of the dominance of the customer effect over the rival effect, and to *increase* the prices of industry 1 because of the dominance of the rival effect. All rival and customer consonance effects are in the expected directions.

Unlike their record in predicting profit experience, the consonance indices of Table 5.5 (but not their effective counterparts) do a good job of predicting the ranking of firms' relative and absolute price effects. Hence, the simpler consonance effect index would seem to be sufficient for structural price changes, though neither index, as we have shown, seems helpful for predicting profit effects. The interfiliations of consonance, therefore, are seen to be quite complex, and not capable of simple projection from measures of direct effects only.

From the structural displacements we conclude that rivalrous consonance in industry 1 functions as a type of tacit collusion, raising profits and prices for all firms in the sector. Although customer consonance restrains price rises somewhat, each firm benefits in profit terms from the fact that its suppliers are strongly dependent upon their purchases and therefore anxious to avoid offending them through high prices. Firm 2 is a particularly fortunate profit beneficiary of these circumstances.

Indeed, relatively speaking, firm 2 -- the firm of intermediate size in the industry -- benefits most from the consonance environment and has most to lose from its disappearance (and most to gain from its extension, as will be seen in section 1.3.3). Firms 1 and 3 are equal in relative benefits, and differ from firm 2 in that the greater part of their enhanced welfare springs from the rivalrous consonance component. Indeed, in relative terms, the net effect of the existence of tacit cooperation among rivals is to benefit the three firms about equally. In absolute terms, of course, the gains are far greater for firm 1, intermediate for firm 2, and least for firm 3.

Firm 3 -- the highest factor cost producer with the smallest market share goal and no industrial sales -- is revealed to be remarkably strong even in the Cournot jungle. Its profit would decline by only 1.19 percent were all consonance protection taken from it, even though it is led to raise its price under the consonance regime by about 2.5 times that of the dominant firm 1 in the face of elastic demand.

Industry 2 suffers mostly -- and surprisingly -- not directly by catering to its heavy dependence on industrial demand for its products, but from the indirect effects of industry 1's price umbrella that reduces its output. It is necessary to add immediately that firm 4 does indeed suffer somewhat profitwise from the customer consonance effect, whereas firm 5 actually benefits slightly, but in both cases negative rival consonance profit effects are far more potent. Both firms are led through concern for customer satisfaction to lower prices by rather large amounts, and firm 5 by twice the amount of firm 4, but because own-price elasticities are large profit implications are those indicated.

Once more the high-cost, low-volume firm, almost completely dependent on industrial demand, proves to be resilient under rivalrous consonance. Firm 5's profits decline by only about 2 percent from its customers' tacit collusion and it manages to carve out a market share in excess of twice its goal.

Lastly, the social effects of rivalrous consonance are both positive and negative but are probably negative on a net basis and in any event are small. The total consonance effect upon sales-weighted industry 1 average price is $4.56, or about .5 percent of Cournot solution price which is 25 percent above marginal cost. Clearly, even in the absence of tacit collusion through consonance, the major deleterious effect socially upon resource allocation has its source in the absence of competition itself.[1] The distributive effect is also rather small, consonance contributing a profit enhancement to the industry of only .73 percent above the Cournot result.

In the case of industry 2, the total sales-weighted consonance price effect is to reduce price by $3.84, or by a mere .36 percent of Cournot solution price. The latter is over 21 percent above competitive price, and hence little social enhancement of efficiency is experienced. Duopoly rent also declines only about 1.65 percent from its nonconsonance Cournot level. Hence, the consonance structure of these interdependent industries does not lead to worrisome social efficiency or distributive effects when compared with the far more fundamentally disturbing control over price that lack of competition gives these firms. For the economy as a whole, the distributive impact of consonance is to raise oligopoly profits by .72 percent.

1.3.3. *Prices and Profits Under Joint Profit Maximization.* Table 5.8 presents price and profit results under joint maximization of profit conditions. Panel a presents

Table 5.8. DECOMPOSITION OF JOINT PROFIT MAXIMIZATION SOLUTIONS: PROFITS AND PRICES

a. Joint Industry Profit Maximization

Firm	Solution	Cournot Solution	Base Case	Value	% of Base Case	% of Cournot Case
1. Prices						
1	$990.66	$943.92	$947.02	+$46.74	+4.94%	+4.95%
2	938.09	890.32	894.34	+47.77	+5.34	+5.37
3	998.42	930.20	937.82	+68.22	+7.27	+7.33
4	938.65	936.95	933.71	+1.70	+.18	+.18
5	1,580.80	1,565.83	1,560.38	+14.97	+.96	+.96
2. Profits						
1	2,945,366	2,807,833	2,841,027	+137,533	+4.84	+4.90
2	1,326,228	1,223,003	1,254,036	+103,225	+8.23	+8.44
3	946,628	963,245	974,854	-16,617	-1.70	-1.73
4	1,062,405	1,223,718	1,204,744	-161,313	-1.34	-1.34
5	349,327	442,217	433,688	-92,890	-2.14	-2.10

b. Joint Industry-Customer Profit Maximization

Firm	Solution	Cournot Solution	Base Case	Value	% of Base Case	% of Cournot Case
1. Prices						
1	966.43	943.92	947.02	+22.51	+2.38	+2.38
2	903.15	890.32	894.34	+12.83	+1.43	+1.44
3	976.29	930.20	937.82	+46.09	+4.91	+4.95
4	870.35	936.95	933.71	-66.60	-7.13	-7.11
5	1,456.78	1,565.83	1,560.38	-109.05	-6.99	-6.97
2. Profits						
1	3,129,675	2,807,833	2,841,027	+321,842	+11.33	+11.46
2	1,617,399	1,223,003	1,254,036	+394,396	+31.45	+32.25
3	1,000,224	963,245	974,854	+36,979	+3.79	+3.84
4	968,283	1,223,718	1,204,744	-255,435	-21.20	-20.87
5	270,540	442,217	433,688	-171,677	-39.59	-38.82

the more realistic case where each industry seeks its own joint profit maximization. Panel b is an economy-wide profit maximization to the limited extent that customers' binary consonance factors as well as rivals' are set equal to 1.[2]

For the simultaneous two-industry Chamberlin case, the intensification of rivalrous consonance and elimination of customer consonance raises prices in industry 1 between 5 and 7.3 percent of both Cournot and base prices and elevates industry 2 prices by less than 1 percent of these bases. Freedom from the need to extend customer consonance and greater protection from rivals benefits firm 2 most profitwise by an amount in excess of 8 percent, but lowers firm 3's profits slightly because of its large price rise. Firm 2, therefore, is marked as the greatest potential beneficiary of a greater general degree of rivalrous consonance, but with firm 1 the greatest profit gainer in absolute terms.

Industry 2, on the other hand, suffers from the enhancement of rivalrous consonance and elimination of customer consonance in industry 1, with the reduced intermediate demand for goods 4 and 5 implied. Slight price rises resulting from own-industry rivalrous consonance intensification compensate somewhat for sales losses, but not sufficiently to eliminate profit losses of between 1 and 2 percent. Firm 4 is the largest loser of profits in absolute amount, but firm 5 loses more relatively. Somewhat surprisingly, however, given industry 2's dependence on industry 1, the former does not suffer grievously from industry 1's cartelization, nor does it benefit greatly from the release of its own burden of extending customer consonance. As the structural displacement analysis of Table 5.6 disclosed, industry 2 is a net loser from rivalrous consonance, and a loser or near-zero gainer from customer consonance. The elimination of the latter and the enhancement of the former lead it to suffer, but much less than would result if they were not compensating.

The extension of other-industry solicitude to customers by including them in the profit functions at own-profit equivalency makes the last point about industry 2 even more dramatically. Firm 5's profits fall almost 40 percent below base case and Cournot case levels as its prices are forced down 7 percent through its industry 1 solicitude. Firm 2's price also declines 7 percent, and, with an absolute profit decline in Table 5.8.b.2 that in percentage terms is about 21 percent below base case and Cournot solutions. The Cournot solution reveals that industry 2 prospers best when left to myopic, self-seeking behavior: any consonance on a joint-industry or inward-looking basis is harmful, at least in the short-run. For it, much maligned Cournot behavior is rational!

Industry 1, though, continues to benefit from industry 2's travails. All three firms damp their price rises above the base case and Cournot levels when customer consonance is introduced, but, as expected, are net beneficiaries, in that the profits of all expand. For firms 1 and 2 the increases are quite large, but firm 3's profit level is not negligible. The structure of the economy is such that industry 1 benefits from enhancements of consonance of either type. Firm 2 is a particularly sensitive beneficiary.

1.4. *Functional Displacements*

With a rather good grip upon the structure of these industries as revealed in the stated goals, consonance relations, base case solution and structural displacements, we now investigate the ex post facto pricing implications of these characteristics of firms' behavior in changing parameter environments. Which firms are more sensitive to rival and supplier cost adjustments? What are the patterns and explanations of price perversity displayed, if any? Is it possible to encapsulate in simple "laws of change" the price reactions to other firms' cost changes from the displayed solutions?

The analysis of these functional questions begins with administering to each firm successively and singly changes in the factor cost term, f_i, of their cost functions in Table 5.1 of ±5, ±10, ±15, and ±20 percent, and then re-solving the model with all other parameters set to base case values. This generated 40 new solutions, and, with the base case solution, 41 "observations" of price behavior for each firm under the different cost configurations. Finally, 8 more solutions were obtained by changing *all* firms' factor costs simultaneously by the indicated percentages, so that 49 instances of pricing reactions to cost changes were analyzed. The price results are displayed in Table 5.9.

The results of Table 5.9 are largely unaffected by constraints. In only 6 of the 49 runs does a price constraint bind -- p_2 is the culprit in 5 instances and p_1 in the other -- and in 17 runs the minimum market share constraint binds p_2. In one case the market share constraint holds p_1 down. Only firm 2's prices are restrained to any great degree, therefore.

Let us consider, first, the results in the fifth panel of Table 5.9, where all firms are undergoing cost inflation or deflation in equal relative degrees. We have increased or decreased firms' factor costs in 5 percent-of-base-case steps, and in Table 5.10 we list (1) the absolute values of the 5 percent factor cost increments or decrements, (2) the values of the price changes as factor costs change by steps of 5 percent of base case factor cost, and (3) the actual incremental cost changes including both factor cost and input price changes.

Note, first, the striking asymmetry of price change in periods of cost deflation compared with periods of cost inflation. Price changes with cost deflation are in every instance except for the first 5 percent cost changes smaller than the corresponding price change with cost rise of equivalent amount. Rivalrous consonance reveals a realistic "price stickiness" in periods of deflation in contrast with price responsiveness in periods of inflation. Moreover, the deflationary data of Table 5.10 show relatively sharp diminishing marginal price reductions to cost reductions as the latter rise. We will indicate in the next paragraph the proximate cause of the phenomenon.

Second, the unusual linearity of price rises to cost increases is an intriguing result for which we gain a partial explanation by studying the pattern of price responses to cost decreases, which does not show such behavior. Note, however, that when factor costs decrease by 5 percent, and p_2 does not strike a lower bound, the same linearity arises. Only when p_2 is prevented from falling by a lower price bound is the linearity disturbed. Hence, under rivalrous consonance with linear sales and marginal cost functions, unconstrained price reactions in periods of universal cost inflation or deflation will reveal linear patterns of price reaction. But why should the "elasticity" of price response to universal cost change be constant? A review of the first-order conditions (11) and (12) of Chapter 2 does not lead to the prima facie expectation that it would. This is an excellent example of the insights that simulative theorizing can yield that are not attainable, or, if attainable, unlikely to be uncovered by classic parametric displacement of unspecified systems.

A third result of some interest, also related to firm 2's lower price bound being operative, is the counterintuitive behavior of p_3 as its factor costs decrease: it falls initially as factor costs fall to .95 and .90 of base case, but then *rises* as further cost cuts occur. We have seen that a close rivalry exists between firms 2 and 3, reflected in high consonance relations. As firm 2's price remains constant and its profit margin widens, its term in the extended rival marginal profit expression becomes larger and hence rivals are led to keep prices higher than they would in the absence of this widening margin. In the case of rivals with high consonance, this can lead to

Table 5.9. PRICES OF FIRMS RESPONDING TO INITIATING FIRM'S FACTOR COST CHANGES, BASE CASE PARAMETERS

Responding Firm/ Initiating Firm Number	5 Percent Reduction					5 Percent Increase				
	1 2	2 3	3 4	4 5	5 6	1 7	2 8	3 9	4 10	5 11
1. 5 % Changes										
1	932.03	946.43	945.89	945.21*	947.30	960.16	948.31	948.24	948.33*	946.75
2	892.35[a]	886.80	892.48[a]	894.18	890.58*	896.00	900.13[a]	896.02	894.50	898.10[a]
3	936.86	937.06	923.16	935.98*	937.38	938.95	939.36	952.58	939.67*	938.27
4	935.19	933.36*	935.14	917.71	932.26	932.16	933.74*	932.24	949.71	935.16
5	1,558.00*	1,564.35	1,559.25	1,558.36	1,532.93	1,562.21*	1,553.89	1,561.22	1,562.4	1587.84
	10 Percent Reduction					10 Percent Increase				
	12	13	14	15	16	17	18	19	20	21
2. 10 % Changes										
1	922.62	945.85	946.33	943.41*	947.57	973.30	951.19	949.45	950.64*	946.95[a]
2	886.88[a]	879.25	887.15[a]	894.02	886.83*	897.65	902.86[a]	897.70	894.66	900.31*
3	937.64	936.30	910.24	934.13*	936.94	940.08	942.64	967.33	941.52*	939.23
4	935.94	933.00*	935.85	917.71	932.26	932.16	933.74*	932.24	949.71	935.16
5	1549.98*	1568.31	1552.47	1556.33	1505.47	1564.04*	1541.79	1562.06	156.43	1613.59
	15 Percent Reduction					15 Percent Increase				
	22	23	24	25	26	27	28	29	30	31
3. 15 % Changes										
1	911.22	945.71	946.76	941.60*	947.85	986.44	954.04	950.66	952.44*	947.70
2	881.43[a]	874.00[b]	881.81[a]	893.86	883.07*	899.31	905.37[a]	899.38	894.82	902.31[a]*
3	938.41	936.31	897.32	932.29*	936.50	941.21	945.93	982.08	943.36*	940.81
4	936.68	933.03*	936.57	885.70	929.36	929.07	932.37	929.29	981.72	937.37
5	1542.04*	1575.90	1545.69	1554.31	1478.01	1565.87*	1529.61	1562.90	1566.45	1637.31

Table 5.9. (continued)

	20 Percent Reduction					20 Percent Increase				
	32	33	34	35	36	37	38	39	40	41
4. 20 % Changes										
1	900.00[b]	946.65	947.20	939.79*	948.12	995.47[a]	956.90	951.88	954.25*	948.71
2	876.08[a]	874.00[b]	876.48[a]	893.70	879.31*	903.89	907.89[a]	901.06	894.98	904.15[a]*
3	939.25	938.10	884.40	930.44*	936.05	945.89	949.21	996.83	945.21*	942.89
4	937.53	933.98*	937.29	869.70	927.91	927.94	931.68*	927.82	997.72	938.18
5	1534.08*	1591.93	1538.92	1552.29	1450.55	1570.72*	1517.48	1563.74	1568.48	1660.95

	-5%	+5%	-10%	+10%	-15%	+15%	-20%	+20%
	42	43	44	45	46	47	48	49
5. All Firms' Factor Cost Change by:								
1	930.55	963.49	919.55	979.97	917.57	996.44	914.84	1012.91
2	879.54	909.14	874.00[a,b]	923.94	874.00[a,b]	938.74	874.00[a,b]	953.54
3	918.89	956.76	907.75	975.69	908.61	994.62	910.47	1013.15
4	918.92	948.49	905.51	963.28	892.60	978.07	879.82	992.85
5	1532.20	1588.56	1518.61	1616.75	1513.44	1644.93	1507.96	1673.12

*Row firm supplier.

_____ Underline indicates perverse result.

[a]Lower price constraint binds.

[b]Minimum market share constraint binds.

price increases, and this happened in our exercise where p_3 rises to protect firm 2's increased profit margin.[3]

The important implication of the linearity hypotheses is that it serves as a measure of responsiveness of firms other than firm 3 to p_2's behavior. In each instance of factor cost reduction in Table 5.10 every firm would achieve the price reductions indicated in the first column of that panel in the absence of the constraint on p_2. Thus, firm 4's actions are hardly modified by p_2's rigidity -- a result that the consonance factors in Table 5.1, the sales function elasticities of Table 5.3, and the effective consonance factors of Table 5.4 would lead us to expect. On the same grounds, we would expect firm 5 to be most ready as its customer's profit margin rose and its rival's fell, to lower price. Why does it limit its customer's competitiveness and its actions so greatly?

Lastly, the strength of the rival component for firm 1 is rather surprising, given its demonstrated relative aloofness from the industry. Nonetheless, it is led through the increase in firm 2's profit margin to forego almost all of its "desired" price reductions in the upper ranges of cost decreases, demonstrating the potential

Table 5.10. FACTOR COST, PRICE, AND TOTAL COST CHANGES, FOR STEPS OF FIVE PERCENT OF BASE CASE FACTOR COST

Firm	Factor Cost 5% Changes	Incremental Price Change Induced by Factor Cost Changes and (Total Cost Increments)							
		-5%	-10%	-15%	-20%	+5%	+10%	+15%	+20%
1	$26.25	-16.47 (-29.21)	-11.00 (-28.93)	-1.98 (-28.83)	-2.73 (-28.81)	+16.47 (+29.21)	+16.48 (29.21)	+16.418 (+29.21)	+16.47 (+29.21)
2	15.90	-14.80 (-23.51)	-5.54 (19.57)	0* (-17.30)	0* (17.38)	+14.80 (+23.51)	+14.80 (+23.51)	+14.80 (+23.51)	+14.80 (+23.51)
3	29.10	-18.93 (-32.31)	-11.14 (-31.92)	+.86 (-31.81)	+1.86 (-31.78)	+18.94 (+32.20)	+18.93 (+32.21)	+18.93 (32.21)	+18.93 (+32.21)
4	32.60	-14.79 (-34.03)	-13.41 (-33.15)	-12.91 (-32.60)	-12.78 (-32.60)	+14.78 +(34.08)	+14.79 (+34.08)	+14.79 (+34.08)	+14.79 (+34.08)
5	58.75	-28.18 (-62.21)	-13.59 (-61.06)	-5.17 (-59.17)	-5.48 (-59.32)	+28.18 (+62.21)	+28.19 (+62.21)	+28.18 (+62.21)	+28.19 (+62.21)

*Price constrained by lower price bound.
___Underline indicates perverse price movement.

impact of even moderate consonance factors when relative profit margins become large.

What these generalized factor cost exercises demonstrate most forcibly is the "distortions" from "rational" optimizing patterns of response even the slightest constraint upon price movement introduces into observed data. Even in the absence of all of the other systematic and random errors introduced into empirical data externally, the functioning of realistic oligopolies under conditions of rivalrous consonance and multiobjective decision making may introduce seeming inconsistencies into the data that regression equations will have difficulty in explaining.

Let us study the profit penalties and percentage of cost rises by which each firm raises its price when those price rises are unconstrained. These data, computed from the rightmost panel of Table 5.10, are given in Table 5.11. The percentages of cost passthrough are similar for all firms in each industry, although as would be expected from our earlier analyses, the common level is lower for industry 2 than for industry 1. Moreover, as the profit data reveal, industry 2 suffers much more from the induced price rises than industry 1, largely from the great reductions in industrial demand for its products. Firm 5 suffers most this way, watching its profits diminish to close to the vanishing point as costs and prices escalate. Firms 1 and 2 are on a par in their ability to conserve profits, while firm 3 suffers distinctly more.

The first four panels of Table 5.9 reveal the price changes that result from factor cost changes for isolated firms. Of the 200 prices registered, 15 cases of an effective lower price bound occur, with p_1 or p_2 the price in question, and 3 cases of a market share constraint binding price occur, with the same two prices at fault. Overall, therefore, a good deal of latitude for free price variation was given in the displacements.

Table 5.11. INDUCED PRICE INCREASES AS PERCENTAGES OF MARGINAL COST INCREASES AND PROFITS AS PERCENTAGES OF BASE CASE PROFIT

Firm	Price Rise As Percent of Marginal Cost Rise	Profits With Factor Cost Increases as Percentage of Base Case Profits			
		+5%	+10%	+15%	+20%
1	56.4%	89.5%	79.6%	70.2%	61.4%
2	63.0	89.1	78.9	69.3	60.3
3	58.6	83.8	69.1	55.7	43.8
4	43.5	81.1	64.3	49.4	36.4
5	45.3	67.5	41.3	21.5	8.14

We have underlined in Table 5.9 the counterintuitive instances of price change and note that in all four panels that form a quite consistent pattern. We distinguish two broad categories of counterintuitive price behavior, depending upon whether the firm that responds perversely to an initiating firm's factor cost change is a rival or a customer.

The cases of counterintuitive rival response are limited to four instances, as shown in Table 5.12. Interestingly, perversity occurs only with quite large factor cost decreases, and involves firm 3 in all cases. The mechanism can be illustrated by the first two examples. A fall in p_1 raises firm 1's sales and permits its supplier firm 4 to raise price. But that firm supplies firm 3 as well, so that it suffers a cost push. Firm 2 is forced to follow firm 1's deep price reduction to preserve market share. The expansion in firm 1's profit margin exerts a positive rival price effect on p_3 and the fall in firm 2's profit margin exerts a negative effect. Reinforced by the small cost effect, the positive price forces dominate weakly the negative, and p_3 rises. The same motivation (less the cost effect) lies behind p_3's perverse movement in the face of a 20 percent cut in firm 2's factor cost, with the roles of firm 1's and 2's profit margins reversed. Finally, a large rise in firm 3's profit margin, not balanced by a smaller fall in firm 2's profit margin, leads p_1 to rise slightly.

Table 5.12. PERVERSE RIVAL FIRM PRICE RESPONSES TO ISOLATED FACTOR COST CHANGES

Initiating Firm	Displacement Number	Percent Change in Initiating Firm's Factor Cost	Responding Firm
1	22,32	-15, -20	3
2	33	-20	3
3	34	-20	1

Table 5.13. PERVERSE SUPPLIER FIRM PRICE RESPONSES TO ISOLATED FACTOR COST CHANGES

Initiating Firm	Displacement Numbers	Percent Change in Initiating Firm's Factor Cost	Responding Firm
1	2,7,12,17,22,27,32,37	-5, +5,-10, +10,-15, +15,-20, +20	4
2	3,8,13,18,23,28,33,38	-5, +5,-10, +10,-15, +15,-20, +20	5
3	4,9,14,19,24,29,34,39	-5, +5,-10, +10,-15, +15,-20, +20	4
5	6,11,16,21,26,36	-5, +5,-10, +10,-15,-20	1

The remainder of the perverse price changes are other-industry where a change in a supplier firm's costs causes counterintuitive price moves in the customer's product. We list them in Table 5.13. We have seen that firm 4's sales are very sensitive to firm 1 and 3 sales and, therefore, price changes. Hence, 16 of the 34 perverse cases involve firm 4's supplier role, in that when customer firms lower price in response to cost reductions its sales curve shifts rightward and, by its reduced elasticity, induces a price rise. For customer price increases, the opposite is true.

In the cases involving firms 2 and 5, with the latter a supplier of the former, the sales sensitivity of firm 5 to firm 4's price is very high (see Table 5.3) and hence shifts the sales function of firm 5 by large amounts. As in the previous case, this leads to movements in p_5 that counter the direction of p_2's changes.

On the other hand, the impact of p_2 on p_4 seems to be a reaction to the rivalrous impacts of p_2's changes on p_1 and p_3. When p_2 rises, p_1 and p_3 tend to rise, reducing their sales and shifting firm 4's sales curve leftward, the resulting increase in elasticity leading to a price fall. The opposite occurs with a cost-induced fall in p_2.

Finally, another nondirect impact of customer-supplier relations occurs in the perverse moves of p_1 with respect to cost changes in p_5. The latter is a customer, not a supplier, of the former firm, and the impacts are small scale. Because firm 2's costs are very susceptible to changes in p_5, its profit margin tends to change substantially with changes in p_5. The perverse reactions of p_1 seem to be weak rival consonance effects of these changes in firm 2's profit margins that are not cancelled out by sales sensitivity to p_2.

1.5. *Patterns of Price Interrelations in the Displacements*

The purpose of simulative theorizing is to gain insights into the structure and functioning of industries or groups of industries considered as sets of interdependent individually motivated firms. Methods must be exploited or developed to cope with a large body of interdependent decisions and to isolate patterns of coassociation within it. Specifically, we have 49 observations of the sets of five prices under different factor (and total) cost configurations -- the base case, 40 isolated factor cost displacements, and 8 joint factor cost displacements. Can we derive from this set of solutions measures of the cost-price and price-price relations among firms with which we have dealt in detail in sections 1.3 and 1.4? Is it possible to isolate "laws of change" that tend to rule among these prices?

Statistical techniques will be used wholly as descriptive devices of course, not as inferential, since no stochastic terms exist in our results. Hence, standard errors, t-values, and the other tools of statistical inference are not relevant to our purposes.

To the economist, the first methodology that suggests itself for these summarizing and integrating analytical tasks is that of multiple regression. We display in Table 5.14 the regression equations obtained by regressing each price against (1) all remaining prices and (2) rivals' prices only. The squares of multiple regression coefficients (R^2) and standard errors of estimate (σ_s) are included as descriptive measures of goodness of fit.

Table 5.14. REGRESSION EQUATIONS OF PRICE ON REMAINING PRICES

Regressand/ Regressors:	Constant	p_1	p_2	p_3	p_4	p_5	R^2	σ_s
p_1	-20.21	---	1.11	-.09	.10[s]	-.02[c]	.634	12.97
p_1	3.89	---	1.13	-.07	---	---	.625	12.85
p_2	191.73	.32	---	.27	.01[c]	.09[s]	.814	6.94
p_2	228.57	.38	---	.32	---	---	.777	7.45
p_3	-130.90	-.12	1.24	---	.12[s]	-.02	.624	14.83
p_3	-105.49	-.09	1.27	---	---	---	.613	14.71
p_4	238.20	.25[c]	.04[s]	.23[c]	---	.13	.326	20.63
p_4	504.15	---	---	---	---	.28	.217	21.51
p_5	-100.55	-.12[s]	1.78[c]	-.10	.30	---	.478	30.99
p_5	818.59	---	---	---	.79	---	.225	36.53

[s]Supplier of row firm.
[c]Customer of row firm.

A quite marked feature of industry 1's regression equations is the lack of variation in rival price regression coefficients as industry 2 prices are eliminated as regressors. Customers' and suppliers' prices have small impacts on industry 1's prices. The small customer consonance effects in prices revealed in Table 5.9's structural displacement results is borne out in the extensive displacement data. As would be expected from that data, the other-industry price impacts on own price are nonnegligible for firms 4 and 5. For firm 4, regression coefficients for customers 1 and 3 are almost twice as large as that for rival 5's price, and for firm 5 customer p_2 has the dominant regression coefficient in the regression equation. Whereas in industry 1 such sensitivity to other-industry prices as exists is dominated by supplier prices, so that the relationship occurs via costs largely, in industry 2 the dominant other-price coefficients are for prices of customers rather than suppliers.

Among industry 1 prices, p_1 is much more sensitive to p_2's movement than p_3's, and, indeed, moves *inversely* to p_3. The effective consonance factors do not lead to this expectation, nor do the consonance factors of Table 5.1. However, Table 5.12 and its accompanying discussion indicate the existence of some perversity occurring for large price decreases and acting through the impact of changes in p_1 on p_2. We suspect, however, that the more basic explanation is that of multicollinearity, since r_{23} reveals high intercorrelation among these regressors in the correlation matrix of Table 5.15. All of our prior analysis points to the expectation that the regressions coefficients for p_2 and p_3 should be positive and more nearly equal. Hence, the

Table 5.15. CORRELATION MATRIX FOR PRICES

	p_1	p_2	p_3	p_4	p_5
p_1	1.00	.789	.586	.481	.521
p_2		1.000	.782	.518	.672
p_3			1.000	.482	.519
p_4				1.000	.468
p_5					1.000

results are to be distrusted, especially as they assert that p_1 will change by more than than the full change in p_2.

Lastly, the weak negative response to changes in customer price p_5 may reflect a real relationship. Customer price regression coefficients will be positive or negative depending largely upon whether customer profit margins tend to move in the same or opposite directions. In the 48 parametric displacements positively and negatively correlated movements were about equal in number for all five firms, so that gauging regression coefficient signs from numbers alone leads to a conclusion that either sign is plausible.[4] But, given the rather high intercorrelation of p_2 and p_5, the resulting coefficients may also be another instance of intercorrelated explanatory variables.

The all-prices equation for p_2 yields the most believable results of all the regressions in Table 5.14. The value of R^2 is high and intercorrelation r_{13} relatively low. The rival price regression coefficients correspond in relative magnitude quite well to consonance factors, elasticities, and effective consonance factors, revealing that p_2 rises or falls by between 25 and 33 percent of the changes in rivals' prices. The customer price coefficient is small, as we would expect from the customer price consonance effect isolated in the structural analysis, and the supplier price coefficient is in line with crude expectations from the cost equation (in monopoly, about half the increased cost of the input, or, from Table 5.1, .13).

The problems with the equation for p_3 are the perverse sign of p_1's regression coefficient and the excessively large value of p_2's. Consonance factors, cross-elasticities, and effective consonance factors argue for greater parity and positivity. The culprit, once more, we suspect, is $r_{12} = .789$.

The equations for industry 2 are even more disappointing, with low R^2 values, high standard errors of estimate, and (in the case of firm 5) implausible regression coefficients with respect to sign and magnitude. Actually, for p_4 the relative magnitudes of the customer price coefficients with respect to each other and the rival price coefficient are plausible, and the supplier price impact also plausible. The explanatory power of the equation, however, is a disappointment. For p_5 the coefficient for p_2 is much too high and the supplier price impacts perversely. As noted, high intercorrelation characterizes the other-industry regressor variables, and multicollinearity's capricious distribution of impacts among them could be the culprit.

Our experience with regression analysis in simulative theorizing as an isolator of underlying patterns of relations among prices set in optimizing rivalrous consonance regimes has been one of disappointment.[5] Of course, it must be stressed once again that we are not employing it in stochastic regimes in which its statistical inferential properties are relevant. Nonetheless, in a quite large number of cases, estimated relationships among prices have not been deemed trustworthy, and multicollinearity is the most likely culprit. From the standpoint of that experience we are highly dubious of the addiction of the economist to the technique for gaining insights into relationships, even for data with well-behaved error terms.

One route that suggests itself as a manner of escaping this troublesome intercorrelation of the regressors is to estimate the "reduced forms" of the system by regressing each price on the costs of the products. This also has the advantage of treating prices as a simultaneously determined endogenous variable set rather than estimating them by ordinary least squares one by one. We will indeed do this in section 1.6 as we seek price-cost patterns, but several objections arise to this as a general means of escaping multicollinearity of prices.

First, costs are not wholly exogenous, containing as they do prices of intermediate inputs. Hence, the resulting equations are not truly "reduced forms". Second, as will be shown in section 1.6, costs are only slightly less correlated among themselves than prices because of their inclusion of price components, so multicollinearity continues to plague the equations. Third, and most importantly, the regression equations do not present the relations of major concern to our analysis -- the interdependence among prices.

If therefore we desire to remain with the task of isolating price interrelationships, what tools exist to combat the troublesome tendency of prices to fluctuate together, masking the direct linkages between prices? The basic problem with regression is the contradiction between the common interpretation of a regression coefficient and the manner of its calculation. It is taken to be the impact of an increment of one unit of the relevant regressor variable upon the regressand, *all other regressor variables held constant*. However, its calculation involves the covariances of every regressor variable with every other. Only if all covariances were zero would the coefficients reflect only the variance of the regressor in question.

One manner of escaping this interdependence of regressors is to use *factor analysis* to construct artificial variables or factors which *are* independent of one another. By grouping the variables into clusters or factors this methodology gives the analyst a clearer picture of which prices are clustered together in close association where each cluster's variation is isolated from all other clusters' covariation. This procedure frequently allows the analyst to concentrate his interest on a smaller number of meaningful covariant clusters than the original number of variables, if collinearity does in fact characterize the data. A seeming sacrifice is the "exactitude" of measurement of covariation by regression coefficients, but we have seen how false and misleading such pretensions can be.

Factor analysis involves manipulating the correlation matrix of Table 5.15 to form orthogonal factors or clusters of associated variables. The resulting "factor loadings" record the correlation coefficients of each of the original variables with the new, independent "variables", or *factors*. For our problem, we isolated 5 factors or "principal components" of the correlation matrix of Table 5.15, and then simplified the structure of the factors by a "varimax rotation", whose orthogonal nature preserves the independence of the factors. The factor loadings of the rotated factors in Table 5.16 present the "factor structure" or decomposition of the correlation matrix.

The factor structure of Table 5.16 permits an additive decomposition of the total variance of each price "explained by" or associated with each independent factor. The three-digit entries in the table are the correlation coefficients of the row price with the relevant factor, and their squares (recorded in parantheses) are the proportions of total variance in the row price observations explained by the factor. The addition of these proportions across the row yields the total explained by any set of factors. Note that the decomposition in Table 5.16 accounts for all the variance in all five prices.

Table 5.16. FACTOR LOADINGS, VARIMAX ROTATED FACTORS, OF PRICES' CORRELATION MATRIX

Prices/Factors	1	2	3	4	5	Cumulative Fraction of Row Price Variance Explained
p_1	.905(.82)	.261(.07)	.221(.05)	.212(.04)	.138(.02)	1.00
p_2	.503(.25)	.491(.24)	.367(.13)	.217(.06)	.569(.32)	1.00
p_3	.262(.07)	.904(.82)	.220(.05)	.214(.04)	.139(.02)	1.00
p_4	.195(.04)	.195(.04)	.194(.04)	.938(.87)	.087(.01)	1.00
p_5	.221(.05)	.219(.05)	.919(.84)	.205(.04)	.126(.02)	1.00
Fraction of Total Variance Explained	.25	.24	.22	.21	.08	

If the paranthesized proportions are summed columnwise and divided by 5.00, the total fractional variances explained for all prices, the contribution of each factor to the explanation of the total variance in all prices is yielded as a fraction. Hence, we conclude that there are four independent associations of prices in our 49 observations of about equal explanatory power, and one quite weak factor in overall power. The four factors together exhaust about 92 percent of the variance among the observations.

One interpretation of the factors is that of "supervariables" that reduce the number of truly functioning, independent forces in the data. This is, of course, the capture of interrelationships among prices: if two prices always moved in perfect lockstep, but independently of the other three prices, a factor would capture that association in near-unity values for the associated two and near-zero values for the others. This would indicate that only four potential independent prices were effectively present in the data. Our factors in Table 5.16 do not permit this ideal structural simplification, but they do reveal interesting insights into the pattern of price variation not obtainable in reliable ways from regression analysis.

By far the greatest amount -- indeed, 82 percent -- of the variation in p_1 is explained by factor 1, which further indicates that p_2 is the only significantly associated price variable. We conclude, then, that factor 1 is the "firms 1-2 rivalry" factor, with firm 1 most affected by firm 2's pricing decisions. Firm 1's pricing decisions are largely unaffected by other interprice relationships, with customer 5 and supplier 4 revealing weak relations. However factor 2 reveals that p_2 is about equally associated with p_3, whose variation is dominated by this association to the the same extent as p_1's. Factor 2 is the "firms 2-3 rivalry" factor, and points up p_2's pivotal and determining role as a transmitter of price forces throughout industry 1. When p_1 changes it affects p_2 via factor 1 and that price transmits the impacts indirectly to p_3. The direct interdependence of p_1 and p_3 is quite small, as their factor 1 and 2 values reveal.

But p_2's role as transmitter does not stop with industry 1. Factor 3 features the interrelationship of p_5 and p_2, with the former price dominantly affected by this association but p_2 only moderately affected. Clearly, this factor features the "firms 5-2 supplier-customer" relationship, and can be so named.

Factors 1, 2, and 3 account for 62 percent of the variation in p_2, but another 32 percent is associated with factor 5. This factor is dubbed the "firm 2 independent" factor, as it is designed to capture the fact that a great deal of p_2's variation after accounting for close relations with firms 1, 3, and 5, is unexplained by other price variances. We will see that we can "close" this explanatory gap by bringing in C_2 so that by anticipating the analysis to follow factor 5 could equally well be termed the "firm 2 cost-price" factor.

Finally, factor 4 is the "firm 4 independence" factor, which, as in the case of factor 5, will be explained by variations in C_4. Indeed, it should be recognized that in the cases of factors 1, 2, and 3, much of the large associations with p_1, p_3, and p_5 respectively will be "explained" by their respective costs when the latter are included in section 1.6.

At the present stage of our factor analysis, the following patterns emerge. An autonomous rise in p_2 acts directly to raise p_1, p_3, and by reducing z_2, to depress p_5. Autonomous rises in p_1 send p_2 up, impacting p_3 positively and p_5 negatively. Autonomous impacts on p_4 have very little direct impact: firm 4 is the most isolated of the five firms in terms of pricing power. Finally, autonomous rises in p_5 raise p_2 and are carried positively to p_1 and p_3. Hence, p_2 and p_5 are vitally involved as the "carriers" of price interdependence, and p_5 largely as a transmitter to firms outside its own industry.

These results reinforce our doubts about the regression equations of Table 5.14. Those for p_1 have too large a coefficient for p_2 and a suspiciously signed coefficient for p_3. On the other hand, the equation for p_2 conforms well to the expectations derived from factor analysis. That for p_3 is deficient as to the sign of the coefficient for p_1 and the size of that for p_2. The estimating equations for p_4 confirm its relative independence from other prices, but we are led to believe that the size of p_2's coefficient is too small. Lastly, the relative independence of p_5 from all prices but p_2 is registered overall in the low R^2 value, but the size of p_2's regression coefficient and the signs of p_1's and p_3's are suspicious in the light of p_2's high correlation with them.

These deficiencies may well be the result of misspecified equations, in that we know the exogenous cost factors have not been included in the system. What we have in fact is a simultaneously determined set of five endogenous variables as near-reduced form functions of the five costs.[6] Unfortunately, these are not the relationships of primary interest of us. We will attempt to relate costs to all prices simultaneously, therefore, with factor analyses, and hope to close that system's explanatory gaps as well as deepen the meaning of the regressions.

1.6. *Patterns of Price-Cost Interrelations in the Displacements*

We display in Table 5.17 the regression equations for prices and costs. The results are more satisfactory than the price-price regressions of Table 5.14 in terms of R^2 values and plausible regression coefficients, but intercorrelation of the regressor variables is present to about the same degree as prices (Table 5.15). The correlation matrix for costs will be found in Table 5.18.

Table 5.17. REGRESSION EQUATIONS OF PRICE ON TOTAL COSTS

Regressand/ Regressors:	Constant	C_1	C_2	C_3	C_4	C_5	R^2	σ_s
p_1	594.44	.45	.10	.01	-.02[s]	-.02[c]	.959	4.42
p_2	540.09	.08	.36	.07	-.03[c]	.00[s]	.896	5.25
p_3	555.23	-.01	.09	.46	-.02[s]	-.01	.935	6.22
p_4	633.64	-.06[c]	-.03[s]	-.05[c]	.50	.02	.999	.72
p_5	1,184.33	.09[s]	-.59[c]	.07	.00	.50	.935	11.06

[s]Supplier of row firm.
[c]Customer of row firm.

Table 5.18. CORRELATION MATRIX FOR COSTS

	C_1	C_2	C_3	C_4	C_5
C_1	1.000	.635	.549	.595	.562
C_2		1.000	.625	.606	.775
C_3			1.000	.591	.541
C_4				1.000	.527
C_5					1.000

Several interesting consistencies are revealed in the regression equations. First, four of the five own-cost passthroughs are close to what we would expect in a monopoly or Cournot context -- one-half the cost increment. Indeed, the values for industry 2 are exactly .5, so that the relative independence of these two firms from other than cost impacts with ceteris paribus changes in their costs or their rivals' costs, are borne out. Rivalry plays a greater role in industry 1's cost adjustments, especially in the case of firm 2, whose role as sensitive transmitter of price impulses we have established in section 1.5.

Second, all customer regression coefficients are negative, which indicates that at the second level of analysis in these industries demand effects swamp customer consonance effects. A ceteris paribus rise in a customer's cost leads to a price rise for that customer of about half the increment. The reduction in the customer's sales shifts the supplier's sales curve downward with attendant downward pressure on price. On the other hand, the shrinkage of the customer's profit margin puts an upward pressure on supplier's price via customer's consonance. The net outcome reflects the resultant of the two forces, and in all cases the downward forces prevailed. But consonance has diminished the price reductions that would have occurred in its absence.

Third, all but one of the supplier regression coefficients are negative and small (2 or 3¢). It is difficult to motivate this, since a ceteris paribus rise in an intermediate good should raise marginal cost in the same manner as a rise in own factor cost, and lead to an approximate passthrough of one half. In this respect, the p_5 supplier coefficient for firm 1's cost is in line with expectations, for a \$1 rise in C_1 should raise p_1 by \$.45, C_5 by .21 x \$.45, or \$.09, and p_5 by .50 x \$.09 = .05. The coefficient of .09 is high but within the limits of accuracy to be expected.

The high R^2 coefficients are suspect from two sources of distortion: because prices contain costs as a large component, costs are correlating with themselves in correlating with prices, and because of the intermediate good contents of costs and consequent price feedback. We can eliminate both sources if we correlate profit margins with factor costs only. By the nature of the factor cost displacements, the correlation matrix for factor costs has off-diagonal elements of .500. The regression equations are recorded in Table 5.19.

Table 5.19. REGRESSION EQUATIONS OF PROFIT MARGINS ON FACTOR COSTS

Regressand/ Regressors:	Constant	f_1	f_2	f_3	f_4	f_5	R^2	σ_s
m_1	550.59	-.54	.06	.02	-.07^s	-.01	.969	4.4
m_2	369.50	.06	-.58	.06	-.02^c	-.07	.962	3.5
m_3	507.21	.01	.05	-.53	-.07^s	-.01	.951	6.2
m_4	580.67	-.06^c	-.04^s	-.05^c	-.51	.02	1.00	.34
m_5	964.05	.03^s	-.58^c	.07	.02	-.56	.979	9.0

^{s}Supplier of row firm.
^{c}Customer of row firm.

The results show an *improvement* in R^2 in every case and are quite similar in regression coefficient structure to the price-total cost regressions of Table 5.17. By definition of profit margin the own factor cost regression coefficients of Table 5.19 should approximate the negative of the complements of the own-cost coefficients of Table 5.17, and this correspondence is closely approached.[7] The negativity of customer coefficients is preserved and the coefficient values are very close to those of Table 5.17. However, supplier coefficients become more negative (less positive in the case of firm 5): rises in supplier prices are predicted to have adverse impacts on profit margins even though price might rise. Finally, the troublesome negative coefficient in firm 3's equation for firm 1's costs has disappeared in favor of a weak rivalrous consonance effect. We must conclude, therefore, that the regression equations of Table 5.17 do in fact yield stable and real relationships, with regressor intercorrelations if they exert any distorting influence biassing supplier cost impacts downward and masking a weak positive correlation between p_3 and C_1.

As a final check of this conclusion we ran a varimax rotation on prices and costs, isolating 5 factors that exhaust all but negligible amounts of variance in the variables. We reproduce the results in Table 5.20. The prior factor analysis of prices alone in Table 5.16 can now be supplemented with the variance explained by factors that were exogeneous in the earlier table. Factor 1 now corresponds to factor 2 in Table 5.16, with C_3 being seen to be the causative factor explaining p_3's variance along with a much weaker coassociation with p_2. Factor 2 reproduces

Table 5.20. FACTOR LOADINGS, VARIMAX ROTATED FACTORS, OF PRICES AND TOTAL COST CORRELATION MATRIX

Variables /Factors	1	2	3	4	5	Cum. Frac. Expl.	σ	Disp. Index
p_1	-.254(.06)	-.887(.79)	.204(.04)	.212(.04)	.228(.05)	.98	.33	.73
p_2	-452(.20)	-.456(.21)	.366(.13)	.197(.04)	.559(.36)	.94	.12	.27
p_3	-.889(.79)	-.238(.06)	.208(.04)	.214(.05)	.217(.05)	.99	.33	.73
p_4	-.182(.03)	-.179(.03)	.210(.04)	.932(.87)	.147(.02)	.99	.38	.84
p_5	-.223(.05)	-.230(.05)	.915(.85)	.187(.03)	.114(.01)	.99	.36	.80
C_1	-.213(.05)	-.890(.79)	.233(.05)	.261(.07)	.174(.03)	.99	.33	.73
C_2	-.299(.09)	-.310(.10)	.345(.12)	.286(.08)	.781(.61)	1.0	.23	.51
C_3	-.890(.79)	-.226(.05)	.212(.04)	.258(.07)	.173(.03)	.98	.33	.73
C_4	-.261(.07)	-.264(.07)	.173(.03)	.897(.81)	.165(.02)	1.0	.34	.76
C_5	-.202(.04)	-.213(.05)	.843(.71)	.235(.06)	.362(.13)	.99	.29	.64
Fraction of Total Variance Explained	.22	.22	.21	.21	.13	.99		

factor 1 in the earlier analysis with the added own-cost association, as do factors 3, 4, and 5 respectively in both tables. None of the earlier interpretations changes, but the previously missing exogenous causal factors are now supplied.

The last two columns of Table 5.20 are measurements of the dispersion of the fractions of total variance explained by the factors over the five factors. To obtain an index of dispersion, we have simply taken the standard deviations, σ, of the row paranthesized values, and have divided each by the value of σ that would be attained if all variation were explained by one factor ($\sigma = .45$). Among the prices, those of industry 2 are seen to be most concentrated in their variation, dominantly with their respective costs and concentrated in their variation, dominantly with their respective costs and with p_4 most isolated, as we would expect from our prior analysis. Note that C_5 has important associations with p_2 via two independent factors, factors 3 and 5, which helps to account for the large regression coefficient for C_2 in the p_5 regression equations. This brings out an important point: in the regression coefficients we find the purported representations of the direct and indirect (via prices) impact of each product cost upon the relevant price. In the factor loadings of Table 5.20, however, these impacts remain separated. This must be remembered in moving from factor to regression analysis or vice versa.

Among industry 1's prices the notable feature is the dispersion of p_2's associations among factors, its role as a transmitter of impulses, and its greater degree of independence from own cost changes. On the other hand, p_1 and p_3 are much more concentrated in their associations with factors.

In the cost sector, as would be expected, the close coassociation of C_2 and C_5 via two factors keeps their dispersion indices lower than the other three costs, which are concentrated upon their own-price factors to about the same degree.

1.7. *A Summation and Conclusion of the Simulative Theorizing Example*

What are the insights given by our extensive exercise in simulative theorizing?

One most important conclusion is that price data generated by an oligopoly or cluster of oligopolies in which firms seek goals that constrain "rational" decision making can yield patterns which are difficult to disentangle. These seeming distortions are made even more puzzling when conjoined with such counteracting forces as customers' consonance and demand effects in determining price reactions. It is not easy to summarize neat laws of pricing behavior among oligopolists *even when one generates data from deductive consonance models.* To work backwards inductively from the price data generated by real world firms to the underlying structural parameters using known statistical techniques to derive such "laws of interdependent pricing" is all but impossible. *The study of realistic oligopoly must begin from deductively specified models tailored to the firms and employ simulative theorizing to permit even moderately generalizable propositions about pricing behavior.*

Industry 1 is a group of firms with moderate consonance relations among rivals and weak consonance considerations given to customers. Firm 2 -- the intermediate size firm in the industry -- is most sensitive to its rivals' prices and serves as a channel to link p_1 and p_3 indirectly to each other. The direct linkage of these two prices is not a dominant factor in the rivalrous consonance relations of the industry. All three firms benefit profitwise from such consonance, with firm 1 -- the dominant firm in terms of market share and in its greater disregard for the consequences of its decisions on rivals' profits -- the greatest absolute gainer, but with firm 2 a nearly-equal beneficiary in relative terms. Firm 3 -- the smallest firm whose sales are limited to nonindustrial customers -- benefits least in both absolute and relative terms. In the neighborhood of the base case rivalrous consonance raises prices somewhat under 1 percent, so that the effective tacit collusion it constitutes is a far less serious social ill than the basic failure of competition to lower price to maginal cost.

Industry 1's customer consonance effects are also one-sided in their beneficiary effects, each firm gaining somewhat from industry 2's deference. Firm 2 is a very large gainer on this account -- to a much greater extent than it benefits from rivalrous consonance. Most of these profit gains result from its actions to temper the price rises rivalrous consonance inspires, and hence to lessen own-profit sacrifices in a region of high own-price elasticity. Firm 2 lowers price by about 20 percent on this account, compared with 7 to 10 percent reductions for its rivals. These pure customer consonance effects tend to be swamped by demand shifts when costs change, but they continue to play their hidden role in affecting price movements.

It is these demand effects of firm 2's sales upon supplier 5's sales that provide the most effective link of industry 1 to industry 2. The latter firm is extremely sensitive to p_2, and that price's role as industry transmitter is enhanced by the impacts it exerts on p_1 and p_3 when p_5 changes. Were we antitrust policy makers, we should evince considerable interest in firm 2's conduct toward supplier 5, given its indicated leverage over that firm, and its competitive policies toward firms 1 and 3, given its strategic role as transmitter of competitive forces in the industry.

On the other hand, firm 3, about which we might appear concerned in viewing the model's specification, turns out to be quite capable of taking care of itself, even in the Cournot jungle. It is, in fact, much more vulnerable to own-cost change in profit terms than its rivals, which are about equally subject to fluctuations, but still earns considerable profit even in the face of large cost increases (Table 5.11).

Industry 2 is a weaker, more vulnerable industry, heavily dependent upon industry 1, and, perhaps, subject to potential monopsonistic pressures[8] from that industry. Customer consonance coefficients and cross-elasticities of demand both reflect this extreme dependence. The net result is large profit losses as a rival effect of the loss of sales from industry 1's price increases and reduced output. These sales reductions are enhanced slightly by the price-increasing pressures of the strong rival consonance factors industry 2 exhibits. However, customer consonance leads both firms to reduce prices substantially, enhancing firm 4's profit sacrifice and leaving firm 5's essentially unchanged. In a word, industry 2's extreme dependence upon industry 1 leads it into a position of extreme vulnerability, but most of this exposure derives from its sales curve rather than customer consonance factors.

Firm 5 reveals a reluctance born of the own-price elasticity of demand to pass through cost increases and maintain profit margins (Table 5.19). Profits decline drastically with factor cost changes, therefore, to a greater extent than firm 4's although they too are more vulnerable than any industry 1 firm (Table 5.11). Firm 4's profit susceptibility is revealed in the greatest insensitivity to cost changes of any of the five firms: our factor analyses reveal its price to be importantly related only to its own cost (Tables 5.16, 5.20). The important distinction here is p_5's great sensitivity to p_2 via its sales curve and its influence on C_2 (Table 5.20, factor 3).

Industry 2, therefore, is on a net basis somewhat disadvantaged by the consonance environment, suffering a fall in profits of 1.6 to 2 percent and reduced prices of .35 percent. The social gain is not an important one, and much of it is garnered by industry 1, of course. It is a far more socially worthwhile goal to act to encourage consonance factors to fall below 0 -- stimulation of active, price-cutting competition -- than to worry about the effects of positive rivalrous consonance's effective tacit collusion or to hope for much from the price-tempering effects of customer consonance.

2. *A SUMMARY AND CONCLUSION ABOUT SECOND-LEVEL ANALYSIS*

We have covered a great deal of ground in Chapters 4 and 5, moving from a reinterpretation of reaction functions in duopoly contexts, as well as the derivation of comparative statics propositions in models with and without binding constraints. These analyses are limited for simplicity to two-firm models, but a brief generalization to n-firm models was sketched.

In the manner of classic parameter displacement analysis, the results are disappointing in terms of meager numbers of unambiguous propositions to guide the policy maker and the restricted applicability of the few theorems derived to epsilon neighborhoods.

Certainly simulative theorizing, which we feature at length in this chapter, is not a perfect answer to these objections, and it contains limitations of its own. We will not repeat these caveats. However, we feel that its use permits deeper and most useful knowledge to be gained into the structure and functioning of oligopolies within their clusters than is attainable by any other method. Its applicability may be limited largely to specific industries and periods, but the very structure of oligopoly guarantees that all useful propositions will have -- and must have -- that quality. In these senses, the metals we work with are base but useful, the Philosophers' Stone that will convert them to imperishable and universally valid gold a vain dream.

1 In this regard we may relate the purely competitive (i.e., zero-profit) solution to rivalrous consonance. The purely competitive price solution is:

$p_1 = 668.86 \qquad p_4 = 719.32$

$p_2 = 673.17 \qquad p_5 - 1{,}315.46.$

$p_3 = 733.06$

We might isolate a "Cournot effect" on prices, defined as the Cournot solution less the purely competitive solution. This would furnish a notion of the importance of small numbers and interdependence as such, apart from tacit collusion or consonance, for prices -- a type of "inescapable" burden of oligopoly. A decomposition of the deviation of base case prices from purely competitive would then be the following:

Price	Base Case Deviation	Cournot Effect		RCE		CCE		Amount	%
		Amount	%	Amount	%	Amount	%		
p_1	+278.16	+275.06	+41.12	+3.40	+.51	-.33	-.05	+.03	---
p_2	+221.17	+217.15	+32.26	+5.23	+.78	-1.24	-.18	+.03	---
p_3	+204.76	+197.14	+26.89	+8.17	+1.11	-.59	-.05	+.04	---
p_4	+214.39	+217.63	+30.25	+.78	+.11	-4.01	-.56	-.01	---
p_5	+244.92	+250.37	+19.03	+3.46	+.26	-8.99	-.68	+.08	+.01

Note the extreme dominance of the Cournot effect, which all but exhausts the social cost of oligopoly. Indeed, in the case of industry 2, consonance reduces that cost.

2 In binary consonance factor terms, joint industry profit maximization makes $\theta_{ir} = 1$, $\theta_{ij \neq r} = 0$. Joint economy profit maximization results when $\theta_{ir} = 1$, $\theta_{ic} = 1$, $\theta_{ij} = 0$.
$j \neq r$
$j \neq c$

3 Note that this is not a case of perverse movement in the sense of Chapter 4.3, (18)-(25), since *both* firms' costs have fallen. The only cases of this Chapter 4 type of perversity occurring among rivals (Displacement numbers 22, 32, 33, and 34) involve one or more constraints binding. See Table 5.12 below.

4 More specifically, if we measure direction of movement from base case values, prices and margins moved together the following percentages of the 48 cases: firms 1, 46 percent; 2, 33 percent; 3, 48 percent; 4, 60 percent; and 5, 58 percent.

5 See also Kuenne, [27].

6 "Near", of course, because the cost contain feedbacks from prices through the intermediate good portions of marginal cost.

7 More exactly, let b_i be the own total cost coefficient and b_f the own factor cost coefficient, a_s the amount of intermediate input per unit of product and p_s its price. Then,

$$b_f = (b_c - 1)(1 + a_s \Delta p_s / \Delta f).$$

8 These would register as negative binary consonance factors.

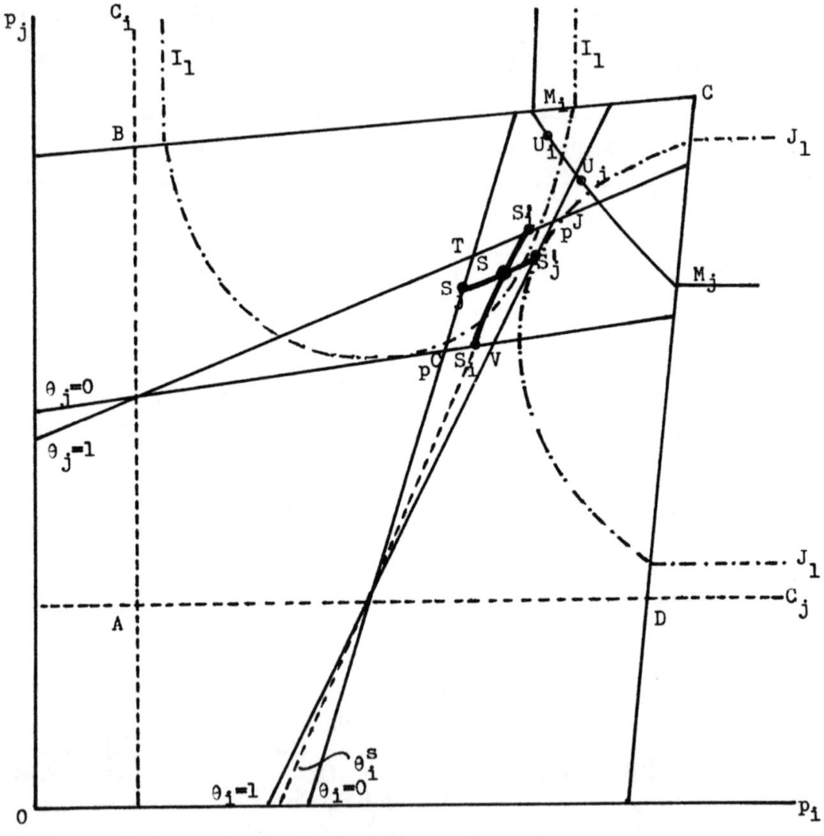

Figure 6.1. ISOPROFIT CONTOURS, REACTION FUNCTIONS, AND SOLUTION REGIONS IN DUOPOLY, WITH LONG-RUN REACTION FUNCTIONS

CHAPTER 6

RIVALROUS CONSONANCE: THEORETICAL CONSIDERATIONS AT THE THIRD LEVEL

1. *THIRD LEVEL ANALYSIS: THE ULTIMATE CHALLENGE*

At the third level of analysis using the rivalrous consonance technique we free the consonance factors and permit them to vary endogenously. In doing so we leave the world of the short- and medium-run and struggle for insights into the long-term evolution of mature oligopolies' power structures and their implications for trends in price levels and structures in the industries. Of course, ambitions must be constrained: we seek glimmerings into the forces that are set in motion by the firms' own optimization actions, but cannot hope to capture the perhaps more important exogenous changes in technology, producT substitutes, management personalities, goals or goal priorities, and so forth.

In the long-term adjustment process, we assume the endogenous movement is dominated by the own-objective component of the short-run objective function. For example, in our familiar case of extended profit maximization, we will assume that each firm will adjust its consonance factors over the long period in such manner as maximizes its own profit, subject to the assumption that rival firms follow reaction functions of the form (30) in Chapter 4.2.1 and such other constraints as the firm sees fit to impose upon itself in the long term.

Implicitly, then, we view the evolution of oligopolistic consonance structures as reflecting firms' perceived self-interests as shaped by their changing circumstances in the market. The pattern of communitarian and egoistic urges slowly alter in the solvents of success or failure, and the consonance factors gradually assume the role of tools to be manipulated in constrained and interdependent fashion for self-aggrandizement. But, in general, they remain positive in a long-term Nash equilibrium, where a sustaining long-term power structure is achieved, or would be in the absence of exogenous disturbances (most particularly, entry of new firms into the industry).

We do not capture in our simple models the rich detail of reality, with its varying successes in research and development, its technological surprises, its management triumphs and disasters, its advertising histories, and, most importantly perhaps and hardly independent of the foregoing, its new entrants. We suspect that insightful modelling of such phenomena will only be achieved with simulation enjoying ex post facto data. Our ambitions are, once more without apology, limited to partial and experimental investigation of the laws of change of industrial power structure, and ultimately their fulfillment must be sought in simulative theorizing. But before we investigate that route, some investment in the abstract will be worthwhile.

2. *DIFFERENTIATED DUOPOLY: THIRD LEVEL ANALYSIS*

2.1. *The Unconstrained Problem*

Let us analyze a differentiated duopoly with short-term reaction functions (under crippled-optimization with extended-profit objective functions)

(1) $p_i = 0.5\, b_{ii}^{-1} [(a_i + b_{ii} C_i - \theta_i b_{ji} C_j) + (b_{ij} + \theta_i b_{ji}) p_j],\ i = 1, 2,\ j \neq i,$

as developed in (3), Chapter 4.1.1. In the long run, firm i chooses p_i in such fashion as to

(2) $\text{Max } Z_i = m_i x_i$

subject to

(3) $C_i = p_j - 0.5\, b_{jj}^{-1} [(a_j + b_{jj} C_j - \theta_j b_{ij} C_i) + (b_{ji} + \theta_j b_{ij}) p_i] = 0.$

For simplicity we omit any subordinate goals the firm may have, but recognize that they probably exist and may be quite different from shorter-term goals that were sought. However, if firm j maximizes extended profits in the short-run subject to a constraint set, then (3) above will contain all of those constraints affecting firm i's long-run behavior. Very speedily, under these conditions, it is necessary to appeal to simulative theorizing techniques and we postpone that.

Performing the constrained maximization (2) - (3) with a Lagrangean form, we obtain from the first-order conditions the system

(4) $$\begin{bmatrix} 2b_{ii} & -b_{ij} & -0.5\, b_{jj}^{-1} (b_{ji} + \theta_j b_{ij}) \\ -(b_{ji} + \theta_j b_{ij}) & 2b_{jj} & 0 \\ b_{ij} & 0 & -1 \end{bmatrix} \begin{bmatrix} p_i^\circ \\ p_j^\circ \\ \lambda^\circ \end{bmatrix} = \begin{bmatrix} a_i + b_{ii} C_i \\ a_j + b_{jj} C_j - \theta_j b_{ij} C_i \\ b_{ij} C_i \end{bmatrix}$$

λ° is simply $\delta Z_i/\delta p_j$, and $[p_i^\circ, p_j^\circ]$ yields the point on firm j's reaction function that maximizes firm i's profit. This is a Stackelberg solution (modified to determine price rather than quantity) when the rival's reaction function has a rivalrous consonance component. That is, firm i simply moves along rival j's reaction function to the p_i that is tangent to its highest own-profit contour.

Let us illustrate this in Figure 6.1*, which is based upon Figure 4.1. The firms' prices are graphed on the axes, with constant marginal costs C_i and C_j depicted as dashed lines. The relevant portion of the diagram is bounded on the right by the linear function that depicts the loci of all **p** such that $x_i = 0$, and from above by the linear function of such loci such that $x_j = 0$. By insisting that both firms make nonnegative profits, we may define our price domain of initial interest as the polygon ABCD.

Within this relevant region, firm i's own-profit contours will be portions of nested ellipses, of which we have drawn one, I_1. Higher profit contours will lie inside I_1, and these ellipses will converge upon a point, M_i, on BC that represents the lowest p_j that yields maximum (i.e., monopoly) profits for firm i. Above BC the contour lines become vertical lines, including the monopoly profit contour. That is, once p_j has reached a level that reduces x_j to zero, if it goes higher it has no further impact on firm i's profits. The analysis of firm j's profit contours is wholly symmetric to that of firm i, of course, except that its ellipses will bow out from right to left, as illustrated by J_1.

Firm i's reaction functions are a family of functions defined for each value of $\theta_i \,\varepsilon\, [0,1]$, as given in slightly rearranged from by (3) of Chapter 4:

(5) $p_i^\circ = 0.5\, b_{ii}^{-1} [(a_i + b_{ii} C_i + b_{ij} p_j) + \theta_i b_{ji} m_j]\,.$

---

* See page 120 for Figure 6.1

In Figure 6.1 we have drawn only those for $\theta_i = 0$ and 1. Note that they (and all other members of the family) intersect at a common p_i on the line C_j; clearly, from (5) when $p_j = C_j$, the consonance term disappears, and the value is a common $p_i = (0.5/b_{ii})(a_i + b_{ii} C_i + b_{ij} C_j)$. A similar analysis holds true for firm j's reaction functions.

Now, suppose $\theta_j = 1$ and firm i follows a Stackelberg strategy. It will move along the relevant reaction function for $\theta_j = 1$ on Figure 6.1 until it finds the p_i that is tangent to the highest I-contour it can attain, say at S_i' on the diagram. *But in terms of rivalrous consonance power structure, this is equivalent to finding a value θ_i such that the reaction function drawn for it intersects the $\theta_j' = 1$ function at S_i', say θ_i^s on Figure 6.1.*[1] In this we move beyond Stackelberg who was bound to only two potential reaction functions -- those for $\theta_i = \theta_j = 0$. Both in the short-run and the long-run rivalrous consonance permits us to study oligopolistic pricing in market structures characterized by a variety of power structures besides the Cournot structure. At the other extreme, for example, is the case where $\theta_i = \theta_j = 1$, which yields the joint profit maximizing solution (the Chamberlin case), as shown at $\mathbf{p}^J$ on Figure 6.1. Since we allow θ_i and θ_j to take any values in the unit square, all short- and long-run industry price equilibria will occur within the polygonal area $\mathbf{p}^C T \mathbf{p}^J V$, and it may be called the *relevant solution domain* for mature oligopolies.

S_i', therefore, will be within this domain, where a reaction function for firm i intersects the boundary $T\mathbf{p}^J$. Given θ_j (=1 in our example), the Stackelberg $\mathbf{p}^\circ$ yielded by (4) when substituted will yield θ_i^1, which defines the reaction function that intersects $T\mathbf{p}^J$ at S_i', as required.

Effectively, firm i has changed its rivalrous consonance factor to accommodate its long-term interest in own-profits. As in the short-run analysis of rivalrous consonance, we do not assert that the firm consciously changes θ_i in an explicit profit maximization. Rather, a whole series of informal and implicit changes will occur as firm i senses firm j's reactions to its pricing experiments, moves to a new price structure that effectively alters its perceived power structure.

But, in similar vein, firm j will now informally sense that firm i's reaction has changed to that defined for θ_i^1, and will seek to

$$(6) \qquad \text{Max } Z_j = m_j (a_j - b_{jj} p_j + b_{ji} p_i)$$

subject to

$$(7) \qquad G_j = p_i - 0.5\, b_{ii}^{-1} [(a_i + b_{ii} C_i - \theta_i^1 b_{ji} C_j) + (b_{ij} + \theta_i^1 b_{ji})\, p_j] = 0\,.$$

This will define a $\mathbf{p}$ lying on firm i's reaction function for θ_i^1 at which firm j's profit is maximized. This is effectively a point on a new firm j reaction function, defined for θ_j^1, that intersects firm i's θ_i^1 function at the new solution.

However, firm i will now maximize Z_i taking firm j's new reaction function as given, to obtain a θ_i^2, and so forth. To see the end of this iterative process, let us allow θ_j to take all values in the interval [0,1] and determine the optimal θ_i from (2) - (3) (and (4)). The locus of intersections of the relevant θ_i reaction functions with the family of firm j functions will be the curve $S_i S_i'$ on Figure 6.1.[2] Similarly, if θ_i takes all values in the unit interval and relevant θ_j^k reaction functions are determined from (6) - (7), the locus $S_j S_j$ is determined. The functions $S_i S_i'$ and $S_j S_j'$ are the *long-term reactions functions* for the firms when sufficient time is allowed to permit power structure adjustments, set in train by own-profit opportunities, to elapse. They will intersect at the *generalized Stackelberg point*, *S*, where a Nash equilibrium leads both firms to accept the status quo.

This long-run price pair, $[p_i^s, p_j^s]$, has some claim to attention in a rivalrous consonance framework as an equilibrium. Within the short-run feasibility region for mature oligopolistic pricing, as defined by $\mathbf{p}^C T \mathbf{p}^J V$, some equilibrium price pair $[p_i^s, p_j^s]$ will exist toward which the internal dynamics of the industry's power structure will impel the firms. The tensions that exist in a rivalrous consonance framework between narrow self interest and communitarian stability exert forces that evolve new power structures until a long-run stability emerges. Once reached, the new power structure satisfies both the short-run and the long-term drives of the rivals, and must be disturbed by exogenous events.[3]

Beyond S lies only the path of collusion. Consider the curve M_iM_j, which is the locus of points of tangency between I- and J-contours -- the "negotiation set". Such points, therefore, denote the maximum profit firm i can make for any given profit of firm j, and vice versa. The end point M_i is firm i's monopoly contour's intersection with BC, the zero profit line for firm j, and thus is the maximum profit attainable by firm i given firm j's profits are zero. At the opposite end M_j has similar meaning. The Chamberlin solution -- $\mathbf{p}^J$ -- lies on the line and is the maximum joint profit attainable.

A firm i wholly under the spur of self advantage will attempt to get as close to M_i on the negotiation curve as it can, and firm j as close to M_j as possible. Thus, if we permit collusion it is necessary to add the negotiation curve M_iM_j to the feasibility region $\mathbf{p}^C T \mathbf{p}^J V$. We do so reluctantly, for, as we noted in Chapter 1, it is difficult to find cases of such game-theoretical behavior among mature oligopolies. But to that literature we can contribute a narrowing of the size of the effective negotiating set through the use of the generalized Stackelberg point, S.

A firm need never settle for a smaller own-profit than that given by its profit contour through S. On Figure 6.1 suppose that the I-contour that passes through S (not drawn) intersects M_iM_j at U_i. Then, firm i's lower bound on negotiating is its profit at this point. It also denotes, therefore, the upper bound on firm j's profits, for the J contour tangent to firm i's lower bound contour at U_i is as close to M_j on M_iM_j as firm i can get. In similar fashion let U_j be the intersection of firm j's S-contour with M_iM_j, and it may be interpreted as firm j's lower bound and firm i's upper bound on profits. Thus, the negotiation set can be limited to the U_iU_j segment of M_iM_j on the basis of the Stackelberg point S.

If we ignore the possibility of such negotiated solutions, it is possible to pare the feasible solution region in the long run. The line S_iS_i' shows the optimal θ_i for any given θ_j, hence in the long run it will never serve firm i's selfish purposes to adopt a θ_i less than that of the reaction function that intersects the reaction function for $\theta_j = 0$ at S_i. Similarly, S_j sets a lower bound on θ_j. If a short-run equilibrium is reached at $\mathbf{p}^\circ$ for $\theta = [0,0]$, it will profit both firms to increase their θ factors until S is reached, at which point both firms lose from uncoordinated moves.

The existence of an interval in which a $\theta_i > 0$ increases firm j's profits for a given θ_j occurs for the following reason. As θ_i rises, θ_j constant, p_i and p_j both rise. As p_i rises in the inelastic portion of the firm i's sales function, its profits grow, and p_j's rise shifts firm i's sales curve outward to enhance the growth. At the relevant Stackelberg point the reduction in profit brought about by the rise in p_i in the elastic portion of the curve is just balanced by the increase in profits caused by the induced sales increase springing from the induced rise in p_j. Beyond this point a further rise in θ_i benefits firm j's profits but harms firm i's, and rivalrous consonance begins in earnest.

Hence, the reduced region of high probability for *short-run* solutions is $SS_i'\mathbf{p}^J S_j'$. For a given θ_j which intersects this set, firm i is led to adopt a θ_i that drives the long-term solution leftward towards S_iS_i' and thereby reduces firm j's profits. Similarly, improving moves by firm j for given firm i reaction functions push solutions downward and lower profits for firm i. Therefore, noncollusive movements in this region cannot benefit both rivals, and duopolistic struggle should drive the solution into this sector. It is in this region that the doctrine of rivalrous consonance has meaning, because only for such solutions need a compromise of profits be truly sought.

In a mature duopoly, therefore, where short-term strategies are being set under rivalrous consonance, but are continuously altered as self-interest leads to experimentation with the power structure over the long term, an inner competitive dynamic is active to compete prices down to levels that can be sustained by a viable power structure. At that generalized Stackelberg price solution each rival extends that degree of consideration to the other's profits that is consistent with its own profit maximum, given the other's similarly motivated consideration.

The generalized Stackelberg point lies at the intersection of the *long-run reaction functions* under rivalrous consonance, which are drawn as S_iS_i' and S_jS_j' in Figure 6.1. They are third-level analytical functions that reflect the variability of θ. That variability captures the changes in communal relations that are set in motion by self-interest within the context of market relations.

2.2. *Multiple Objectives and Constraints*

The impact of the introduction of constraint sets on short-run reactions was analyzed in Chapter 4.2. In the long run, of course, these constraint sets may be quite different in content. Market share goals may be dropped as profit motives become stronger. Price change bounds may be widened or removed. Capacity should no longer be limitational. On the other hand, the constraint sets may contain a larger "communitarian" bearing than their short-run counterparts. As the primary goal -- captured in the objective function -- becomes more own-profit oriented, the self-imposed limitations on egoistic behavior in the interests of long-run industry stability may best be introduced in the constraint sets. For example, own-profit upper bounds may be set; or upper bounds on price may be imposed to deter the entry of new firms, perhaps to protect weaker rivals; or a lower bound on the consonance factor may be set to protect the rival.

Such constraints, of course, form a constraint set, to which is added the rival's short term reaction function, and own-profits are maximized subject to it. For example, for firm i, the model, if it contained all constraints suggested, would be

(8) $\text{Max } Z_i = m_i x_i$

subject to

(9)
1. $p_j - 0.5\, b_{jj}\, [(a_j + b_{jj} C_j - \theta_j b_{ij} C_i) + (b_{ji} + \theta_j b_{ij})\, p_i] = 0$
2. $m_i x_i - L_i^+ \leq 0$
3. $p_i - T_i^+ \leq 0$
4. $L_i^- - \theta_i = L_i^- - (b_{ii} m_i - x_i)/b_{ji} m_j \leq 0$
5. $x_i - a_i + b_{ii} p_i - b_{jj} p_j = 0$
6. $p_i, p_j \geq 0$.

Together with an analogous model for firm j, the long-run rivalrous consonance system is complete, and may be solved by the crippled optimization techniques discussed in Chapter 3 and employed in Chapter 4. Using exterior penalty function techniques, SUMT is capable of solving problems with constraint sets containing both inequalities and equalities.[4]

If (8) and (9) are solved independently of firm j's model, and θ_j is moved parametrically in the interval [0,1], firm i's long-run reaction function is derived. The manner in which each of constraints 9-2--9-4 will affect its shape if they bind separately is shown in Figure 6.2. If (8) and (9) are solved jointly with firm j's analogous model, the iterative solutions will converge on the generalized Stackelberg point.

2.3. *Mathematical Properties*

The Stackelberg problem (2)-(3) is a constrained maximum that seeks firm i's maximum own-profit subject to p_i and p_j lying on firm j's reaction function. Second-order sufficient conditions for a local maximum are that the determinant of the bordered Hessian

$$(10)\qquad \mathbf{H} = \begin{bmatrix} 0 & (b_{ji} + \theta_j b_{ij}) & -2b_{jj} \\ (b_{ji} + \theta_j b_{ij}) & -2b_{ii} & b_{ij} \\ -2b_{jj} & b_{ij} & 0 \end{bmatrix}$$

be positive; that is, that

$$(11)\qquad 2b_{ii} b_{jj} > b_{ij} (b_{ji} + \theta_j b_{ij}).$$

Where own-price elasticities are stronger than other-price elasticities, we expect this condition to hold for all $\theta_j \varepsilon[0,1]$, and henceforth will assume it true.[5] Thus, even though the isoprofit contours of Figure 6.1 may not be everywhere jointly concave in **p**, a local profit maximum for firm i will be attained where the isoprofit contours are tangent to a reaction function for firm j, as they are at generalized Stackelberg optima.

When the constraint set is expanded to include inequalities in the recognition of other objectives, the problem may well become a nonconvex programming model. The firm j reaction curve equality constraint limits any feasibility region to that linear function. The danger is that constraint functions that are not convex functions (in our maximization problem) may result in a feasible region that is not connected, hence, not convex. That is, the feasible region *may* be disconnected segments of the firm j reaction function. When the inequality constraint functions are convex, of course, the problem does not arise.

In the illustrative model (8) - (9), the profit constraint (9.2) is the problem, because firm i's own-profit function is not concave in p_i and p_j. This may be seen from its unbordered Hessian which is obtaining by eliminating the first row and column of **H** in (10). Considering only this own-profit constraint and firm j's reaction function constraint, Figure 6.3 illustrates the nature of the difficulty. The isoprofit contour drawn is the upper bound on firm i's profit that is permitted, L_i^+, and R_j is firm j's reaction function. The feasible region, therefore, consists of those portions of R_j that intersect lower isoprofit contours than L_i^+, or the disconnected linear segments F^1 and F^2. The optimal solutions in this cut-down problem lie either at $\mathbf{p}^1$ or $\mathbf{p}^2$, although in the larger problem other constraints might eliminate one or both of them from the optimal set. Because both (9.3) and (9.4) are linear in p_i and p_j, their lower contour sets are convex and hence their intersection with (9.1) will be convex. Of course, in all of the modelling we assume that the feasible region is not empty.

In general, therefore, rivalrous consonance modelling must confront the likelihood of nonconvex programming modelling at the third level, as a reflection of the realistic decision making of mature oligopolies. Local optima in such cases are the best that can be hoped for, but the justification for the modelling is by now familar: reality does not conform to the analytical convenience of the economist, nor does it

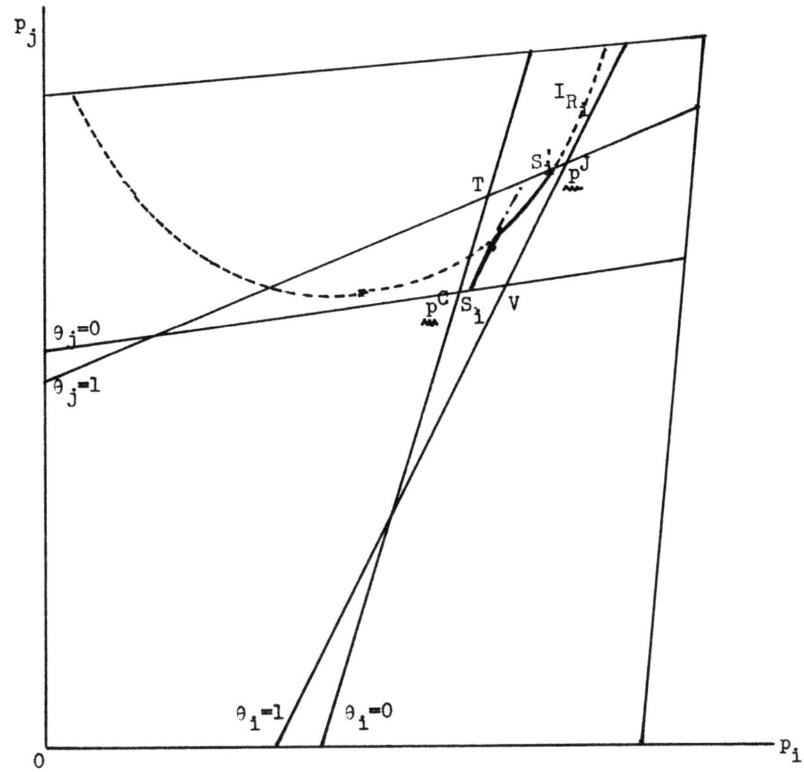

Figure 6.2. FIRM i's LONG-RUN REACTION FUNCTION WITH SEPARATE CONSTRAINTS BINDING

a. Profit Constraint Binds

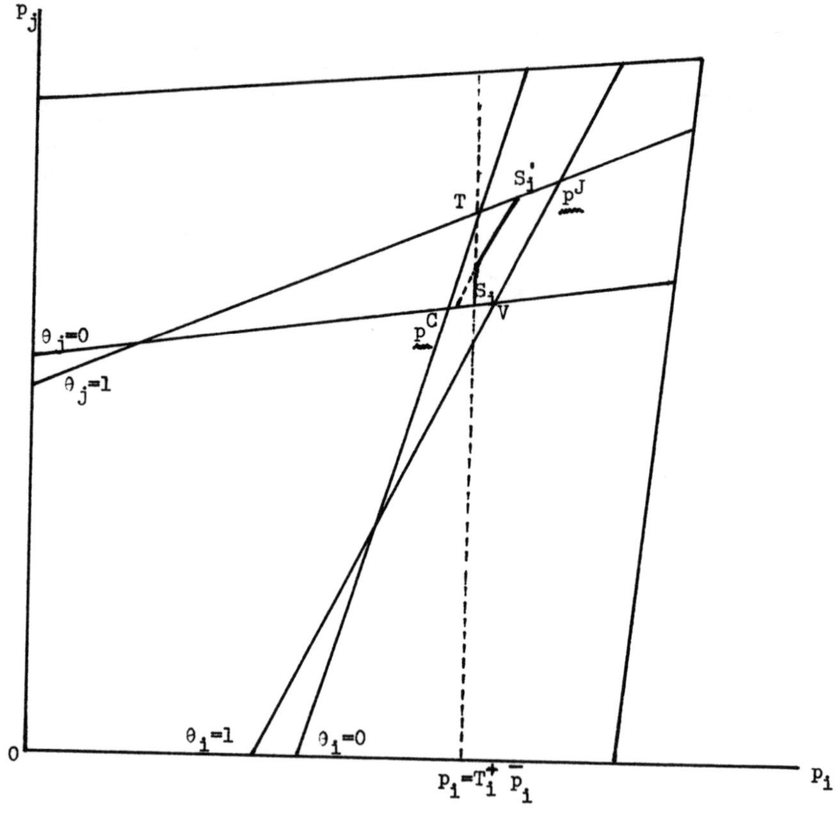

Figure 6.2. FIRM i's LONG-RUN REACTION FUNCTION WITH SEPARATE CONSTRAINTS BINDING

b. Price Constraint Binds

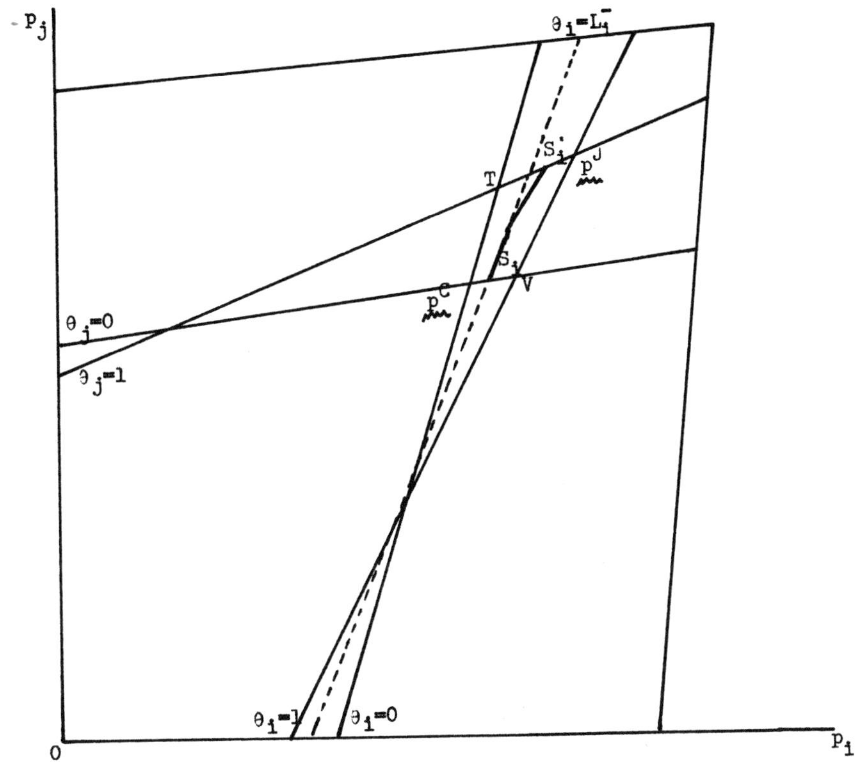

Figure 6.2. FIRM i's LONG-RUN REACTION FUNCTION WITH SEPARATE CONSTRAINTS BINDING

c. Consonance Factor Constraint Binds

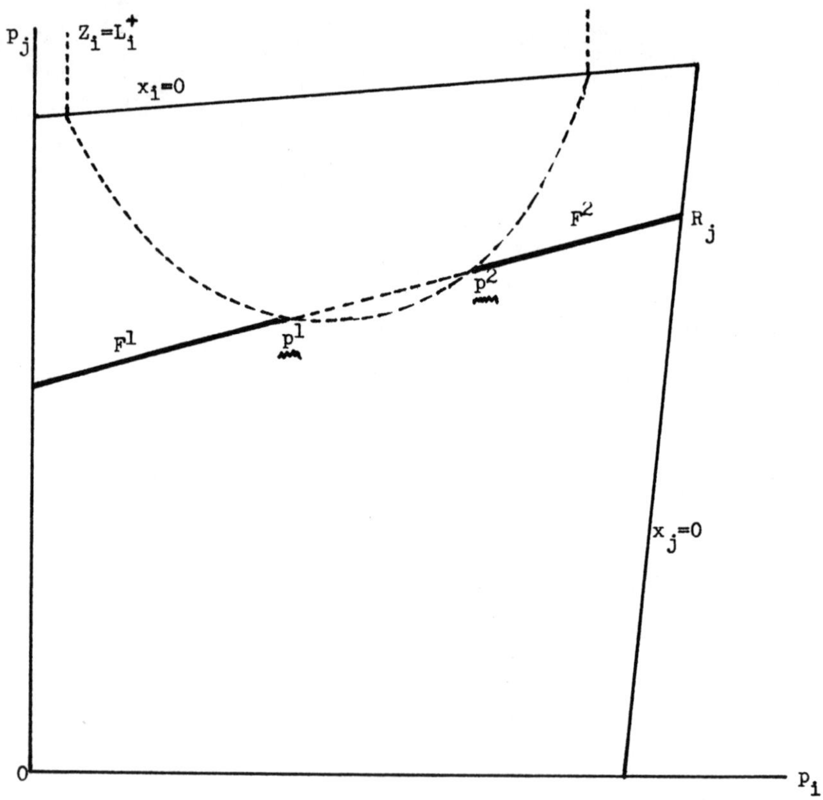

Figure 6.3. A DISCONNECTED FEASIBLE REGION

guarantee the oligopolistic decision maker a global constrained optimum even when he may be actively seeking it.

Classic displacement analysis of the unconstrained generalized Stackelberg problem yields

$$d\theta_i/d\theta_j = (2b_{ij}\, b_{ii}\, m_i)/(2b_{ii}\, b_{jj} - b_{ij}\,(b_{ji} + \theta_j\, b_{ij}))\, m_j \tag{12}$$

which, given positive profit margins and the sufficient condition (11), will be positive. Hence, the positive sloped S_iS_i' long-run reaction function of Figure 6.1, and, by extension, the positively-sloped S_jS_j'. Also, of course, $dp_i/d\theta_j > 0$ is implied by the same conditions. Finally, $d^2\theta_i/d\theta_j^2 < 0$, making S_iS_i' a concave function as drawn.

3. *DIFFERENTIATED OLIGOPOLY: THIRD-LEVEL ANALYSIS*

3.1. *The Theoretical Basis*

The generalization of the duopoly rivalrous consonance model to n rivals was done in Chapter 4.2 and for the unconstrained model the reaction function was shown to generalize to

$$p_i = 0.5\, b_{ii}^{-1}\,[\sum_{j\neq i}(b_{ij} + \theta_{ij}\, b_{ji})\, p_j + (a_i + b_{ii}\, C_i - \sum_{j\neq i}\theta_{ij}\, b_{ji}\, C_j)], \quad i = 1, 2, \ldots, n. \tag{13}$$

Hence, the generalized Stackelberg problem for the oligopolisitic industry is, for firm i,

$$\text{Max } Z_i = x_i\, m_i \tag{14}$$

subject to

$$G_k = p_k - 0.5\, b_{kk}^{-1}\,[\sum_{j\neq k}(b_{kj} + \theta_{kj}\, b_{jk})\, p_j + (a_k + b_{kk}\, C_k - \sum_{j\neq k}\theta_{kj}\, b_{jk}\, C_j)] = 0, \quad k = 1, 2, i\text{-}1, i+1, \ldots, n \tag{15}$$

$$\mathbf{p}_i \geq 0\,, \tag{16}$$

where the subscript i identifies the price vector as relevant to firm i's optimum. The solution defines a $\mathbf{p}_i^o$ lying on rivals' reaction functions for their given θ_{kj}.

If $\mathbf{p}_i^o$ be substituted in (13), we derive

$$\sum_{j\neq i} b_{ji}\, m_j^o\, \overset{1}{\theta}_{ij} = b_{ii}\, m_i^o - x_i^o\,, \qquad \overset{1}{\theta}_{ij}\,\varepsilon\,[0,1]\,. \tag{17}$$

Thus, in the n-rival case, unlike duopoly, a unique $\overset{1}{\theta}_i$ cannot be associated with firm i's multifirm generalized Stackelberg solution. In Chapter 7 we will address the problem of determining the consonance factors, but we anticipate that treatment to assert -- in extension of the discussion in Chapter 1 -- that this is consistent with our theory. The *structure* of an oligopolistic industry's rivalrous consonance is determined by a host of largely industry-specific factors that are not captured by narrow, own-profit maximization, and will not be changed wholly by it. However, what we do expect to be altered in the long-run by selfish profit considerations is the firm's *overall* willingness to accommodate itself to the *group* of rivals it faces.

Consider the initial θ_i. We may define the *structure* of the firm's rivalrous consonance by computing firm i's *aggregate consonance factor*,

$$\theta_i = \sum_{j \neq i} \theta_{ij} ,$$

and determining

$$k_{ij} = \theta_{ij}/\theta_i .$$

The vector $\mathbf{k}_i$ specifies the structure of firm i's rivalrous consonance whose determinants will be discussed in Chapter 7. For the present we will assume that this structure is fixed in the long-run, and that only θ_i is changed as a firm seeks to alter its own-profit advantage. Hence, we assume that (17) may be written

$$(18) \qquad \overset{1}{\theta_i} = (b_{ii}\, m_i - x_i^{\circ})/(\sum_{j \neq i} b_{ji}\, m_j^{\circ} k_{ij}) ,$$

so that only the aggregate consonance factor is changed in the present modelling, its structure remaining constant.

Successive iterative solution of (14) and (15) for each rival will converge to the generalized Stackelberg price vector, $\mathbf{p}^S$, with associated aggregate consonance factors, θ_i, i = 1, 2, . . ., n, which, with the fixed power structures, define the long-run binary consonance factors. If the solution variables affect the determinants of the structures of the consonance coefficients, those are recalculated in preparation for the short-run solutions of Chapters 2-5. This feedback is considered in Chapter 7's treatment of the determination of rivalrous consonance structures.

The generalization of the second-order sufficient condition of (10) to industries with n > 2 yields complicated expressions for evaluation that require numerical specification. The bordered Hessian for firm i's Stackelberg optimum with n firms in the industry may be written

$$(19) \qquad \mathbf{H} = \begin{bmatrix} \mathbf{0} & \mathbf{L}_{jk}^{*} \\ \mathbf{L}_{jk}^{*} & \mathbf{L}_{ij} \end{bmatrix}, \qquad \begin{array}{l} j \neq i , \\ k = 1, 2, \ldots, n , \end{array}$$

where:

- $\mathbf{0}$ is an n-1 x n-1 null matrix;
- $\mathbf{L}_{jk}^{*}$ is an n-1 x n matrix, with each row the gradient vector of a rival j's reaction function, with elements $(b_{jk} + \theta_{jk}\, b_{kj})$ for $k \neq j$, $-2b_{jj}$ otherwise;
- $\mathbf{L}_{ij}$ is an n x n Hessian with zeroes everywhere but in the ith row and column. In the ith row the elements for $k \neq i$ are b_{ik}, and for k = i, $-2b_{ii}$. The ith column is the transpose of this vector.

The necessary and sufficient condition for $\mathbf{L}_{ij}$ to be negative definite for dp_k satisfying the n-1 reaction function constraints is that the determinant of the bordered Hessian in (19) have the sign $(-1)^n$. This, in turn, is a second-order sufficient condition for firm i to reach a local constrained profit maximum.

3.2. *A Simulative Theorizing Analysis*

Even without the addition of constraint sets of the type (9-2,3,4), long-run reaction functions for realistically-sized oligopoly industries or industry groups become too complex for analytical solution. Therefore, a resort to simulative theorizing becomes imperative in order to determine such functions and the generalized Stackelberg solution toward which the industry or industries may be drawn in the long run.

We shall apply such methods to the case of Chapter 5's two-industry example whose short-run structural implications were analyzed at great length in that chapter. It will be assumed that in the long run firms do not adopt the short-run constraint sets used there, and, for the purposes of this analysis we will assume no long-term replacement constraints are adopted. Hence, the question is posed: if the two industries retain the demand and cost functions and the consonance factors of Table 5.1 and start from the base case solution of Table 5.2, what would be the generalized Stackelberg solution at their intersection? What aggregate consonance factors would be implied by this long-run solution?

Table 6.1 translates the base case θ_{ij} into their equivalent $k_{ij}\,\theta_i$ forms for long-run analysis. The short-run reaction functions will *variable* aggregate consonance factors are reproduced in Table 6.2 along with the aggregate consonance factors.

Table 6.1. AGGREGATE CONSONANCE FACTORS, θ_i, AND STRUCTURAL COEFFICIENTS, k_{ij}, BASE CASE

Firm	θ_{ij}					θ_i	k_{ij}				
	1	2	3	4	5		1	2	3	4	5
1	---	.09	.07	0	.03	.19	--	.47	.37	0	.16
2	.13	---	.14	.08	0	.35	.37	---	.40	.23	0
3	.15	.15	---	0	0	.30	.50	.50	---	0	0
4	.07	0	.05	---	.17	.29	.24	0	.17	---	.59
5	0	.10	0	.19	---	.29	0	.34	0	.66	---

3.2.1 *The Stackelberg Solution.* In Table 6.3 we state the generalized Stackelberg solution and compare it with the base case and three relevant structural solutions: the Cournot case, reflecting a zero level of rivalrous consonance; the joint profit maximization solution on a narrow own-industry basis, in which all rival θ_{ij} are unity but all customer θ_{ij} are zero; and the joint profit maximization solution involving both industries on a limited basis where all θ_{ij} for rivals and customers are unity. These structural cases provide lower and upper bounds on plausible long-term consonance and help to give perspective to the intermediate Stackelberg solution. The base case provides the starting point for the long-term Stackelberg process.

The relationship revealed in the analysis of Chapter 5 between industries 1 and 2 is also manifested in the longer run. Although the Stackelberg process is more egoistically driven, in general consonance relations are enhanced, and industry 2 profits suffer slightly as the role of consonance increases in the setting of prices. Compared with the base case, industry 2's profits decline 2.5 percent while industry

Table 6.2. SHORT-RUN REACTION FUNCTIONS AND AGGREGATE FACTORS, INDUSTRY 1 AND 2

1. Reaction Functions

1. $p_1 = (77{,}927.5\text{-}4{,}870.5592\theta_1 + (6.25+5.65687\theta_1)\, p_2+(9.62+2.99644\theta_1)\, p_3+ (11.056 - .74386\theta_1)\, p_4 - (2.50+.51925\theta_1)\, p_5)/(104.76+.19891\theta_1)$

2. $p_2 = (55{,}712.42\text{-}4{,}771.2709\theta_2+(10.98+2.51306\theta_2)\, p_1+(11.49+3.7547\theta_2)\, p_3 - (3.19\text{-}.23778\theta_2)\, p_4+(15.0763\text{-}.07015\theta_2)\, p_5)/(109.38+.14444\theta_2)$

3. $p_3 = (53{,}959.00\text{-}4{,}352.16\theta_3+(8.38+4.81\theta_3)\, p_1+(8.99+5.745\theta_3)\, p_2+(8.82\text{-}.962\theta_3)\, p_4 - (1.55115\theta_3)\, p_5)/84.00$

4. $p_4 = (63{,}979.76\text{-}5{,}460.6795\theta_4\text{-}(8.72\text{-}2.01231\theta_4)\, p_1+(6.328\text{-}.62094\theta_4)\, p_2\text{-}(6.90\text{-}1.03764\theta_4)\, p_3+(3.05+1.7484\theta_4)\, p_5)/(63.76+.05568\theta_4)$

5. $p_5 = (39{,}853.00\text{-}4{,}863.861\theta_5+(5.4632\text{-}1.00796\theta_5)\, p_1 - (14.77\text{-}4.92464\theta_5)\, p_2+(3.10\text{-}1.05478\theta_5)\, p_3+(2.76+2.30584\theta_5)\, p_4)/(23.84+.05692\theta_5)$

2. Aggregate Consonance Factor Functions

1. $\theta_1 = (77{,}927.5\text{-}104.76p_1+6.25p_2+9.62p_3+11.056p_4\text{-}2.50p_5)/(4{,}870.5592+.19891p_1\text{-}5.65687p_2\text{-}2.99644p_3+.74386p_4+.51925p_5)$

2. $\theta_2 = (55{,}712.42+10.98p_1\text{-}109.38p_2+11.49p_3+15.0763p_5)/(4{,}771.2709\text{-}2.51306p_1+.14444p_2\text{-}3.7547p_3\text{-}.23778p_4+.07015p_5)$

3. $\theta_3 = (53{,}959.00+8.38p_1+8.99p_2\text{-}84.00p_3+8.82p_4)/(4{,}352.16\text{-}4.81p_1\text{-}5.745p_2+.962p_4+1.55115p_5)$

4. $\theta_4 = (63{,}979.76\text{-}8.72p_1+6.328p_2\text{-}6.90p_3\text{-}63.76p_4+3.05p_5)/(5{,}460.6795\text{-}2.01231p_1+.62094p_2\text{-}1.03764p_3+.05568p_4\text{-}1.7484p_5)$

5. $\theta_5 = (39{,}853.00+5.4632p_1\text{-}14.77p_2+3.10p_3+2.76p_4\text{-}23.84p_5)/(4{,}863.861+1.00796p_1\text{-}4.92464p_2+1.05478p_3\text{-}2.30584p_4+.05692p_5)$

1's rise 1.2 percent. Nonetheless, industry 2's profits are higher than they would be in either of the two upper bound cases, in which either its welfare is sacrified to that of industry 1's or that industry's prices rise so high as to reduce its sales and therefore industry 2's intermediate sales to very low levels. The lesson is most starkly revealed in the Cournot solution: industry 2 does best when (1) it is not forced to consider industry 1's profits in its decision making, and (2) the enhanced competitiveness reduces industry 1's prices and increases its sales.

Of course, industry 1 offers the mirror image, benefiting from the lessened competition among its rivals and the vassalage of its suppliers that consonance brings. The Stackelberg solution enhances its profits above the base case and Cournot case, but they remain below the upper bounds. It benefits firm by firm as industry 2 loses, firm by firm, by moving from base case to the Stackelberg solution.

At first appearance this may be somewhat paradoxical because the aggregate consonance factors rise substantially for firms 1 and 2 and it declines only slightly for firm 3. Because larger consonance coefficients are associated with altruistic urges in the industry, this appears counterintuitive. However, the theory of section 2.1 suggest a region of the solution domain where rises in θ_i will benefit all rivals. Moreover, as the analysis of Chapter 5 revealed, rivalrous consonance in this

Table 6.3. GENERALIZED STACKELBERG, BASE CASE, AND STRUCTURAL SOLUTIONS

Variable	Base Case	Cournot	Joint Profit-- Both Industries	Joint Profit-- Own Industry	Stackelberg
p_1	947.02	943.92	966.43	990.66	952.77
p_2	894.34	890.32	903.15	938.09	903.15
p_3	937.82	930.20	976.29	998.42	938.90
p_4	933.71	936.95	870.35	938.65	933.59
p_5	1,560.38	1,565.83	1,456.78	1,580.80	1,550.63
π_1	2,841,027	2,807,833	3,129,675	2,945,366	2,859,773
π_2	1,254,036	1,223,003	1,617,399	1,326,228	1,278,507
π_3	974,854	963,245	1,000,224	946,628	994,790
π_4	1,204,744	1,223,718	968,283	1,062,405	1,187,798
π_5	433,688	442,217	270,540	349,327	409,284
z_1	12,075	12,127	11,706	10,598	11,864
z_2	8,019	8,178	8,432	6,862	7,680
z_3	6,103	6,361	4,729	4,317	6,135
z_4	6,266	6,246	7,563	5,509	4,729
z_5	2,325	2,296	3,432	1,766	2,231
M_1	.46	.45	.47	.49	.47
M_2	.31	.31	.34	.32	.30
M_3	.23	.24	.19	.08	.23
M_4	.73	.73	.69	.76	.68
M_5	.27	.27	.31	.24	.32
θ_1	.19	0	5	2	.56
θ_2	.35	0	5	2	1.27
θ_3	.30	0	2	2	.27
θ_4	.29	0	3	1	.24
θ_5	.29	0	2	1	.79

Table 6.3. GENERALIZED STACKELBERG, BASE CASE, AND STRUCTURAL SOLUTIONS

K	1	2	2	2	5
1	--	.26	.21	0	.09
2	.47	--	.51	.29	0
3	.14	.14	--	0	0
4	.06	0	.04	--	.14
5	0	.27	0	.52	--

particular situation is strongly associated with tacit collusion among industry 1 rivals.

In industry 2, firm 5 raises its consonance factor substantially above base case levels in attaining the Stackelberg solution, but firm 4 reduces its moderately. Firm 5 is much more dependent on its customer, firm 2, than firm 4 is upon firms 1 and 3. Since firm 2 raises its price and profit margin substantially, firm 5 is forced to enhance the degree of customer consonance extended it. From Table 6.2, the expression for θ_5 reveals that the sign of $d\theta_5/dp_2$ is opposite in sign to the denominator of that expression, which is strongly positive for all five solutions given in Table 6.3. Therefore, p_2 falls to raise θ_5.

It is interesting to see that the Stackelberg solution leads to prices that are far short of those that would be established under own-industry profit maximization. The enhanced tacit collusion reflected in the general enhanced consonance that characterizes the Stackelberg solution is distinctly less than "perfect" collusion would imply, as would be expected in the end result of a process where own-profit egoism is given a greater role.

4. *CONCLUSION*

In this chapter we have completed the purely theoretical development of rival consonance analysis by developing the third level of analysis that permits the aggregate consonance factors to vary over the long run in response to own-profit seeking, with or without a subordinate goal constraint set. We have shown that there exists at least one Nash equilibrium -- a generalized Stackelberg point -- at which firms in the long run are simultaneously maximizing own- and extended profits. This point has an interest as a point of long-run attraction to oligopolistic rivals under conditions of fixed relative power structure among the rivals and customers, but in which the *general* willingness to extend consideration to competitors' and customers' profits (i.e., the aggregate consonance factors) may vary.

There remains one task in this initial presentation of rivalrous consonance theory which is of an impirical nature. It is the confrontation of the difficult task of isolating firms' aggregate consonance factors and industries' power structures. We will consider it in Chapter 7.

1 At this point we depart from Stackelberg, in whose analyses firm i did not have a reaction function.

2 It is a tedious but conceptually simple task to demonstrate that for any $\theta_j \varepsilon [0,1]$, the Stackelberg p_i will lie between the p_i defined by the intersection of the firm j reaction function for θ_j and firm i's reaction function for $\theta_i = 0$ (as a lower bound) and $\theta_i = 1$ (as an upper bound). The two p_i^θ values determined by these intersections are given in Chapter 4, (9), and the Stackelberg p_i is given by (4) above. A comparison reveals the intermediate nature of the latter, as drawn in Figure 6.1.

3 By Brouwer's Fixed Point Theorem, at least one equilibrium pair $[p_i^S, p_j^S]$ will exist. From Figure 6.1, pi and p_j are clearly bounded by the region $\mathbf{p}^C T \mathbf{p}^J V$, which is a convex set for linear reaction functions. From (4) and its counterpart for firm j functions can be defined that map $[p_i, p_j]$ into itself. Those functions are continuous and defined over the closed, bounded and convex set defined above. Hence, at least one $\mathbf{p}^\circ$ must exist that maps into itself -- a fixed point in the mapping that is S on Figure 6.1.

4 See Fiacco and McCormick, [11], pp. 59-71, 102-110.

5 This is a stronger assumption than follows from the concavity assumption in (6) of Chapter 4.1.

CHAPTER 7

ISOLATING THE POWER STRUCTURE OF AN OLIGOPOLY

In previous chapters we have assumed the existence of a power structure or, more broadly, a web of live-and-let-live considerations extended by oligopolistic firms to rivals and customers in their decision making. The motivation for such conditioning of firms' strategies ranges from the pure egoistic fear of retribution to the pure altruism of communitarianism. The sociology of a mature oligopolistic industry simply cannot be adequately explained in the economist's conventional framework of a search for egoistic advantage even when this is altered by the incorporation of mutual interdependence. In the short-run, at least, the desire for a stable, peaceful, and predictable industry price structure may be a closer approximation to realistic goals than the ceaseless struggle for profit improvement of conventional oligopoly theory. Even in the long-run, when own-profit search may become a predominant goal, its accommodation within a rivalrous framework will require a de facto consonance structure.

One implication of this adoption of the rivalrous consonance framework is that the economist should devote more attention to the work of the sociologist and social psychologist, who have developed frameworks for analyzing social interaction. It is difficult to understand how a deeper and more sophisticated analysis of interfirm relationships can be developed if the insights from these fields continue to be ignored by the theorist in a short-sighted allegiance to simple behavioral assumptions in pursuit of an universal theory of oligopoly.

A second implication is that methods must be sought to encapsulate that complex web of interfirm interaction in a θ matrix. We have treated θ as composed of two constituents for a typical firm i: a measure of the total or overall extension of concern for rivals or customers, as summarized in the aggregate consonance factor, θ_i, and the relative power structure among firms, k_{ij}, where $\theta_{ij} = k_{ij}\,\theta_i$. In this chapter we will explore methods of deriving θ_i and $\mathbf{K}$ from objective and subjective evidence in the industry.

Our procedures are admittedly heuristic and, inescapably, subjective. They are initial efforts in an endeavor that is foreign to economics -- "inexact" or "fuzzy" measurement -- and which are extremely in need of improvement and sophistication. They are presented, hopefully, as "seed" efforts to stimulate methodological progress in a branch of empirical work that has been slighted as impure and to attempt the conversion of theorists to the view that such paths must be explored if oligopoly theory is to progress beyond its present sterility. Indeed, the point will be made that we accept such heuristic methods routinely in extremely important areas of our daily decision making, yet spurn them as unworthy in approaching theoretical analysis. The theorist has accepted the proposition that ordinal measurement is frequently sufficiently unique for his purposes. He has yet to take the much more difficult step of accepting "quasi-measurement" of intangibles as an access to the only promising paths to such goals as oligopoly analysis.

1. *A STANDARD STATISTICAL APPROACH*

A first standard approach that suggests itself for the isolation of θ is the regression-implemented econometric model. The technique seems extremely well suited to the task because the theoretical model to be fitted is well-defined and yields an exactly identified set of structural equations. When the n-firm rivalrous consonance reaction functions of system (30) in Chapter 4 are modified to include customer consonance as well as rivalrous consonance, they may be written, after transposing variables as

$$(1) \qquad b_{ii}\, m_i = z_i + \Sigma_r\, \theta_{ir}\, b_{ri}\, m_r + \Sigma_c\, \theta_{ic}\, (b_{ci}\, m_c - v_{ic}\, z_c)\,,$$

where

1. r is a summation index for firm i's rivals;
2. c is a summation index for customers of firm i;
3. v_{ic} is the amount of product i used per unit of customer c's product, derived from the unit cost functions $C_c = f_c + v_{ic}\, p_i$;
4. z_k are the reduced form demand functions, incorporating consumer and intermediate demand, whose coefficients are b_{kj};
5. m_k is profit margin $p_k - f_k - v_{jk}\, p_j$.

Given a body of price-sales-cost observations for industries under analysis, let us define

1. $X_i = b_{ii}\, m_i$
2. $Z_i = z_i$
3. $XA_i = X_i - Z_i$
4. $Y_{ir} = b_{ri}\, m_r$
5. $Y_{ic} = b_{ci}\, m_c - v_{ic}\, z_i$.

Then, we may assert two alternative hypotheses:

$$(2) \qquad 1.\ X_i = \beta_{ii}\, Z_i + \Sigma_r\, \beta_{ir}\, Y_{ir} + \Sigma_c\, \beta_{ic}\, Y_{ic} + \varepsilon_i$$

$$i = 1, 2, \ldots, n$$

$$2.\ XA_i = \Sigma_r\, \beta_{ir}\, Y_{ir} + \Sigma_c\, \beta_{ic}\, Y_{ic} + \mu_i\,,$$

where θ_{ik} is to be an estimate of β_{ik}, $\beta_{ii} = 1$, and the ε_i and μ_i are assumed to be, taken separately, normally and independently distributed with zero mean and common variance.

The skepticism we revealed in Chapter 5 about the usefulness of regression analysis in disentangling the complicated interrelationships of oligopolistic decision making is not lessened by experience in the present task. Consider, for example, the laboratory example that exists in the 49 factor cost displacements conducted in Chapter 5 for our two-industry model, with results summarized in Table 5.9. All of these "observations" were generated from an absolutely fixed θ, with ε_i and μ_i the result of rounding errors only in the instances where no constraints bind. However, we know that in 21 of the solutions prices were constrained by one or more binding constraints. Hence, the error terms will contain components from these sources.

The destructive influences of these disturbances to the hypothesized relationships of (2) may be readily shown by fitting estimating equations for the five firms to the 49 observations. Table 7.1 contains the relevant statistics and the population values of the studies.

Table 7.1. REGRESSION EQUATIONS FOR ILLUSTRATIVE FIVE FIRMS, 49 DISPLACEMENT OBSERVATIONS

	Equation	
1.	X1 = 1.19Z1 - 2.29Y12 + 1.32Y13 + 5.12Y15, R^2 = .960	θ_{12} = .09, θ_{15} = .03
	X1A = -1.09Y12 + 1.54Y13 + 3.28Y15, R^2 = .666	θ_{13} = .07
2.	X2 = 1.42Z2 - .98Y21 - .32Y23 + 57.98Y24, R^2 = .792	θ_{21} = .13, θ_{24} = .09
	X2A = .49Y21 + .21Y23 + 36.61Y24, R^2 = .380	θ_{23} = .14
3.	X3 = .91Z3 + .71Y31 - .14Y32, R^2 = .783	θ_{31} = .15
	X3A = .60Y31 - .28Y32, R^2 = .195	θ_{32} = .15
4.	X4 = 1.02Z4 + .40Y45 + .15Y41 + .10Y43, R^2 = .995	θ_{45} = .17, θ_{41} = .07
	X4A = .43Y45 + .11Y41 + .06Y43, R^2 = .415	θ_{43} = .05
5.	X5 = 1.0125 + 1.69Y54 + .53Y52, R^2 = .733	θ_{54} = .19, θ_{52} = .10
	X5A = 1.70Y54 + .52Y52, R^2 = .100	

None of these estimating equations yields satisfactory estimates of the consonance coefficients despite some large coefficients of multiple determination. That this is wholly due to the effects of the binding constraints is demonstrated in Table 7.2, which reproduces the regression equations obtained from the 28 observations in which constraints did not bind.

Table 7.2. REGRESSION EQUATIONS FOR ILLUSTRATIVE FIVE FIRMS, 28 UNCONSTRAINED DISPLACEMENT OBSERVATIONS

1. X1 = 1.00Z1 + .10Y12 + .07Y13 + .02Y15, R^2 = 1.000
   X1A = .09Y12 + .07Y13 + .04Y15, R^2 = .789

2. X2 = 1.00Z2 + .12Y21 + .13Y23 + .01Y24, R^2 = 1.000
   X2A = .13Y21 + .14Y23 + .12Y24, R^2 = .987

3. X3 = 1.00Z3 + .15Y31 + .14Y32, R^2 = 1.000
   X3A = .15Y31 + .15Y32, R^2 = .998

4. X4 = 1.00Z4 + .17Y45 + .07Y41 + .05Y43, R^2 = 1.000
   X4A = .17Y45 + .07Y41 + .05Y43, R^2 = .997

5. X5 = 1.00Z5 + .19Y54 + .10Y52, R^2 = 1.000
   X5A = .19Y54 + .10Y52, R^2 = .984

The exact relations that underlie the 28 observations have been all but perfectly estimated by the equations, wholly validating, of course, the "hypotheses" of (2), with a slight edge for accuracy accorded to the (2.2) formulation. In a realistic rivalrous and customer consonance solution, therefore, when θ is reasonably stable over the period of analysis, isolation of the consonance matrix by standard regression techniques will depend heavily upon the ability to separate those solutions (if any) in which constraints do not bind for any firm from those in which one or more do restrain prices. It is not to be expected that this discrimination can be made ex post facto, and if the experience under the otherwise ideal conditions of the 49 observations is not misleading, when substantial constraint binding does occur -- and we expect it to be the general case -- regression analysis will fail or mislead us. This expectation is enhanced by the existence of other realistic divergences from the ideal, such as shifting θ_{ij}, faulty price-sales-cost data, failure of firms to set optimum prices through faulty knowledge or altered expectations, and so forth.

Therefore, although these standard regression methods are available as tools, it is to be expected that they will have to be supplemented by deductive techniques and statistical applications made on simpler and more selective bases.

2. *SOME PRELIMINARIES ON THE THEORY OF MEASUREMENT*

It will be useful to investigate the basis for the puritanical reluctance to undertake fuzzy measurement in the theory of measurement. With the conditions for "exact" measurement before us, it will be possible to display the departures that many social variables or attributes possess that make conformance to such conditions difficult or impossible.

Formal measurement of the degree to which empirical objects possess a given property entails two problems, whose solutions imply the proof of two types of theorem.[1] We discuss each in turn briefly.

2.1. *The Representation Problem*

The first problem is that of establishing that the *empirical relational system* relevant to the given property possesses a similar structure (is "isomorphic" or "homomorphic") to a relational system defined (for practical purposes) on the real number line. The empirical relational system is simply (1) the set of objects possessing the property to be measured, (2) the stated property, and (3) one or more relations between objects with respect to the property. For example, let the set A be a group of firms in an industry, the property of interest annual sales revenue, and the relation chosen the binary relation "≥", or "at least as large as". The empirical relational system may then be defined as

$$\mathrm{A} = [\mathrm{A}, \mathrm{S}, \geq], \tag{3}$$

where S denotes sales revenues.

It is possible with such a system to place the firms in descending sequence of revenues through simple pairwise comparisons, with firms of equal sales revenue in the same group as their fellows. To "measure" the empirical objects with respect to the property, however, a numerical relational system

$$\mathrm{N} = [\mathrm{N}, \mathrm{R}_1, \mathrm{R}_2, \ldots], \tag{4}$$

on the set of real numbers N and employing the indicated relation(s) R_i (in our case, "≥"), must be established, and a function f defined to map the elements in A onto N in a one-to-one (isomorphic, i.e., no ties) or, when f^{-1} is not one-to-one, in a homomorphic (permitting ties) manner, such that $f(a) \geq f(a')$ if $a \geq a'$. For our case, the numerical relational system

$$\mathrm{N} = [\text{positive integers}, \geq] \tag{5}$$

is homomorphic to the elements of A, and

(6) $N = [\text{positive integers}, >]$

is isomorphic to the sequenced groups of equal-sales-revenue firms. Hence f is defined as a functional assignment of integers to the sets of objects such that firms with larger revenues get larger numbers than firms with smaller revenues and equal-revenue firms get the same number. The representational problem is solved when the proof that N is isomorphic or homomorphic to A is completed.

2.2. *The Uniqueness Problem*

The three-tuple [A, N, f] defines a *scale* of measurement characterized by its "uniqueness", which is to say by the kinds of transformation of f that do not affect the structure or "exactness" of the measurement. To economists, three types of scales so characterized have been of theoretical interest:

1. *Uniqueness up to a monotonic transformation.* We are accustomed to this degree of uniqueness which merely preserves ranking in ordinal utility functions.
2. *Uniqueness up to a linear transformation.* The measurement of time and temperature are classic examples of this scale. The nonexistence of a natural zero origin for the ordinary (non-Kelvin) measurement of temperature means that an arbitrary origin can be chosen (say 32°F for the freezing point of water) and an arbitrary value chosen higher on the scale (say 212°F for the boiling point of water), with the interval between divided into equal units. Such measurement yields meaningful *intervals*, and measurement specialists term such scales *interval scales*, but ratios of such measurements are not meaningful (e.g., 212°F/32°F ≠ 100°C/0°C).
3. *Uniqueness up to a similarity transformation.* When a scale possesses a natural zero origin any function f derived differs from all potentially derivable f^* only in the choice of unit; i.e., $f^* = b \cdot f$, $b > 0$. Such a scale is characterized by the meaningfulness of ratios, and is termed a *ratio scale* for this reason.

In summary, exact measurement techniques rest upon the clear and precise definition of the property being measured; the choice of appropriate relations; the proof that an empirical relational system has an exactly defined structural similarity to a numerical relational system; and the proof of a uniqueness theorem to establish the scale type.

2.3. *The Practicalities of Scaling in the Social Sciences*

In the social sciences frequent occasions arise when one or more of these procedures are impossible, and progress in quantification depends upon the use of techniques with only an empirically-demonstrated validity. For example, psychologists seek insights into attitudes, ask subjects to scale handwriting in terms of "pleasingness", and require raters to score candidates in such qualities as "cooperativeness", "leadership", and "acting ability". None of these properties is truly susceptible of exact definition, nor capable of meeting the other preconditions for rigorous measurement discussed above.

The methods we shall employ in obtaining θ_i and **K** are those of "subjective estimate"[3] or "quasi-measurement", a blend of the scientific and the intuitive. The use of such "inexact" or "fuzzy measurement" for practical scaling purposes has a long history in such fields as psychology and education, and we may appeal for an extended example to a familiar procedure: grading in or being graded by an educational system in many course dimensions. Consider the scoring of students' achievements in a course of study on a scale from 0 to 100. The characteristic to be "measured" is notable for its lack of precise definition: it is a connotative quality, drawing upon the experience, intuition, and introspection of the grader for meaningfulness. Attempts to give it simple meaning lead one to balk: for example, conversion to the proportion of objective questions answered correctly in a series of examinations leads to the objection that there is no readily plausible relation between percentage points on the correct-answer scale and percentage points of achievement.

What degree of uniqueness does such a student scoring system have? Is it at best unique up to a monotonic transformation? If so, the usual arithmetic operations performed upon such grades are illegal; they cannot be added to other grades or averaged or weighted. Are they equivalent to points on an interval scale, so that the 0 mark corresponds to no natural origin but distances between individual on the scale are meaningful? This would permit us to perform arithmetic operations of the weighted-average variety, in certain circumstances, but would forbid such procedures as standardizing grades by the use of standard deviations. Or is the 0 on the scale indeed a natural zero in some definable sense, and do we in fact have a ratio scale: is a student who earns 90 considered to have achieved 90 percent of a definable range of 100 units, and a student who received a grade of 45 in that sense only half the beneficiary?

To ask these questions is to seek for a clear definition of the characteristic, a representation theorem, and a uniqueness theorem. In all respects that search will fail. We are enmeshed in "quasi" or "inexact" measurement which possesses only a surface resemblance to exact measurement. Is it, therefore, a useless or misleading procedure which would be best discontinued?

It is suggested that an interpretation of the following type will validate the procedure as a useful exercise. A teacher acquires through experience and training a good conception of the performance of an idealized student who has passed through the course or some segment of it with no practicably measurable accretion of knowledge. This idealized notion of null accomplishment he placed at the zero mark of his scale, and we interpret it as a "natural" zero for the individual grader. On the other hand, the idealized student who has mastered the material in a manner that could not be effectively surpassed in the time available is also present in the teacher's professional subconscious, and anchors the scale at the 100 mark. Hence, the grading scale may be interpreted as *percentages of effective range (ER) of accomplishment* and may be manipulated is a ratio scale.

If the "standards" of a teacher -- the idealized definitions at 0 and 100 -- are similar in some inevitably intuitive sense to the standards of other teachers, the grades may be averaged among courses over the academic lifetime of the student with meaningful results. Decisions of great importance to individuals, universities, and societies are made on the basis of such scaling and in the faith that their assimilated uniqueness is that of a ratio scale. The indefinable quality of academic excellence or achievement is scored in a "measurement" procedure reflecting intuitive-introspective knowledge, without formal proofs of representation or uniqueness, and with no scale validations by means of controlled stimuli.

3. *INEXACT OR QUASI-MEASUREMENT AND THE POWER STRUCTURE*

The problem we face in defining the consonance or power structure of an industry is to compute, for each firm i, the proportion, k_{ij}, of its aggregate consonance factor, θ_i, that is bestowed upon rival or customer j in firm i's pricing decisions. The binary consonance coefficients are then obtained after θ_i is determined from the first-order extended profit conditions for firm i, as we will demonstrate in section 3.6; that is, $\theta_{ij} = \mathbf{k}_{ij}\,\theta_i$.

The approach to be followed assumes that the k_{ij} are determinable by (1) scaling firm i's and j's locations on individual quality scales that range from 0 to 1.00, and

(2) weighting each such "measurement" by the degree of importance given the quality by the industry in the evolution of its power structure. The task is admittedly judgmental, subjective, and "unscientific" in the sense of section 1, but also in the same senses that educational grading is. The defense of the procedures is, therefore, the same as that for educational grading: it seems impossible to make progress in defining an essential structural element of the process under analysis (oligopoly theory, in our case) in their absence. The essential empirical validation of these quasi-measurement procedures that has been established by years of at least toleration in the educational sector lies ahead of us in the field of oligopoly theory.

We distinguish two groups of firces that act to determine the consonance structure: market factors and nonmarket factors. We discuss each in turn.

3.1. *Market Factors in the Determination of Power Structure*

In the cases of its rivals, firm i will be more ready on market advantage grounds alone to sacrifice own profit by raising p_i above the maximum own-profit elasticity, ε_{ii}, and when rival j's cross-elasticity, ε_{ji}, is small, so that it doesn't benefit greatly from the price rise. It will also be readier to grant consideration to firm j if the (absolute) value of ε_{jj} is large, so that firm j is strongly tempted to keep its price lower and thereby reduce firm i's sales, and if ε_{ij} is large, so that p_j has a large potential impact on firm i's sales.

Using recently observed price data and the computed sales functions to determine elasticity approximations in relevant price domains, we compute the rival market component as

$$(7) \qquad RMC_{ij} = (\varepsilon_{jj} + \varepsilon_{ij})/(\varepsilon_{ii} + \varepsilon_{ji}) \,,$$

and it will be used to index the strength of these market demand forces.

For customers we assume that the market's contribution to the willingness of firm i to lower p_i below its own-profit level varies with the relative impacts upon its own and its customers' profit margins. The greater the impact a reduction in p_i has upon the customers' profit margins and the less upon its own the greater the market contribution to the customers' consonance factors. We index these forces by computing the ratio of the p_i elasticity of the customer's profit margin, m_j, to the own-price elasticity of m_i:

$$(8) \qquad CMC_{ij} = (\delta m_j/\delta p_i)(p_i/m_j)/(\delta m_i/\delta p_i)(p_i/m_i) = v_{ij}\,(m_i/m_j) \,.$$

To obtain the final scalings for firm i's market factor contributions to its power structure perceptions we normalize to obtain market components

$$(9) \qquad W_{ij} = [RMC_{ij}\,(\text{or})\,CMC_{ij}]/[\Sigma_r RMC_{ir} + \Sigma_c CMC_{ic}] \,.$$

As an example of the procedure we compute the W_{ij} for the two-industry example we have used in Chapters 5 and 6 for simulation theorizing. We have used elasticities and prices for the base case solution in computing these market components, and display them in Table 7.3.

Table 7.3. MARKET COMPONENTS (W_{ij}) FOR ILLUSTRATIVE INDUSTRIES

Firm i/ Firm j	1			2			3		
	RMC_{ij}	CMC_{ij}	W_{ij}	RMC_{ij}	CMC_{ij}	W_{ij}	RMC_{ij}	CMC_{ij}	W_{ij}
1	--	---	---	1.24	---	.44	1.33	---	.47
2	.81	---	.43	---	---	---	.99	---	.53
3	.75	---	.43	1.01	---	.57	---	---	---
4	---	.16	.09	---	---	---	---	.25	.13
5	---	---	---	---	.22	.25	---	---	---

Firm i/ Firm j	4			5		
	RMC_{ij}	CMC_{ij}	W_{ij}	RMC_{ij}	CMC_{ij}	W_{ij}
1	---	---	---	---	.26	.09
2	---	.08	.04	---	---	---
3	---	---	---	---	---	---
4	---	---	---	1.49	---	.78
5	.67	---	.75	---	---	---

3.2. *Nonmarket Factors in the Determination of Power Structure*

It is to be expected that market factors will play a large role in the determination of power structure in the short run, but by no means an exclusive role. We have stressed in this work the important role of the industry community in oligopolistic functioning and its tempering of the narrowly self-seeking urges so dear to conventional economic theory in its preoccupation with competition. The discernment of the nonmarket factors that are active in any particular industry is dependent upon the knowledge of the industry's history and mores, and their enumeration is difficult to generalize. Moreover, the problems of measurement or quasi-measurement loom more disturbingly because such factors are frequently attributes or characteristics of rather subtle and subjective natures. Our analysis of the two-industry example that follows is meant to illustrate some of these qualities and quantification difficulties.

In the determination of consonance among rivals and customers four types of qualities are encountered and must be scaled:

1. qualities that are measurable with a cardinal degree of uniqueness in natural units;
2. qualities that differ ordinally among firms in an absolute sense;
3. qualities that differ ordinally among firms in a relative sense;
4. qualities that are attributes, or 0-1 qualities.

In each case our approach is to locate firms on a scale between 0 and 1 with the purpose of deriving "distances" between pairs of firms in each quality dimension.

3.2.1. *Cardinally Measurable Qualities.* If a quality is capable of measurement with uniqueness up to a multiplicative constant (a similarity transformation) our task is easy. Certainly one index of power in an industry is annual sales (z_i), which may be scaled simply by conversion to proportionate market share. Similar power measures are profit shares (π_i), or asset shares, or capacity shares, and so forth. Although each of these indexes has a certain ability to command respect in the industry community, profit share would seem to reflect both sales and financial prowess and be the preferred measure. Table 7.4 lists base case solution profit shares for each industry, with scaling a natural consequence of a ratio scale.

In gauging the power of customers a similarly measurable index is the proportion of each firm's sales accounted for by each industrial customer. We list these in Table 7.5:

Table 7.4. PROFIT SHARES, π_i, BASE CASE SOLUTION

Industry	Firm (i)	π_i
1	1	.56
	2	.25
	3	.19
2	4	.74
	5	.26

Table 7.5. SALES SHARES, s_i, OF EACH FIRM TO INDUSTRIAL CUSTOMERS, BASE CASE

Firm	Customers	s_i
1	5	.04
2	4	.08
3	--	0
4	1	.39
	3	.20
5	2	.93

3.2.2. *Ordinal Qualities Differing Absolutely Among Firms.* A quality which can be viewed as being associated with a given firm in greater or lesser intensity, though objective measurement techniques do not exist to calibrate that intensity in other-than-ordinal manners, we shall speak of as differing *absolutely* among firms. One such quality of great importance in dictating power structure in an industry is the perceived willingness or propensity of firms to use price as an aggressive competitive weapon, perhaps in following a penetration pricing strategy or in a desire to exploit its perceived marketing advantages or to overcome marketing disadvantages.

Our approach, as analysts outside the industries, studying the record of their pricing histories, is to construct a subjective probability distribution over the placement of each firm on a 0 to 1 scale of price aggressiveness. At the 0 end of the scale we envision a firm whose pricing record is wholly reactive and sluggish, evincing no tendency to use this competitive tool except in self-defense. At the other extreme our mind's-eye envisages a firm whose short-run policy features frequent price cutting unrelated to prior competitor moves or to cost decreases to a degree which would constitute an effective, practical upper limit. The calibrations we seek place firms on a probabilistic basis somewhere within the limits of this *effective range* (ER) scale.

For each firm we derive three scaling points:

1. L: a lower bound of intensity below which we are in effect certain the firm's price aggressiveness does not lie;
2. H: an upper bound of intensity above which we believe the firm does not lie;
3. M: the best point location on the scale we can make of the most likely value of a pure aggressiveness of the firm.

Obtaining such subjective estimates permits the analyst to take into account the uncertainty he feels concerning his scaling as well as his best judgment of a firm's score from the revealed record.

To obtain a single scale value reflecting this dispersion, we assume that L and H are endpoints of a domain over which the subjective probability distribution that characterizes the analyst's judgment is defined, and for ease of handling we shall assume that the form of the distribution is that of a beta distribution:

$$(10) \qquad \beta(x) = A\,(x - L)^{\alpha}\,(H - x)^{\beta}\,,$$

where

$$A = [\Gamma(\alpha + \beta + 2)]/[\Gamma(\alpha + 1)\,\Gamma(\beta + 1)\,(H - L)^{\alpha + \beta + 1}]\,.$$

Further, we assume M is the mode of (10) -- the most probable value -- and will use the expected value of $\beta(x)$ as the firm's scale value for price aggressiveness. For a beta distribution

$$(11) \qquad E(x) = (L + (\alpha + \beta)\,M + H)/(\alpha + \beta + 2)\,,$$

and, by maximizing (10) with respect to x,

$$(12) \qquad M = (\alpha H + \beta L)/(\alpha + \beta).$$

As an approximation of E(x) the following methodology is adopted. Define $Z = \alpha + \beta$, so that from (12) we derive

$$(13) \qquad \alpha = Z[(M\text{-}L)/(H\text{-}L)] = ZK,$$

where K is the expression in parantheses. From (13) we may rewrite (11) to be

(14) $E(x) = (L+ZM+H)/(Z+2)$.

The task is now one of estimating Z, for which we need another independent relation, which we find in the expression for the variance of the beta distribution:

(15) $$\sigma^2 = [(H\text{-}L)^2 (\alpha+1)(\beta+1)]/[\alpha+\beta+2)^2 (\alpha+\beta+3)]$$
$$= [(H\text{-}L)^2 (Z^2K\text{-}Z^2K^2+Z+1)]/[(Z+2)^2 (Z+3)] .$$

The value (H-L) we know to be the domain of the distribution, and we will assume that the beta distribution follows closely the normal distribution in that practically all of its domain is included in an interval of 6σ. This is exactly true only for three sets of values $[\alpha,\beta]$, but it is a reasonably good approximation for the range of Z values that will concern us.[3] From (15), under the assumption $(H\text{-}L) = 6\sigma$.

(16) $$[Z^2(K\text{-}K^2)+Z+1]/[(Z+2)^2 (Z+3)] = 1/36 ,$$

which yields Z as a function of K. For the range of values for K and Z which are relevant for the unimodal beta distributions of our analysis, we list in Table 7.6 the relation between σ and (H-L) as well as V*, the value of (H-L) at which the 6σ relation holds exactly. In our experience with similar experiments[4], K in the range of .30 to .50 and Z in the 3 to 4 range have proved to be most relevant, and the spread between H and L of 30 to 40 a quite frequent range. The estimate of range as 6σ, therefore, seems workably accurate.

Table 7.6. RELATION BETWEEN σ AND (H-L) AND V*

	Z	σ	V*
1. K = .25 or .75	2	.22(H-L)	27
	3	.14(H-L)	43
	4	.17(H-L)	35
	5	.37(H-L)	16
2. K = .50	2	.22(H-L)	27
	3	.19(H-L)	30
	4	.19(H-L)	32
	5	.12(H-L)	50

From (13) it may be seen that for a reasonably symmetrical distribution K should approximate .50, hence $K\text{-}K^2 \approx 0.25$. If we solve (16) for these values we find $Z \approx 6$, so that (11) may be written

(17) $E(x) = (L+6M+H)/8$,

which could be used as an approximation to the expected value. We will sharpen this approximation as follows. Z reaches a maximum for K = 0.50 and a minimum for K = 0 or 1, at which latter values Z ≈ 2.85. Further, when K = .25 or .75, Z ≈ 4.80. By fitting a least squares regression to these three points we obtain

$$(18) \qquad Z \approx 2.85 + 9.30G - 6.00G^2, \qquad G = \begin{cases} K, \text{ for } K \leq .50 \\ (1\text{-}K), \text{ for } K > .50 \end{cases},$$

which we substitute into (14) to obtain a better estimate of E(x) than that yielded by (17). This estimate is the scale value we seek.

To illustrate the technique we studied the generalized cost change displacements of Table 5.9.5 for the five firms under study. We felt that such data would be most analogous to the historical record that would be available in an actual analysis. For each of the generalized factor cost changes we computed percentage changes from base case prices. Then for each pair of equi-percentage changes (±5 percent, etc.) we studied the degree of asymmetry of price rises to price declines as an index of pricing aggressiveness. It is recognized, of course, that such asymmetry may reflect a high degree of rivalrous consonance in a firm's price behavior, and therefore index a motivation exactly opposite to that we are associating with this quality. However, in periods of *generalized* cost change, where all profit margins should be rising and falling together, the effects of rivalrous consonance should be minimized.

On the basis of a study of these data, the subjective scaling estimates for pricing aggressiveness that we arrived at (from the "historical record") are given in Table 7.7, along with calculation of the expected values of such indices. On the basis of this evidence alone we suspect that firms 2 and 5 will be price leaders in their industries, with the latter firm much less aggressive in that leadership position than the former. Firm 1 is marked as a rather more passive or adaptive producer than might be expected from its sales leadership.

Table 7.7. HYPOTHETICAL SCALINGS OF PRICING AGGRESSIVENESS OF FIRMS 1-5, WITH COMPUTATION OF EXPECTED VALUES

Firms	Scalings:					
	L	M	H	K	Z	E(x)
1	.57	.61	.65	.50	6.00	.61
2	.75	.81	.90	.40	5.61	.81
3	.66	.74	.85	.42	5.70	.74
4	.37	.38	.39	.50	6.00	.38
5	.62	.66	.70	.50	6.00	.66

Of course, in an actual analysis of an industry we would have a great deal more concrete evidence on which to base our scalings. It will generally be possible to mark the instances each firm takes the lead in raising or lowering prices, its initiation of rebate or other discounting techniques, or the degree of emphasis upon price in its advertising. This body of objective and subjective evidence can only be brought into usable confluence by such controlled scaling techniques as that demonstrated.

3.2.3. *Ordinal Qualities Differing Relatively Among Firms.* By this admittedly puzzling title we mean to differentiate qualities that must be or are best anchored upon one firm, with other firms' scalings measuring departures from it. For example, a quality that affects the willingness of firms to extend consonance consideration to its rivals or customers is the "distance" a firm's management perceives other firms' managements to be from itself. That distancing may be a subtle amalgam of similarity or dissimilarity in management techniques, recruitment sources, and style; the relations among management personnel between firms; a perceived similarity or dissimilarity in the product quality goals of rivals; the perceived treatment a firm has received from other firms' management practices, in the case of customers, perhaps, in times of scarcity of materials; similarity or dissimilarity in "industry citizenship", or attitudes of restraint in competitive ardor in periods of excess supply or in exploiting the misfortunes of other firms; and degree of respect for leading industry innovation and product improvement versus "copycat" strategies orientation. All of these and others unmentioned -- the category is extremely industry specific -- may enter into the distancing perceptions of each firm in the relevant industries. We calibrate these distances for each firm by placing it at 0 on a scale and placing rivals and customers at points up to 1.00 as an upper bound using the L-M-H techniques discussed in the previous section.

This type of measurement employing quarternary relations in its empirical relation system -- "the difference between A and B is no greater than the difference between C and D: true or false?" -- is frequently used in psychological scaling theory, usually with a controllable stimulus which varies continuously or in small discrete steps over the entire continuum of the scale. For example, suppose the stimulus is the frequency of a tone in cycles per second, and the scale is being constructed for the subject's awareness of pitch. Arbitrary maximum and minimum frequencies are selected to anchor the scale, and the subject is asked to choose a frequency that bisects the whole interval. He is then asked to choose a frequency that bisects the interval between the minimum point of the scale and the midpoint, and so forth. The equal-interval assumption permits a scale unique up to a linear or similarity transformation, depending upon one's interpretation of the 0 origin.

Note the fact that this procedure in psychometrics depends solely upon this discernment that the distance of a variable stimulus from one end-point is greater than, equal to, or less than the distance to the other end-point. This is the basis for the frequent assertion that cardinal measurement depends upon the ability to rank differences between stimuli values, but the crucial ability to control the stimuli in continuous or quasi-continuous ways over the whole continuum is often omitted.

Of course, "management distance" is not an operationally-definable concept, and our attitude to it is the practical one of Luce and Galanter:

> "The word [distance] used in the instructions is vague and it is left that way because neither the experimenter nor the subject can verbalize very precisely what he means by it. Nonetheless, subjects respond non-randomly when instructed in this way. That reproducible data can arise from a vague criterion should not surprise us when we think how often we use equally vague criteria in every day life, but in the long run a science is not likely to let reproducibility alone substitute for well analyzed and controlled experimental design."[5]

Moreover, we must face the complications of uncontrolled stimuli and the need to imagine a polar antithesis. But the only scientific manner to proceed in the face of an unscientific problem is to experiment to see if indeed such measures are useful in understanding oligopolisitic behavior.

In that spirit, therefore, suppose that after due deliberation the scalings of Table 7.8 are derived. Note that we have assumed that firm i's perception of its distance to firm j is the same as firm j's perception of firm i's. This is not necessary, of course, if sufficient expertise and evidence is available to discriminate between the two firms' possibly variant perceptions.

Table 7.8. HYPOTHETICAL SCALINGS OF MANAGEMENT DISTANCES FOR FIRMS 1-5, WITH COMPUTATION OF EXPECTED VALUES

Firms/ Firms	1			2			3			4			5			Expected Value				
	L	M	H	L	M	H	L	M	H	L	M	H	L	M	H	1	2	3	4	5
1	---	---	---	.70	.80	.85	.36	.42	.50	---	---	---	.18	.25	.38	--	.79	.42	--	.26
2	.70	.80	.85	---	---	---	.45	.60	.70	.45	.60	.70	---	---	---	.79	--	.59	.75	--
3	.36	.42	.50	.45	.60	.70	---	---	---	---	---	---	---	---	---	.26	.59	--	--	--
4	.50	.55	.59	---	---	---	.65	.70	.75	---	---	---	.72	.74	.76	.55	---	.70	--	.74
5	---	---	---	.33	.35	.42	---	---	---	.72	.74	.76	---	---	---	--	.36	--	.74	--

3.2.4. *Qualities That Are Attributes.* In the case of pure attributes -- qualities which are present or absent and in which no gradations are possible -- we place firms either at 0 or 1 on the quality scale in a binary fashion.

As an example relevant to our current power structure task, we answer the question "Does firm i compete with firm j in other product markets?", with the assumption that if firm i does it will be more inclined to extend consideration to firm j.[6] A 0-1 no-yes response is recorded in Table 7.9.

Table 7.9. HYPOTHETICAL SCALINGS OF OTHER-GOOD COMPETITION FOR FIRMS 1-5

Firm/ Firm	1	2	3	4	5
1	--	1	0	--	1
2	1	--	1	0	--
3	0	1	--	--	--
4	1	--	0	--	0
5	--	0	--	0	--

3.3. *Normalization of Factors on Row-Wise Base*

Because the computation of the k_{ij} power structure factors is a comparison of factor scores across the ith row, and because the *relative* scores on each factor count in comparisons among firms, in general we normalize each factor to sum to 1 when they do not. Moreover, it will be convenient to treat such normalized scores as positively related to market power. Therefore, when a normalized factor is negatively related to the k_{ij} we substitute its complement.

We have isolated six factors as important to the determination of market structure in these industries:

1. market factors
2. profit shares
3. sales shares from industrial customers
4. pricing aggressiveness
5. management distances
6. other goods competition

The market factors and sales shares have already been normalized rowwise. Profit shares and other goods competition scores are normalized by dividing by row sums. Because pricing aggressiveness must retain the intensity of that quality for each rival *relative to the row firm's* intensity, the final scores are obtained by dividing each score by the industry total score. Row by row, therefore, they will not sum to 1. Finally, management distances are normalized by dividing scores by row sums, but, because k_{ij} are negatively related to distance, these normalized values are subtracted from 1 before the final normalized scalings are computed by division by the new row sums.

The final factor scores are listed in Table 7.10.

3.4. *Cross-Factor Analysis: Deriving Factor Weights*

In order to combine the normalized factor scores into the k_{ij} we seek it will be necessary to obtain weighted averages of them row by row. The next step, therefore, must be an operational method of computing the relative weights for the factors. In this enterprise it is once again necessary to formalize inevitably subjective evidence of industry attitudes, as possessed by a panel of industry experts or by the individual analyst. This is merely to say that we are in another phase of quasi-measurement.

We use a cross-factor matrix method that assures the comparison of every factor with every other factor in the determination of the weights, yet reduces such comparisons to pairwise decisions. An n x n matrix of the n factors is established as a tableau, as in Table 7.11 for the six factors we have isolated. The diagonal elements are ignored, and only those cells above the main diagonal need to considered. Across row i, factor i is compared successively with factors j, k, . . ., and we index the importance of factors j, k, . . . in the relevant cells.

We grade factor i versus factor j on the basis of scores from 0 to 4 according to the following scheme:

- 4: factor i is much more important than factor j in determining power structure in these industries;
- 3: factor i is more important than factor j;
- 2: factor i and factor j are of equal importance;
- 1: factor j is more important than factor i;
- 0: factor j is much more important than factor i.

Table 7.10. FINAL FACTOR SCORES FOR POWER STRUCTURE CALCULATION, FIRMS 1-5

Row Firm/Factors		Firms				
		1	2	3	4	5
1	1. Market	---	.44	.47	---	.09
	2. Profit	---	.57	.43	---	---
	3. Sales	---	---	---	---	.04
	4. Aggressiveness	---	.38	.34	---	---
	5. Distances	---	.23	.36	---	.41
	6. Other Goods	---	.50	---	---	.50
2	1. Market	.43	---	.53	.04	---
	2. Profit	.75	---	.25	---	---
	3. Sales	---	---	---	.08	---
	4. Aggressiveness	.28	---	.34	---	---
	5. Distances	.31	---	.37	.32	---
	6. Other Goods	.50	---	.50	---	---
3	1. Market	.43	.57	---	---	---
	2. Profit	.69	.31	---	---	---
	3. Sales	---	---	---	---	---
	4. Aggressiveness	.28	.38	---	---	---
	5. Distances	.69	.31	---	---	---
	6. Other Goods	---	1.00	---	---	---
4	1. Market	.09	---	.13	---	.78
	2. Profit	---	---	---	---	1.00
	3. Sales	.39	---	.20	---	---
	4. Aggressiveness	---	---	---	---	.37
	5. Distances	.36	---	.33	---	.31
	6. Other Goods	1.00	---	---	---	---
5	1. Market	---	.25	---	.75	---
	2. Profit	---	---	---	1.00	---
	3. Sales	---	.93	---	---	---
	4. Aggressiveness	---	---	---	.63	---
	5. Distances	---	.67	---	.33	---
	6. Other Goods	---	---	---	---	---

Table 7.11. THE CROSS-FACTOR MATRIX

Factor (i)/Factor j	1	2	3	4	5	6
1. Market	--	3	4	3	4	4
2. Profit Share	1	--	3	2	3	3
3. Industrial Sales	0	1	--	2	3	2
4. Pricing Agressiveness	1	2	2	-	3	2
5. Management Distances	0	1	1	1	--	2
6. Other Goods Competition	0	1	2	2	2	--

The cells below the main diagonal may be filled in because the value in cell (i,j) plus that in cell (j,i) must sum to 4. Our estimates of the index values are found in Table 7.11.

The straightforward manner of obtaining factor weights -- we shall call it Method 1 -- is to obtain row sums from Table 7.8 and normalize them as ratios to the sum of the row sums. These sums and their normalized values are given in the Method 1 columns. A difficulty with this method is that no factor can have a weight exceeding 2/n, where n is the number of factors. Method 2 assumes that the importance of a factor rises as the *square* of its index value, and obtains its weights by normalizing the row sums of the squares of the values recorded. This permits the maximum weight to attain a value of (4/(n + 2)). Method 3 compromises the weighting systems of Methods 1 and 2 by taking a simple average of their weights. The results of Methods 2 and 3 for our illustrative problem are found in Table 7.12.

Table 7.12. ALTERNATIVE FACTOR WEIGHTS

Factor	Method 1		Method 2		Method 3 Weights
	Row Sums	Weight	Row Sums	Weight	
1	18	.30	66	.42	.36
2	12	.20	32	.21	.20
3	8	.13	18	.11	.12
4	10	.17	22	.14	.16
5	5	.08	7	.04	.06
6	7	.12	13	.08	.10
Totals	60	1.00	158	1.00	1.00

3.5. *The Power Structure: An Initial Estimate*

We derive the power structure for all three weight systems by multiplying the final factor scores of Table 7.10 by the relevant weights in Table 7.9 and normalizing on row sums. The results are contained in Table 7.13.

Table 7.13. ESTIMATED POWER STRUCTURE FACTORS, k_{ij}, FOR FIRMS 1-5, FOR THREE ALTERNATIVE WEIGHTING STRUCTURES

Firms/ Firms	1. Method 1 Weights				
	1	2	3	4	5
1	--	.47	.37	--	.16
2	.50	--	.44	.06	--
3	.46	.54	--	--	--
4	.27	--	.11	--	.62
5	--	.28	--	.72	--

	2. Method 2 Weights				
	1	2	3	4	5
1	--	.48	.40	--	.12
2	.50	--	.45	.05	--
3	.46	.54	--	--	--
4	.21	--	.10	--	.69
5	--	.27	--	.73	--

	3. Method 3 Weights				
	1	2	3	4	5
1	--	.48	.39	--	.13
2	.50	--	.45	.05	--
3	.46	.54	--	--	--
4	.23	--	.11	--	.66
5	--	.29	--	.71	--

	4. "Actual" Power Structure				
	1	2	3	4	5
1	--	.47	.37	--	.16
2	.37	--	.40	.23	--
3	.50	.50	--	--	--
4	.24	--	.17	--	.59
5	--	.34	--	.66	--

For our example the three methods yield essentially the same results: the root-mean-square deviations from the "actual" power structure used in Chapters 5 and 6 are .019, .022, and .020 respectively. Note that, in general (indeed, with the single exception of firm 5) our methods underestimate the degree of consonance extended customers by these industries. Nonetheless, they do seem to be workably acceptable approximations to the power structure "actually" present in the short-run and long-term industry analyses of Chapters 5 and 6. Nonetheless, attempts will be made to correct and refine them in section 5.

4. *THE AGGREGATE CONSONANCE FACTORS*

To complete the initial determination of θ we must compute $\theta_i = \Sigma_j \theta_{ij}$ for each firm i, a parameter we have termed the "aggregate consonance factor" because it estimates the firm's own-profit valuation of n-1 dollars of profit spread equally over all other firms.

4.1. *Using the Reaction Functions*

A first approximation to the θ_i may be obtained from the power structure estimates in panels 1-3 of Table 7.13 and the reaction functions of (1). We may rewrite the latter in general form as

$$\theta_i = (b_{ii} m_i - z_i)/[\Sigma_r k_{ir} b_{ri} m_r + \Sigma_c k_{ic} (b_{ci} m_c - v_{ic} z_i)] . \tag{19}$$

Through the judicious choice of price-output-cost solutions from available observations, therefore, it is possible to make estimates of the underlying θ_i.

The nature of the "judiciousness" has been indicated in section 1. Solutions should be chosen insofar as possible in which it is believed the role of firms' goals other than extended-profit maximization was minimal. This may be difficult, admittedly, in which case appeals to many different solutions and averages may be necessary.

For our illustrative case, we shall use (1) the base case, (2) an average of all 49 displacement operations discussed in section 1, and (3) an average of the 28 displacement solutions in which constraints were not operative. We have used the averages of XA_i, Z_i, Y_{ir}, and Y_{ic} as defined there for the computations. The results for Methods 1, 2, and 3 power structures in Table 7.13 are displayed in Table 7.14.

Note once more the relative impotence of standard regression analysis to lift from data which are only slightly disturbed by the cross-currents of binding constraints the underlying and strong pattern of causation. This is revealed in the results of the 49-observation sample, which is the type of sample data we would have in an actual analysis. For all three weighting methods the θ_i estimates are quite misleading, even in Industry 1 where the power structure coefficients are close to the actual values. Only when the distortions are eliminated by our illegitimate omniscience do the θ-coefficients approach the values implied by the k-coefficients of Table 7.13.

It would seem more promising in the pursuit of realistic field industry studies to spend time isolating one or a few solutions in the period under analysis in which objective function goals operated to determine solutions in relative freedom from interference by the constraints of other goals and power structures where static. This may admittedly be difficult to do, and minimally will require a thorough grasp of the pricing experience and recent history of the industry. However, the concentration of research effort upon a thorough study of a few instances, perhaps supplemented by field interviews with industry officials with relevance to those periods offers greater hope of uncovering the consonance structure than rather mindless processing of all available observations.

Table 7.14. ESTIMATED AGGREGATE CONSONANCE FACTORS, θ_i, FOR FIRMS 1-5, FOR THREE ALTERNATIVE POWER STRUCTURE ESTIMATES

Firm i	Method 1 Weights	Method 2 Weights	Method 3 Weights	"Actual" θ_i
1. Base Case Solutions				
1	.19	.18	.18	.19
2	.30	.29	.29	.35
3	.30	.30	.30	.30
4	.31	.54	.42	.29
5	.58	.68	.65	.29
2. 49-Observation Average				
1	.33	.32	.32	.19
2	.25	.25	.24	.35
3	.41	.41	.41	.30
4	.25	.43	.33	.29
5	.73	.86	.63	.29
3. 28-Observation Average				
1	.19	.18	.18	.19
2	.30	.29	.29	.35
3	.30	.30	.30	.30
4	.31	.55	.42	.39
5	.55	.64	.49	.29

The imprecision of the methods, the data, and, indeed, the concepts themselves, must be honestly accepted. The chances are highly likely that the attitudes and behaviors that define a consonance structure are not rigidly fixed from pricing period to pricing period, but are in constant flux about some fuzzy core of consistency. Our estimates must reflect this imprecision, and we will be wise to be resigned to that need. Hence, we will seek to estimate a *bracket* of θ_i values for each firm -- a *lower bound* (L_i), an *upper bound* (U_i), and an intermediate (I_i) value.

For our "experiment" in determining the aggregate consonance coefficients we chose 4 of the 49 "observations" of Table 5.9's displacement solutions at random (numbers 16, 30, 4, and 13) using the power structure derived by Method 3 weights in Table 7.13. The resulting θ_i estimates, along with base case results are recorded in Table 7.15.

To eliminate extreme items, we trim the lowest and highest of the five estimates for each θ_i where deemed advisable and average the remaining intermediate estimates of the four remaining to get an intermediate value. The results are given in

Table 7.15. AGGREGATE CONSONANCE COEFFICIENTS FOR BASE CASE AND FOUR COST DISPLACEMENT SOLUTION SETS

Firm	Base Case	Observation Number			
		16	30	4	13
1	.18	.19	.19	.19	.18
2	.29	.29	.29	.28	.29
3	.30	.30	.30	.31	.30
4	.54	.80	.56	.54	.56
5	.65	.63	.51	.78	.61

Table 7.16. If we use the Method 3 k_{ij} estimates of Table 7.13, and use the cost structures for the base case, the three sets of θ_i estimates yield the price solutions of Table 7.17. Mean-square deviations from the base case solution are also given.

Table 7.16. LOWER AND UPPER BOUNDS AND INTERMEDIATE VALUES FOR θ_i, DERIVED FROM SAMPLE SOLUTIONS

Aggregate Consonance Factor (θ_i)	Base Case	Lower Bound (L_i)	Intermediate Value (I_i)	Upper Bound (U_i)
1	.18	.18	.19	.19
2	.28	.28	.29	.29
3	.30	.30	.30	.31
4	.54	.54	.55	.56
5	.65	.61	.63	.65

A first observation is that the price estimates are surprisingly close to the "actual" prices, given our "illegitimate" knowledge of the actual consonance factors that generated the base case solution. Industry 2 prices are consistently underestimated, the degree of error rising with θ_4 and θ_5. Hence, we are led to suspect the estimates obtained are too large -- a hypothesis supported by the mean-square deviations. On the other hand, Industry 1 price estimates are too close to actual values to give much indication of bias. The improvement in p_2's intermediate factor estimate with a slight rise in θ_2 may indicate an underestimate, but Industry 1 prices are affected primarily by its customers' demands and suppliers' prices rather than its firms' consonance factors in these examples.

Since the four sets of θ_i estimates are so close together and yield such similar prices, we will select the base case values as initial θ_i estimates, because they are associated with what we would view in the real world studies as the most accurate

Table 7.17. IMPLIED PRICE SOLUTIONS OF θ_i AND METHOD 3 k_{ij} ESTIMATES WITH BASE CASE COST STRUCTURES

Price	"Actual" Base Case Solution	Lower Bound Factors (L_i)	Intermediate Factors (I_i)	Upper Bound Factors (U_i)
p_1	$947.02	$946.97	$946.94	$946.98
p_2	894.34	894.18	894.28	894.13
p_3	937.82	937.69	937.67	937.87
p_4	933.71	933.18	932.81	932.77
p_5	1,560.38	1,559.09	1,558.80	1,557.51
Mean Square Deviation		.631	.817	1.354

observation. Were the price solutions sensitive to the L, I, and U parameter changes we would proceed into section 5 with 3 sets of θ_i estimates.

Although encouraging, the deductive derivation of K structure with implied θ_i yields some internal evidence that improvement in both aspects of consonance structure is possible. In section 5 we will proceed to derive improved and corrected estimates of both parameter sets using the filtered observations 4, 13, and 30, as well as the base case.

5. *THE REFINEMENT OF ESTIMATES OF* **K** *AND* θ_i *STRUCTURES*

As a first step to refinement of these parameters we will combine the reaction function forms of (19) with the relevant data of Table 5.1 to obtain the general reaction functions for the firms:

(20)

1. $\theta_1^{-1} = (10.98m_2 k_{12} + 8.38m_3 k_{13} + 2.96m_5 k_{15} - .21z_5 k_{15})/(52.3m_1 - z_1)$
2. $\theta_2^{-1} = (6.25m_1 k_{21} + 8.99m_3 k_{23} + 3.14m_4 k_{24} - .10z_4 k_{24})/(54.69m_2 - z_2)$
3. $\theta_3^{-1} = (9.62m_1 k_{31} + 11.49m_2 k_{32})/(42.00m_3 - z_3)$
4. $\theta_4^{-1} = (.58m_1 k_{41} + 2.76m_5 k_{45} - .20z_1 k_{41} - .21z_3 k_{43})/(31.88m_4 - z_4)$
5. $\theta_5^{-1} = (.10m_2 k_{52} + 3.05m_4 k_{54} - .27z_2 k_{52})/(11.92m_5 - z_5)$.

When the m_i and z_i relevant to the solutions of the base case and observations 4, 13, and 30 are substituted in (20), 4 specific reaction functions linking m_i to θ_i are derived for each firm. It is upon these functions that the refining operations will be performed.

Our techniques will attempt simultaneous determinations of **K** and θ_i through a search for consensual stability for their values in solutions to the reaction functions. Three questions will be addressed to the functions:

(1) if the θ_i values were equalized for each firm i in a subset of the observed reaction functions for firm i, what would the K matrix and θ_i be?

(2) if the K matrix were the initial estimates (those for Method 3 in Table 7.13), what θ_i would be implied by each reaction function?

(3) if the θ_i were set equal to a consensual value, what K structure would emerge?

The motivation of the questions is the same. If the four observations were generated by firms with stable power structures and aggregate consonance factors, these parameters should emerge when the m_i and z_i for the observations are substituted into the reaction function. Enforcing this equality in asking question 1, we permit θ_i to vary among subsets of reaction functions but be equal within any subset. This permits a set of θ_i and **K** structure to emerge. For those cases in which no acceptable θ_i emerges, we seek one by substituting the initial K structures into the reaction functions. Finally, we search these results for a consensual θ_i among the subset solutions and impose it upon other subsets to observe whether the same K structure emerges, as that present in the prior analyses. From study the three sets of results for similarities, we finally synthesize refined estimates of **K** and θ_j. The goal of this chapter will then have been reached.

5.1. *Variable θ_i Analysis*

As noted, we have four reaction functions for each firm derived from the four solutions we have decided upon. For those firms with three k_{ij} values (firms 1, 2, and 4), subsets of 3 such functions plus the constraint that the k_{ij} and the common θ_i. Hence four such solutions can be obtained from all combinations of the observations. In the case of those firms with only two k_{ij} values (firms 3 and 5), subsets of two reaction functions plus the normalization constraint will determine six solutions.

The resulting solutions are reproduced in Table 7.18. A study of the results as a whole reveals that observation 4 is suspect as a solution that is unconstrained by secondary objectives. (Actually, we know that a lower bound on p_2 is operative -- the only constraint that binds in the three observation solutions). Of the 15 subsets in which it is a member, negative or otherwise implausible or nonconsensual k_{ij} or θ_i values are obtained 12 times. Hence, this observation contributes negatively to our search, and in a realistic analysis we would eliminate it, but for the illustrative purposes of our exercise it will be retained.

Even when those subsets containing observation 4 are eliminated, the results are a bit disappointing. For firm 1, the remaining subset (B/13/30) yields an implausibly high customer value for k_{15}. Firm 2, for the same subset, does yield a tentatively plausible solution. On the other hand, four of the six subsets -- one of them involving observation 4 -- are consensual and plausible for firm 3. Observation 4 also is contained in the two subsets for firm 4 that are accepted; the solution for B/13/30 is rejected for implausibly high k_{43}. Lastly, the analysis yields three consensual and plausible parameter sets for firm 5. The solution for subset 4/30 is on the borderline of plausibility, but its nonconsensus θ_5 value leads us at this stage to reject it.

We emerge from this analysis with three consensual θ_i estimates, but fail to obtain one for firm 1 or firm 2, with, however, one acceptable solution for the latter firm.

5.2. *Fixed* **K** *Analysis*

Let us now address the second question to the data for those firms that do not have a consensual θ_i: if the **K** structure is frozen at its initial values, what θ_i values would the reaction functions for the four cases generate? The results are listed in Table 7.19.

Table 7.18. VARIABLE θ_i SOLUTIONS FOR SUBGROUPS OF REACTION FUNCTIONS DEFINED BY THE BASE CASE AND OBSERVATIONS 4, 13, AND 30

Included Functions	k_{i1}	k_{i2}	k_{i3}	k_{i4}	k_{i5}	Implied θ_i	Accept/ Reject	Consensua θ_i
Firm 1								
B/4/13	---	-.05	.17	---	.98	-36.46	R	None
B/4/30	---	.08	-.08	---	1.00	2.62	R	
B/13/30	---	.25	.17	---	.58	.36	R	
4/13/30	---	-.11	.04	---	1.07	-3.42	R	
Firm 2								
B/4/13	-3.79	---	-.46	5.25	---	-.06	R	None
B/4/30	-.71	---	-.02	1.73	---	-.36	R	
B/13/30	.42	---	.37	.21	---	.34	A	
4/13/30	-3.79	---	-.46	5.25	---	-.06	R	
Firm 3								
B/4	-56.44	57.44	---	---	---	.06	R	.30
B/13	.49	.51	---	---	---	.30	A	
B/30	.59	.41	---	---	---	.29	A	
4/13	.65	.35	---	---	---	.29	A	
4/30	1.83	-.83	---	---	---	.23	R	
13/30	.50	.50	---	---	---	.30	A	
Firm 4								
B/4/13	.27	---	.14	---	.59	.28	A	.30
B/4/30	.26	---	.12	---	.62	.31	A	
B/13/30	.05	---	.48	---	.47	.27	R	
4/13/30	.25	---	1.14	---	-.39	.07	R	
Firm 5								
B/4	---	.17	---	.83	---	-.88	R	.30
B/13	---	.33	---	.67	---	.31	A	
B/30	---	.34	---	.66	---	.29	A	
4/13	---	.66	---	.34	---	.09	R	
4/30	---	.40	---	.60	---	.21	R	
13/30	---	.34	---	.66	---	.29	A	

Table 7.19. ESTIMATES OF θ_i FROM FINAL **K**

Reaction Functions	FIRM:	
	1	2
Base Case	.18	.30
4	.15*	.29
13	.18	.30
30	.18	.30
Mean (Excluding Starred Items)	.18	.30
Final Estimate	.18	.31

Because observation 4 is suspect, we have eliminated θ_i's for its reaction functions when nonconsensual before averaging. The means are displayed in Table 7.19.

The observation values are all but identical for firms 1 and 2 when observation 4 is eliminated. If we compare the means with the results of Table 7.18 we can gain greater insight into their conformance to "reality".

For firm 1, no acceptable solution was found in the four subsets of Table 7.18: hence, we will tentatively adopt the mean $\theta_1 = .18$ from Table 7.16 as the best estimate we can make of that parameter at this point.

In the case of firm 2, one solution from Table 7.15 is plausible, both with respect to θ_2 and the k_{2i}. We will average in its θ_2 value (.34) with the four of Table 7.16 to get a final estimate of $\theta_2 = .31$.

We now have a complete set of modified but tentative θ_i: the consensual values of Table 7.18 and, in their absence, the fixed-K analysis values of Table 7.19. They will be adopted as new parameters with which to enter the last analytical task.

5.3. *Fixed θ Analysis*

It is to be hoped that a final basis of choice for the θ_i and final **K** estimates will emerge from the third and last of our refining procedures. In it, we force subsets of the base case and observation reaction functions to equal the θ_i-estimates of section 5.2 in order to observe the behavior of the k_{ij} so obtained. If consensus estimates can be obtained that are plausible for the consensus θ estimates, final power structure coefficients k_{ij} can be computed. For those firms with 3 such coefficients, subsets of two reaction functions plus the normalizing constraint are used. This constraint, that forces the sum of the k_{ij} to be 1 over all j, and one reaction function will suffice for firms with only two k_{ij}. The results of the analyses are summarized in Table 7.20.

5.4. *A Synthesis*

On the basis of the deductive initial estimates and the three analyses based upon a limited number of homogeneous solutions, we must now synthesize revised estimates of **K** and θ_i. The latter have already been chosen, and are repeated in Table 7.21. It remains, therefore, to derive **K**.

For firm 1, we have rejected all variable -θ_i estimates of Table 7.18; hence, we must base our revised estimates on the means of k_{12}, k_{13}, and k_{15} in the three acceptable

Table 7.20. ESTIMATES OF **K** FROM FIXED θ_i

Firm i Subsets	θ_i	k_{i1}	k_{i2}	k_{i3}	k_{i4}	k_{i5}	Accept/ Reject
1	.18						
B/4		---	1.82	-1.32	---	.50	R
B/13		---	.50	.37	---	.13	A
B/30		---	.51	.36	---	.13	A
4/13		---	1.13	-.51	---	.38	R
4/30		---	.95	-.32	---	.36	R
13/30		---	.51	.36	---	.13	A
2	.31						
B/4		.82	---	.04	.14	---	R
B/13		.48	---	.39	.13	---	A
B/30		.48	---	.38	.14	---	A
4/13		.81	---	.05	.14	---	R
4/30		.78	---	.07	.14	---	R
13/30		.60	---	.26	.14	---	A
3	.30						
B		.45	.55	---	---	---	A
4		.51	.49	---	---	---	A
13		.42	.58	---	---	---	A
30		.45	.55	---	---	---	A
4	.30						
B/4		.27	---	.12	---	.61	A
B/13		1.41	---	-1.65	---	1.24	R
B/30		.20	---	.22	---	.58	A
4/13		.27	---	.11	---	.61	A
4/30		.26	---	.13	---	.61	A
13/30		.04	---	.48	---	.48	R
5	.30						
B		---	.34	---	---	.66	A
4		--	.35	---	---	.65	A
13		---	.34	---	---	.66	A
30		---	.33	---	---	.67	A

Table 7.21. REVISED ESTIMATES OF K AND θ_i

Firm i	Initial θ_i	Initial k_{ij}	Initial θ_{ij}	Revised θ_i	Revised k_{ij}	Revised θ_{ij}	Actual θ_i	Actual k_{ij}	Actual θ_{ij}	Mean-Square Dev. from Actual: Init	Mean-Square Dev. from Actual: Rev
1	.18			.18			.19			.006	.006
k_{12}		.48	.09		.50	.09		.47	.09		
k_{13}		.39	.07		.37	.07		.37	.07		
k_{15}		.13	.02		.13	.02		.16	.03		
2	.28			.31			.35			.041	.027
k_{21}		.50	.14		.50	.15		.37	.13		
k_{23}		.45	.13		.35	.11		.40	.14		
k_{24}		.05	.01		.15	.05		.23	.08		
3	.30			.30			.30			.010	0.00
k_{31}		.46	.14		.51	.15		.50	.15		
k_{32}		.54	.16		.49	.15		.50	.15		
4	.54			.30			.29			.114	.010
k_{41}		.23	.12		.26	.08		.24	.07		
k_{43}		.11	.06		.14	.04		.17	.05		
k_{45}		.66	.36		.60	.18		.59	.17		
5	.65			.30			.29			.201	.010
k_{52}		.29	.19		.34	.10		.34	.10		
k_{54}		.71	.46		.66	.20		.66	.19		
All Firms										.098	.014

solutions of the fixed-θ_i estimates of Table 7.20. These are duly recorded in Table 7.21. For firm 2 we average the k values for the accepted values for Tables 7.18 and 7.20, a total of four. Eight acceptable solutions have been averaged for firm 3, and six for firm 4. In the case of firm 5, Tables 7.18 and 7.20 contribute fully seven acceptable subset solutions for averaging. All of the k_{ij} and θ_{ij} have also been recorded in Table 7.21.

It will be noted that the revised θ_{ij} estimates yield substantial improvements over the initial θ_{ij} for industry 2. For firms 4 and 5 θ_i is very sensitive to small changes in the θ_{ij}, rendering consonance factor estimation difficult. Nonetheless we have succeeded in making excellent approaches to the actual values of the θ_{ij}.

For industry 1, the initial estimates of θ_{ij} for firms 1 and 3 were so accurate that little room for improvement existed. The least accurate estimation occurs for firm

2, for which we have not been able to approach θ_2 sufficiently closely to permit the level of accuracy in projecting θ_{2j} that we achieved in the other four cases. Even so, the revisions have reduced the mean-square error somewhat under that revealed by the initial estimates.

Over the five firms (and 13 θ_{ij}) as a whole, mean-square deviations of θ_{ij} estimates from actual values were reduced from .098 for the initial estimates to .014 for the revised estimates. Of course, our possession of this knowledge is not legitimate, and besides, the matter of approximation accuracy is more directly and relevantly addressed in terms of the accuracy of the price solutions yielded by the θ_{ij} estimates.

We compute the solutions for the base case and observations 4, 13, and 30 for initial and revised θ, with p_2 at its lower bound in all cases for observation 4. These solutions are then compared with their "actual" values from which mean-square deviations are computed for comparison. The results are displayed in Table 7.22.

A first observation is that the estimates using the initial consonance factors were surprisingly close to the actual values. They departed from these actual consonance structure solution values between .04 and .07 percentage points between solutions, with an average of .05 percentage points over the 19 price estimates. In absolute terms the errors averaged between 44¢ and 85¢ over the solutions, with a 19-item mean of 61¢. Given the deductive content of the analysis that projected the initial K-structure, and the large overestimate of industry 2's aggregate consonance factors, these seem quite close. Equally importantly, in every one of the 19 unconstrained price movements the signs of the price deviations from the base case to the several displacement observations were identical to the actual solution movements of the same prices. Hence, the initial estimates preserve the signs in the face of parameter displacements and would yield these qualitative insights into the two industries' behaviors.

However, the revised consonance structure estimates lead to marked improvements in the price estimates. Percentage errors decline to between .01 and .04 between solutions with an average over the 19 price observations of .02 percent. In absolute terms this translates to between 11¢ and 39¢ with a mean of 23¢. The solutions are sign-preserving with displacements with one exception -- that of p_2 in observation 30, which moves in a contrary direction to actual movements. The tendency in the revised θ estimates is to underestimate industry 1 prices, because of the failure to approach the true θ_2 as closely as other θ_i's have been estimated.

6. *CONCLUSION*

These preliminary experiments, as well as an extensive empirical investigation of the structure of the Organization of Petroleum Exporting Countries in the period 1974--1980 (Kuenne [31], [33]), lead to the conclusion that operational methods of this type can deliver adequate depictions of industrial consonance structures. Of course, we cannot hope for general results as closely approximative as those we have just examined, since the price data in the latter were generated from rigidly fixed θ, albeit with some "noise" from binding constraints. However, no doubt refinements and improvements in techniques will provide greater power than those employed above. Most compelling, however, for urging the adoption and polishing of such techniques is their indispensability if oligopoly theory is to make progress. The isolation of quantitatively specified, detailed, and empirically validated power structure is a sine qua non of useful oligopoly analysis.

Table 7.22. SOLUTIONS FOR BASE CASE AND OBSERVATIONS 4, 13, AND 30 WITH INITIAL, REVISED, AND ACTUAL θ

	p_1	p_2	p_3	p_4	p_5	Deviations from Actual: Mean Sq. Dev.	Abs. Mean Dev.	Abs. % Mean Dev.
1. Base Case								
1. Initial	$946.93	$894.17	$937.69	$933.12	$1,558.89	.724	.494	.040
2. Revised	946.94	894.16	937.75	933.61	1,560.48	.113	.106	.011
3. Actual	947.02	894.34	937.82	933.71	1,560.38			
2. Observation 4								
1. Initial	945.69	892.48	923.05	934.63	1,558.32	.485*	.438*	.037*
2. Revised	945.72	892.48	923.08	935.17	1,559.64	.217*	.168*	.014*
3. Actual	945.89	892.48	923.16	935.14	1,559.25	*Divisor of con-	of 4 used strained	because p_2
3. Observation 13								
1. Initial	945.77	878.99	936.19	932.43	1,566.11	1.025	.644	.050
2. Revised	945.71	878.98	935.56	932.97	1,568.38	.359	.250	.026
3. Actual	945.85	879.25	936.30	933.00	1,568.31			
4. Observation 30								
1. Initial	952.37	894.50	943.21	981.08	1,563.40	1.403	.846	.046
2. Revised	952.63	893.94	943.19	981.53	1,565.95	.474	.386	.038
3. Actual	952.44	894.82	943.36	981.72	1,566.45			
Total for All Observation:		Initial				.991	.614	.048
		Revised				.326	.231	.023

1 I draw heavily upon the work of S. S. Stevens, [44] and Patrick Suppes and Joseph L. Zinnes, [45].

2 Warren S. Torgeson, [50], p. 62.

3 The relation is exact for [α, β] equal to [$2+\sqrt{2}$, $2-\sqrt{2}$], [$2-\sqrt{2}$, $2+\sqrt{2}$], and [3,3].

4 See Kuenne, [28].

5 R. D. Luce and E. Galanter, [36], p. 251.

6 The competition among conglomerates in a large number of product markets has played a large role in the development of "live-and-let-live" theorizing. See Corwin Edwards [10] and D. Kantarelis, [19] and [20].

BIBLIOGRAPHY

[1] Andrews, P. W. S., *Manufacturing Business*, Longmans, London, 1949.

[2] Archibald, G. C., "The Qualitative Content of Maximizing Models," *Journal of Political Economy*, 73 (1965), pp. 27-36.

[3] Bain, Joe S., *Barriers to New Competition*, Harvard University Press, Cambridge, Mass., 1956.

[4] Baumol, William, John C. Panzar, and Robert D. Willig, *Contestable Markets and the Theory of Industry Structure*, Harcourt, Brace, Jovanavich, New York, 1982.

[5] Bishop, Robert, "Duopoly: Collusion or Warfare?", *American Economic Review*, L (1960), pp. 933-961.

[6] Bresnahan, Timothy F., "Duopoly Models With Consistent Conjectures," *American Economic Review*, LXXXI (1981), pp. 934-945.

[7] Chamberlin, Edward H., *The Theory of Monopolistic Competition*, Harvard University Press, Cambridge, Mass., Sixth Edition, 1948.

[8] Cyert, Richard M. and M. H. DeGroot, "Multiperiod Decision Models With Alternating Choice as a Solution to the Duopoly Problem," *Quarterly Journal of Economics*, 84 (1970), pp. 410-429.

[9] ______________________, "An Analysis of Cooperation and Learning in a Duopoly Context," *American Economic Review*, LXIII (1973), pp. 24-37.

[10] Edwards, Corwin D., "Conglomerate Bigness as a Source of Power," in *Business Concentration and Price Policy*, Princeton University Press, Princeton, N. J., 1955.

[11] Fiacco, Anthony V. and Garth McCormick, *Nonlinear Programming: Sequential Unconstrained Minimization Technique*, John Wiley, New York, 1967.

[12] Fog, Bjarke, *Industrial Pricing Policies: An Analysis of Pricing Policies of Danish Manufacturers*, North-Holland, Amsterdam, 1960.

[13] Friedman, James, "Reaction Function and the Theory of Duopoly," *Review of Economic Studies*, 35 (1968), pp. 257-272.

[14] ______________, "Individual Behavior in Oligopolistic Markets: An Experimental Study," *Yale Economic Studies*, 3(1963), pp. 359-417.

[15] ____________, *Oligopoly and the Theory of Games*, North-Holland, Amsterdam, 1977.

[16] Hoggatt, Austin C., "Response of Paid Student Subjects to Differential Behavior of Robots in Bifurcated Duopoly Games," *Review of Economic Studies*, 36 (1969), pp. 417-432.

[17] ____________, "Measuring the Cooperativeness of Behavior in Quantity Variation Duopoly Games," *Behavioral Science*, 12 (1967), pp. 109-121.

[18] Johnsen, Erik, *Studies in Multiobjective Decision Models*, Studentlitteratur, Lund, 1968.

[19] Kantarelis, Demetrius, *Live and Let Live Behavior of Oligopolists in a Multidimensional Setting With Demand Fluctuations*, Ph. D. Dissertation, Clark University, 1983.

[20] ____________ and Emiel C. H. Veendorp, "Live and Let Live Behavior in a Multi-Market Setting With Demand Fluctuations," reproduced, April, 1983.

[21] Kaplan, A. D. H., Joel B. Dirlam, and Robert F. Lanzillotti, *Pricing in Big Business: A Case Approach*, Brookings, Washington, D. C., 1958.

[22] Kaysen, Carl, "The Corporation: How Much Power? What Scope?", Ch. 5 in Edward S. Mason, *The Corporation in Modern Ssociety*, Harvard University Press, Cambridge, Mass., 1959, pp. 85-105.

[23] Koopmans, Tjalling C., *Three Essays on the State of Economic Science*, McGraw-Hill, New York, 1957.

[24] Kuenne, Robert E., *The Theory of General Economic Equilibrium*, Princeton University Press, Princeton, N. J., 1963.

[25] ____________, "Quality Space, Interproduct Competition, and General Equilibrium Theory," Chapter 10 in Robert E. Kuenne, ed., *Monopolistic Competition Theory: Studies in Impact*, John Wiley, New York, 1967.

[26] ____________, "Towards a Usable General Theory of Oligopoly," *De Economist*, 122 (1974), pp. 471-502.

[27] ____________, "Towards an Operational General Equilibrium Theory With Oligopoly: Some Experimental Results and Conjectures," *Kyklos*, 27 (1974), pp. 792-820.

[28] ____________, "Interproduct Distances in a Quality-Space: Inexact Measurement in Differentiated Oligopoly Analysis," *Applied Economics*, 6 (1974), pp. 255-273.

[29] ____________, "General Oligopolistic Equilibrium: A Crippled Optimization Approach," in *Pioneering Economics: Essays in Honor of Giovanni Demaria*, Cedam, Padua, 1978, pp. 537-577.

[30] ____________, "A Short-Run Demand Analysis of the OPEC Cartel," *Journal of Business Administration*, 10 (1978-1979), pp. 129-164, reprinted in *The Logistics and Transportation Review*, 17 (1981), pp. 231-265.

[31] ____________, "Rivalrous Consonance and the Power Structure of OPEC," *Kyklos*, 32 (1979), pp. 695-717.

[32] ____________, "Duopoly Reaction Functions Under Crippled Optimization Regimes," *Oxford Economic Papers*, 32 (1980), pp. 224-240.

[33] ____________, "The GENESYS Model of OPEC, 1974-1980: Structural Insights From a Non-Forecasting Model," *Energy Economics*, 4 (1982), pp. 146-158.

[34] Lanzillotti, Robert F., "Pricing Objectives in Large Companies," *American Economic Review*, XLIX (1959), pp. 921-940.

[35] Luce, R. Duncan, R. Bush, and Eugene Galanter, *Handbook of Mathematical Psychology*, I, John Wiley, New York, 1963.

[36] Luce, R. Duncan and Eugene Galanter, "Psychophysical Scaling", in [34].

[37] Marschak, Thomas and Reinhard Selten, *General Equilibrium With Price Making Firms*, Springer-Verlag, Berlin, 1974.

[38] Negishi, Takashi, "Monopolistic Competition and General Equilibrium" *Review of Economic Studies*, 28 (1961), pp. 196-201.

[39] Nicholson, Michael, *Oligopoly and Conflict*, Liverpool University Press, Liverpool, 1972.

[40] Samuelson, Paul A., *Foundations of Economic Analysis*, Harvard University Press, Cambridge, Mass., 1948.

[41] Shubik, Martin, *Strategy and Market Structure*, John Wiley, New York, 1959.

[42] Simon, Herbert A., *Administrative Behavior*, Third Edition, Free Press, New York, 1976.

[43] Stevens, S. S., ed., *Handbook of Experimental Psychology*, John Wiley, New York, 1951.

[44] ____________, "Mathematics, Measurement, and Psychophysics," Ch. 1 in [43].

[45] Suppes, Patrick and Joseph L. Zinnes, "Basic Measurement Theory," Ch. 1 [35].

[46] Sylos-Labini, Paolo, *Oligopoly and Technical Progress*, Harvard University Press, Cambridge, Mass., 1969.

[47] Telser, Lester, *Competition, Collusion, and Game Theory*, Aldine-Atherton, Chicago, 1972.

[48] Thin, Tun, *Theory of Markets*, Harvard University Press, Cambridge, Mass., 1960.

[49] Thompson, Arthur A., Jr., *Economics of the Firm: Theory and Practice*, Prentice-Hall, Englewood Cliffs, N. J., 1973.

[50] Torgeson, Warren S., *Theory and Methods of Scaling*, John Wiley, New York, 1958.

[51] Wärneryd, S., Ch. 3 in [18].

[52] Williamson, Oliver, *The Economics of Discretionary Behavior: Managerial Objectives in a Theory of the Firm*, Prentice-Hall, Englewood Cliffs, N. J., 1964.

INDEX